THE DYNAMICS OF INTERNATIONAL NEGOTIATION

This book explores the dynamics of international negotiations from the perspectives of researchers and practical negotiators. Reinforcing the idea that the study of negotiation is not merely an academic endeavor, the essays reflect the author's lifetime experiences as a negotiation researcher and provider of analytical support to international negotiation teams. Addressing a wide range of critical issues, such as creativity and experimentation, psychological dynamics, avoiding incomplete agreements, engineering the negotiation context, reframing negotiations for development conflicts, understanding what matters when implementing agreements, utilizing decision support systems, engaging new actors, and expanding core values, each chapter opens new doors on our conceptual and practical understanding of international negotiations. The author introduces new ways of understanding and explaining the negotiation process from different intellectual perspectives. The goal of this book is to resolve many critical unanswered questions by stimulating new research on these dynamics and developing new approaches that can help negotiation practitioners be more effective. The book will be used in university courses on international negotiation and conflict resolution, and provide a useful resource for researchers, policymakers, practitioners, NGOs, donor organizations, and grant-giving organizations.

Bertram I. Spector has more than 40 years of experience conducting and directing research, training, and technical assistance programs internationally, specializing in the international negotiation and anti-corruption fields. He has been the Editor-in-Chief of an international peer-reviewed academic journal, *International Negotiation: A Journal of Theory and Practice*, since its inception in 1996. Dr. Spector is author of *Negotiating Peace and Confronting Corruption: Challenges for Post-Conflict Societies* (US Institute of Peace 2011), and co-editor of *Getting It Done: Post-Agreement Negotiation and International Regimes* (US Institute of Peace 2003), among many other books and journal articles.

"This is a wonderful book. It meets the unusual challenge of packaging a broad grasp of established wisdom on international negotiation with lights and insights into hidden angles and creative innovation, wrapped up in a highly readable style. For a quarter century the author has sifted through all the scholarship on the topic as editor of the top journal on international negotiation and so is on top of current trends and new discoveries, combined with his own research and imagination. The result is a book that is perfect for classrooms but also enjoyable for enlightening reading."

I. William Zartman, *Jacob Blaustein Distinguished Professor Emeritus of International Organization and Conflict Resolution, The Johns Hopkins University, School of Advanced International Studies (SAIS)*

"This book is a collection of essays that clearly and brilliantly examines the state of the domain. It covers an impressive number of topics. It should be used as a reference book for a couple of decades. This contribution is especially important for research and also for implementation because it opens new doors for effective international negotiation. It is a most inspiring work for the potential it carries with it."

Guy-Olivier Faure, *Vice President of the Executive Board of CERIS-ULB, the Diplomatic School, Brussels, Belgium*

THE DYNAMICS OF INTERNATIONAL NEGOTIATION

Essays on Theory and Practice

Bertram I. Spector

Cover image: © Getty Images

First published 2023
by Routledge
4 Park Square, Milton Park, Abingdon, Oxon OX14 4RN

and by Routledge
605 Third Avenue, New York, NY 10158

Routledge is an imprint of the Taylor & Francis Group, an informa business

© 2023 Bertram I. Spector

The right of Bertram I. Spector to be identified as author of this work has been asserted in accordance with sections 77 and 78 of the Copyright, Designs and Patents Act 1988.

All rights reserved. No part of this book may be reprinted or reproduced or utilized in any form or by any electronic, mechanical, or other means, now known or hereafter invented, including photocopying and recording, or in any information storage or retrieval system, without permission in writing from the publishers.

Trademark notice: Product or corporate names may be trademarks or registered trademarks, and are used only for identification and explanation without intent to infringe.

British Library Cataloguing-in-Publication Data
A catalogue record for this book is available from the British Library

Library of Congress Cataloging-in-Publication Data
A catalog record has been requested for this book

ISBN: 978-1-032-32298-8 (hbk)
ISBN: 978-1-032-32310-7 (pbk)
ISBN: 978-1-003-31440-0 (ebk)

DOI: 10.4324/9781003314400

Typeset in Bembo
by KnowledgeWorks Global Ltd.

For my children – Sam and Naomi
and my grandchildren – Moriah, Vivian, Naftali, and Sylvie.
May they live in peaceful times, where problems – even the most complex ones – can be managed and resolved through smartly applied negotiation processes.

CONTENTS

List of Figures   *ix*
List of Tables   *x*
Preface   *xi*

1 The Dynamics of International Negotiation   1

2 Negotiation Is a Creative Experiment   10

3 Engineering Negotiation Situations for Improved Outcomes   25

4 The Psychology of Negotiation   34

5 The Negotiability of Nations   57

6 Incomplete International Negotiations: Adding Implementation Formulas   63

7 What Matters When Implementing Negotiated Agreements?   75

8 Decision Support Systems: Getting Negotiators to Use Them   91

9 Citizen Negotiation: Adding New Voices   111

10 Negotiated Rulemaking   120

11 Paradiplomacy and the Democratization of International Negotiation   129

12 Values in Negotiation: The Case of International Development Assistance   141

13 Negotiating for Good, Negotiating for Bad   150

14 Reframing Negotiation to Avert Development Conflicts   156

15 Evolutionary Negotiation   165

16 Future Paths   174

Bibliography   *180*
Index   *191*

LIST OF FIGURES

1.1	The Dynamics of International Negotiation	3
4.1	Psychological Model of Two-Person Negotiations (from the perspective of Negotiator A)	35
4.2	Map for the Camp Game	36
4.3	Final Path Model: Creative Cooperative Behavior	43
4.4	Final Path Model: Active Cooperative Behavior	44
4.5	Final Path Model: Passive Cooperative Behavior	45
4.6	Final Path Model: Active Hostile Behavior	46
4.7	Psychological Impacts on the Choice of Bargaining Strategy	51
4.8	Revised Psychological Model of Two-Person Negotiations	53
5.1	Negotiability Dimensions for Seven Countries	60

LIST OF TABLES

3.1	Sampling of Analogies Used in the Slovakia-Hungary Hydroelectric Project Experiment	31
4.1	Bargaining Strategies	39
4.2	Definitions of Murray's Manifest Needs as Employed in Stein's Self-Description Questionnaire	41
4.3	The Effects of Personality Pairing on Bargaining Behavior Types (in %)	48
5.1	Dimensions and Measures of Negotiability	59
7.1	Differences in Ratification Rates for All Nations and Those with Stated Environmental Priorities	82
7.2	National Priorities by Sector (% of Countries Stating High Priorities)	83
7.3	Differences in Ratification Rate for Countries that have Performed Current Concrete Activities by Sector	84
7.4	Differences in Ratification Rate for Countries with Any Planned Activities by Sector	84
7.5	Percent of Activities Pursued Across All Sectors	85
7.6	Domestic Incapacity and Developmental Level (% of Countries)	86
7.7	Differences in Ratification Rate for Countries with High Levels of Incapacity	86
7.8	Sources of Domestic Incapacity (in %)	87
7.9	Percent of Stated Problems by Post-Agreement Phase	87

PREFACE

It seems so obvious. If there are peaceful ways to solve major international problems or avert violent conflicts, why don't leaders always take advantage of them? If these peaceful mechanisms are successful, the potential for substantial death and destruction will have been avoided, and countries will move forward with more positive political, social, and economic development programs instead. If these peaceful entry points don't work out, at least leaders can tell their constituents that they tried as best they could to manage or resolve the conflicts in the least damaging way. But unfortunately, choosing conflictual paths are all too common, not giving peaceful options much of a chance. It must be embedded in our DNA.

What peaceful options are available? The most obvious is negotiating with the other parties. International negotiation usually manifests as power-based dialogues where each party seeks to achieve its interests and goals by using strategies and tactics that they believe will influence the other parties to make compromises in search of a mutually acceptable agreement. Like any other conflict management or conflict resolution approach, how one perceives negotiation and how one applies it makes all the difference in the outcomes.

A country's leadership can view entering into negotiation in a positive or negative light. From a positive perspective, choosing the negotiation option can certainly be seen as the approach that saves lives and reduces the inevitable destruction that would result from pursuing a violent path. It can also be seen as the principled approach – where you take the initiative to discuss your interests and goals with the other side and try to persuade them to take a peaceful approach as well to resolve the issues at hand.

From a negative perspective, pursuing the negotiation option could be viewed as a sign of weakness – where you are not willing to fight for your country's interests, but you are willing to make concessions to the other. These negative perceptions can be influenced by cultural and historical tendencies, by perceptions of the other side's willingness or reluctance to negotiate the issues at hand in good faith, and by their likelihood to live up to their commitments and implement negotiated provisions if an agreement is reached.

Whether the negotiation option is selected or not also depends on how capable or ready the country is to follow a negotiation approach. Do they have the capacity to prepare properly for negotiations by developing a strong strategy, projecting short-term and long-term goals, and assessing the other parties' interests and intentions? Do they have the training and experience to recognize the best opportunities for negotiation, primarily when the conflict appears to have reached a mutually hurting stalemate? Can the parties identify a way out of the conflict – a plan that achieves their goals? Do they have the capacity to negotiate effectively – to develop and apply persuasive strategies and tactics, to adjust these approaches as needed, to know when to make demands and when to concede, and how to develop formulas and details for successful negotiated solutions?

Despite the growing literature on international negotiation, there are still many questions about how to best conduct negotiation and achieve mutually acceptable outcomes. While we know a lot about the many dynamic factors that influence the path that negotiations may take, there are still a lot of unknowns. These gaps in knowledge spurred me to write the essays in this book. How can you approach the negotiation process as a creative experiment that views different strategies as hypothetical mechanisms to produce meaningful solutions to complex problems? How can you engineer the bargaining context to improve the chances of successful agreements? How can you understand and apply psychological dynamics in the negotiation process to overcome impasse and reach outcomes? How can you best understand who you are negotiating with – their capacity, trustworthiness, and interest in the negotiation process? How can you develop preemptive strategies to ensure the faithful implementation of negotiated provisions after the negotiation is completed? How can you address problems that can affect the implementation of negotiated agreements? How can information, analytical tools and information technology best be used to support practical negotiations? How can all affected stakeholders be engaged to negotiate rules and regulations that their societies need to move forward in a fair and just fashion? How can civil society participate in international negotiation along with government so that all interests are represented? How can non-central government actors be engaged in international negotiation to best address issues that are local and regional in nature, producing fairer and more sustainable outcomes? How do values resonate with international negotiation goals and processes; rather than win-win or win-lose outcomes, is it possible to negotiate out of empathy and altruism for the other party, resulting in a "caring-win" outcome? How can unintended bad consequences from negotiated agreements be avoided; can negotiation strategies be reframed to "do no harm"? How can the negotiation process be prevented from serving negative goals, such as international money laundering? How can complex international negotiations that yield only incremental results and require multiple follow-up negotiations to achieve their ultimate objectives best be conceived and applied, given their prolonged time requirements?

I have been the Editor-in-Chief of *International Negotiation: A Journal of Theory and Practice* for many years. This has brought me in contact with the best thinkers in the international negotiation field. Prior to that, I was very fortunate to have been selected as the Project Director of the Processes of International Negotiation (PIN) project at the International Institute for Applied Systems Analysis (IIASA) in Laxenburg, Austria. This negotiation project was originally envisioned by Howard Raiffa when he served as the first Director of the Institute from 1972–75, and it was finally established in 1986. During my three-year assignment from 1990–93, I was privileged to work with the PIN Steering Committee members, implementing many research programs with the participation of our worldwide network of negotiation scholars. PIN produced many in depth books on under-researched topics concerning international negotiation, extending analysis, developing new areas of inquiry, and building strong personal relationships in this field of study. During my tenure, I was able to conduct research on negotiating international regimes, post-agreement negotiation, environmental negotiation, multilateral negotiation, and negotiation support tools, among other. Importantly, the focus of PIN's work was always to provide a link between research and practice – to facilitate more effective real-world applications of international negotiation processes. Back in the Washington, DC area after PIN, I was again pleased to become part of the Washington Interest in Negotiation (WIN) Group that met at the Johns Hopkins University School of Advanced International Studies on a regular basis, a forum that facilitated the sharing of ideas and research findings.

I am forever grateful to three of my professors in graduate school at New York University. Bill Zartman introduced me to the field of international negotiation as he proceeded to revolutionize its study by introducing such central concepts as ripeness theory, hurting stalemates, formulas and details, forward-looking and backward-looking outcomes, preventive diplomacy, and the effects of power asymmetry, among many more. He has continued to be a valuable mentor. Courses I took with Moe Stein began my interest in the psychological factors that are so central to understanding the negotiation process – the effects of perception and personality. Most importantly, his research on stimulating creativity became a major element in how I have conceived of transforming conflicts into agreements among negotiators. Bob Burrowes introduced me to statistical and experimental methods in political science. My work with him on several research grants made me aware of new ways of analyzing and explaining political and behavioral change at a time when such quantitative tools were just getting introduced into political science research. I was lucky to have found such great thinkers and mentors at an early stage in my career.

I dedicate this book to my children and grandchildren, hoping that they can live their lives in peaceful times, and when problems arise, negotiation processes are used to resolve them quickly and effectively.

1
THE DYNAMICS OF INTERNATIONAL NEGOTIATION

In a smart, rational, and empathetic world, how could the choice between waging war that kills thousands and destroys civilizations versus managing conflicts through peaceful discussions not steer toward the nonviolent option? Unfortunately, most humans – at least the ones that lead nations – must not be too smart, rational, or empathetic. Conflict, violence, and warfare have been so commonplace in the human experience from the beginning of time. But hiding in the background has always been the alternative: resolving differences and managing conflicts peacefully through negotiation. Most parties can transform their disagreements and achieve much of what they want through nonviolent means if they prioritize brains over brawn.

There are many ways to examine international negotiations. Since 1996, I have been the Editor-in-Chief of *International Negotiation: A Journal of Theory and Practice* which publishes original research, and practical and theoretical pieces by academics and practitioners on the intricacies of the negotiation process – what makes it work well, what inhibits effectiveness, and how its application can be improved to ensure better outcomes. We have published special thematic issues and unsolicited articles that examine a very wide range of topics: coordination in negotiation; ethics in negotiation; the impacts of culture and ethnicity; negotiation styles; inclusivity in negotiations; Track Two diplomacy; mediation; innovative negotiation tools; reframing formulas; preventive diplomacy; post-agreement negotiation and regimes; research methods; teaching and training approaches; negotiations about trade and the economy, international development, sustainable development, peace processes, multinational issues, weapons of mass destruction, and security; and negotiating with terrorists, colonialists, riparian states, and international businesses; among many others. These studies have opened up so many new ways to understand and explain the negotiation process, with all of its many moving parts. At the same time, most of these studies, even the best ones, leave me with lingering questions that remain unsolved. There is always more to discover.

The Negotiation System

The negotiation system is often analyzed in relation to its building blocks: structure, process, strategy, actors, and outcomes.[1] This unlocks the doors to many topics for research on how this behavioral process operates. First, from a *structural perspective*, one needs to examine the number of parties interacting in negotiation; multilateral engagements are often more complex than bilateral talks. Sometimes, a third party plays the role of mediator, which also changes the chemistry of the interactions. Each party wields power that is used to convince the other sides to come to agreement; power can be symmetrical or asymmetrical among the parties, leading to very different types of interactions. This power can be derived from different sources – financial, technological, military, cultural – which can also impact the negotiations. Another structural element involves the issues under discussion; collaborative problem-solving issues will yield a very different type of negotiation environment than one that is seeking to end a violent conflict situation among parties. And the context is a critical structural factor influencing how the negotiations proceed. Bargaining conducted in the midst of violence or peace, prosperity or financial stress, or a health pandemic or humanitarian disaster, for instance, will feel the influence of these contextual pressures and support mechanisms differently.

Second, the *negotiating process* examines the sequence of activities that make up the negotiation experience. It is usually discussed as a multi-staged effort that exhibits patterns of information exchange, communications, and influencing. The progressive stages of the process include pre-negotiation, negotiation, implementation, post-negotiation, and renegotiation. Third, selecting one's *strategies* in negotiation is a critical decision. It determines the extent to which one will go to compete, concede, or problem-solve with the other negotiating partners. The primary approach through which strategies are pursued is persuasion – making demands and counteroffers – and hoping these tactics will result in dialogue that encourages the parties to make concessions and find common ground. Fourth, the *actors* in negotiation bring the process down to the human level, where the openness, personality, inventiveness, flexibility, interpersonal sensitivity, patience, and tenacity of the individual make a big difference in how the process moves forward. And the last building block, *outcomes*, represents the results and impacts of the negotiation process, which can be represented, alternatively, by an agreement and the implementation of an agreement, or the failure to reach either of these solutions. All of these components of the process have fostered volumes of creative research.

What makes the study of the negotiation system so exciting is that it can be examined from many different intellectual perspectives and disciplines: history, the law, politics, economics, psychology, sociology, business, and communications are among the key specialty areas. Each of these disciplines introduces additional ways of dissecting, understanding, and explaining the negotiation process from their own viewpoints. For example, a political science lens would focus on the interests of the parties, their power relationship, and the use of power tactics. With a psychological lens, one would look at negotiator perceptions of the other parties, negotiator personalities, leadership, and social interactions. An economic perspective would focus on cost-benefit and risk analyses of the issues being negotiated.

The Dynamics

The trajectory of the negotiation system, in any particular case, is influenced by many factors. These are the critical elements that push negotiations toward an agreement or breakdown. They can include, for example, contextual considerations, human factors, creative thinking, and essential values brought to the table by negotiators. Altogether, the interplay of these factors can explain the dynamics within which international negotiations proceed and how effective they are in achieving acceptable outcomes. These dynamics make negotiations complex, are subject to infinite possibilities, and, as a result, are difficult to predict. Figure 1.1 presents many of these dynamic factors that are discussed in this book's essays. They are among the most important drivers of international negotiation, but there are certainly many more that can be examined.

Creativity

Creative ideas and strategies can be injected into the negotiation system to find mutually acceptable solutions by trying something new and different. The

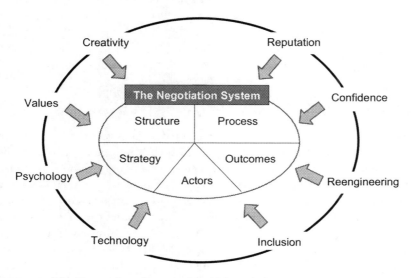

FIGURE 1.1 The Dynamics of International Negotiation.

negotiators who use these experimental approaches are willing to take risks with their fresh approaches to problem-solving. The hope is that their creativity will trigger new and desired responses in contrast to traditional and expected approaches.

Reengineering

A critical goal of the negotiation process is to transform a violent or threatening situation into a peaceful problem-solving dialogue. Introducing new ways to reframe or reengineer the situation can sometimes accomplish this type of adjustment. For example, negotiators can bring in new actors, such as mediators or facilitators, to change the nature and structure of the dialogue. As well, issues where parties are at a stalemate can be reframed into smaller subproblems that might be easier to address and solve.

Another reason to reengineer the negotiation system is to address the need for adjustment over time in negotiated agreements that might become outdated. Negotiations that establish international regimes often accept the fact that changes to agreed provisions are likely to be required over time, and, as a result, they incorporate mechanisms in the regime to do just that. But most negotiated agreements do not include such adjustment structures. This is where reengineering approaches can have an impact. There are several stages through which negotiations progress, and some might be more appropriate than others to inject these adjustment loops.

As well, while the negotiation system is typically used to end conflicts and solve problems among states in a peaceful way, the system can also be used for bad purposes, such as promoting transboundary corruption or the use of delay tactics that allow parties to rearm themselves. The system can be reengineered to constrain its use for such adverse pursuits. Targeted changes to the negotiation system under these circumstances can have a major impact on shutting down such negative applications.

Psychology

The impact of the human factor on negotiation dynamics is infinite. The process is significantly influenced by the perceptions held by each negotiator of the other side's strategies and the overall context. Perceptions of power symmetry versus asymmetry can also impact strategies and the propensity to compromise. And personality can also drive behavior, attitudes, and actions taken at the negotiation table. The mix of negotiator personalities around the table is a major dynamic influencing the progress of talks; highly aggressive negotiators can quickly cause the talks to stalemate, while collaborative actors can find it easier to reach accommodation, and a mix of aggressive with collaborative negotiators can yield a win-lose outcome.

Reputation

All countries have a negotiation reputation: how they have behaved in previous negotiations. Contributing to their reputation is the capacity, training, and experience of their individual negotiators, the country's cultural orientation to negotiation, and also the history of how they used process and strategy in past cases. In the pre-negotiation phase, these reputational factors are surely examined by the other parties and taken into account as they prepare their own strategies. Despite a party's reputation in past negotiations, they can certainly make major adjustments to surprise their opponents.

Confidence

A major influencing factor in the way the negotiation system proceeds is the degree of confidence that the parties have in one another to follow-through on any promises made in an ultimate agreement. Can the other side really be trusted? Hopefully, the negotiation dialogue builds such confidence. But sometimes, it is more convincing if there is a solid plan of action negotiated along with the rest of the agreement on how, when, and who will implement the agreement once it is signed. This is a missing piece in many negotiated outcomes: there is no negotiated plan for implementation and thereby no certainty that the agreed provisions will indeed be executed as intended. Finding concrete ways to build this confidence and trust – that the investments made in the negotiation system are worth the effort – are important motivators to reach agreement.

Technology

Decision support tools and the Internet are two ways that information technology has become a new and important factor that influences the way the negotiation system operates. This technology provides critical information, analysis, projections, and communication channels to negotiators that have not been available previously. Especially during the COVID-19 pandemic, web-based platforms have been employed creatively to facilitate international negotiation sessions that would otherwise have been postponed. Perhaps they will continue to be used, even after the pandemic restrictions are lifted, for financial and environmental reasons. But these web communications platforms are lacking in one major feature: they eliminate the direct human interaction that has always been so essential to the negotiation process. In addition, analytical support tools certainly can be very useful for designing more informed strategies and formulas for negotiation, but they need to be accepted and understood by the practitioners, not only by the analytical staff. So, the technological impact on the negotiation system is a developing matter and one that is likely to be of increasing importance as time progresses.

Inclusion

The inclusion of new and different types of actors in international negotiations has had a significant impact on the system. In a domain that has traditionally seen only government-to-government interactions, citizen groups and businesses are now being accepted on negotiating teams, depending on the sectors and issues under discussion. Especially when the subject of the negotiation directly targets these actors – or they are seen as the likely implementers of agreed provisions – their active engagement at the time of negotiation makes a lot of sense so that their ideas are incorporated and their buy-in is confirmed. International negotiations are also being conducted at new levels, not only among central governments. Local or regional governments are being empowered by the central state to negotiate issues across state boundaries that will affect them directly, but perhaps not impact other parts of their countries. Bringing these new actors to the table in a very active fashion can influence the negotiation system at its core: who is included, how they are selected and trained, and what is their role and limits. These new negotiation actors, with their new interests and orientations, will certainly have a significant impact on the system.

Values

Negotiators come to the table with certain values that can impact how they interact, the strategies they choose, and their likelihood of being able to reach reasonable compromises. Sometimes, these values are culturally influenced. Self-interest is typically high on everybody's list, but values such as justice, fairness, and equity are also often prevalent, understanding that the journey to most agreements requires that all parties feel they have achieved something that they want from the negotiation. Depending on the subject of the negotiation, additional values may be critical. If the negotiation concerns humanitarian emergencies or a fragile or post-conflict context, for example, values that elevate empathy and altruism might be appropriate. How these caring and compassionate values are brought to the fore and how they are manifested in negotiating positions, strategies, and formulas can seriously impact the trajectory of the negotiation process in new and unexpected ways.

All of these factors can be used by negotiators to influence the dynamics of bargaining. How, when, and why they are applied are a matter of choice by the negotiators and their teams. But the nature and extent of their impact and influence on the talks and their outcome are still a matter for research to determine.

My Perspective

Over the course of my career, I have never been a professional negotiator. However, I have studied many negotiations and analyzed the process, and in some cases provided direct analytical support to real negotiating teams. My doctoral dissertation at New York University, on the impacts of power, perception, and personality on the negotiation process and outcome, was strongly influenced by the ideas and mentorship of I. William Zartman, Morris Stein, and Robert Burrowes. My thesis assessed the extent to which political and psychological factors play important roles in promoting positive outcomes in negotiation episodes, using an experimental bargaining simulation. In the late 1970s, working on contracts for the United States Department of State and Department of Defense with a small group of creative researchers, I conducted statistical analyses and developed forecasting models that supported government planning for upcoming Middle East peace negotiations that led to the Camp David Accords in 1978 and subsequent peace talks concerning the Israeli-Palestinian conflict.

In the early 1990s, I served for three years as the Project Leader for the Processes of International Negotiation (PIN) project at the International Institute for Applied Systems Analysis in Laxenburg, Austria. The project took deep dives into many core negotiation concepts and processes to expand upon previous thinking by establishing international research networks that yielded a resurgence of studies and books on many key analytical and practical negotiation issues. It also served as an analytical resource for UN-sponsored international environmental negotiations taking place at that time.

In the mid-1990s through 2020, I conducted applied research projects for the United States Agency for International Development and the United Kingdom's Department for International Development, primarily on anti-corruption reform efforts in developing countries. As a part of these projects, I was able to conduct training workshops on negotiation and mediation mechanisms for local activist groups in several countries as relevant tools to ensure civil society inclusion in policy reform and get local governments to practice collaborative problem-solving to improve accountability and transparency in their decision-making and service delivery. And then, starting in 1996 to the present, as founding Editor-in-Chief of the journal *International Negotiation*, I supported the development of many thematic issues that focused on topics in need of further research.

Each of these experiences and projects opened up new questions for me about the negotiation system. They each reinforced the idea that the study of negotiation is not merely an academic endeavor, but it has serious practical implications as well. How to make the transition from theory to practice is difficult, as many policymakers and negotiators do not keep up with the research community's efforts. This book examines the state of the field writ broadly, focusing on particular negotiation dynamics where a lot of research has been conducted, but where there are still many questions to be resolved and ideas to be analyzed in support of enhancing theory as well as practice.

Yet Unanswered Questions

Given the wide breadth of issues, domains, frameworks, and approaches, the dynamics of the international negotiation system still leave a wide door open for study. The essays in this book examine these dynamics and seek to extend these key negotiation drivers to stimulate further research and analysis that can help both academics and practitioners in their difficult work.

In Chapter 2, the negotiation system is explored as a unique platform upon which practitioners can try out creative solutions and assess the viability of "what if" hypotheses to resolve problems and manage conflicts. Negotiation, after all, *is* an experiment.

The possibilities for practical negotiators to engineer their situation, especially one that is at a stalemate, to break open the talks in a new way and reach a mutually acceptable solution, are enticing. Chapter 3 assesses various situational levers and creativity heuristics that negotiators can apply to transform an impasse into an agreement.

Chapter 4 examines the impact of psychological factors on the negotiation process. Negotiator personalities, perceptions, and the use of power are assessed using data from simulation experiments. The results are enlightening but suggest additional research paths that need to be pursued.

One of the principal tasks in the pre-negotiation phase is to assess the other parties before anyone gets to the negotiating table. How able and reliable are the other nations? Chapter 5 looks at some straightforward ways of assessing and measuring their negotiation capacity and the ease with which countries practice negotiations – what we call a "negotiability" quotient.

Many international negotiations can be assessed to be failures because they missed out on some important provisions – especially, explicit formulas on how to implement the negotiated agreement. Chapter 6 examines how the negotiation process should ensure that such provisions are designed as part of every negotiated agreement.

After a negotiation agreement is reached, how it is implemented is a critical process unto itself. Chapter 7 addresses the role of power asymmetry and other factors that push the implementation of negotiated provisions forward or place obstacles in the way of implementation.

The information age has introduced targeted decision support systems for policymakers and negotiators, but the problem is in getting these innovative tools accepted and used by practitioners. Chapter 8 examines how these special tools can be engineered and introduced to ensure their application.

In Chapter 9, we examine how citizens and businesses in many countries can be incorporated into the negotiation process as active stakeholders in negotiated rulemaking efforts. Cultural and administrative issues may hinder the efficacy of this mechanism, but steps can be taken to enhance its implementation.

Chapter 10 examines the growing inclusion of civil society in advocacy efforts in developing countries, and how negotiation and mediation approaches can be used to enhance their effectiveness vis-à-vis their local governments.

Non-central governments are increasingly given the authority and legitimacy to conduct negotiations with their counterparts from other countries to resolve problems that affect their citizens on either side of the border. Chapter 11 explores these paradiplomatic efforts to assess how different they are from traditional international negotiations and what can be learned to strengthen them in the future.

Core values that drive international negotiation processes can lead to justice and fairness in the process and outcome – win-win solutions – though too often, self-interested values result in win-lose solutions. There are yet other negotiation contexts where altruistic values ought to be front and center, such as humanitarian negotiations, that should result in a "care-win" outcome, but these sometimes get diverted by self-interest. Chapter 12 examines what can be done under these conditions.

Despite the pledge to "do no harm," negotiations that aim to strengthen developing nations by providing foreign aid sometimes result in inequitable development trajectories that produce instability and violent conflict in the recipient countries. Chapter 13 assesses how such negotiations need to be more sensitive to these unanticipated outcomes by adjusting negotiation strategies and ensuring inclusive participation by all stakeholders.

The process of negotiation is typically applied to solve problems and manage or resolve conflicts; that is its good side. But sometimes, the process has also been harnessed to support negative goals that prolong conflict or promote corruption. Chapter 14 analyzes these tensions.

Most negotiation processes do not end after one round of talks. Most, especially in the international realm, go through a series of iterations – the making of agreements, adjustments to those agreements, and entire renegotiations as the context changes over time. Chapter 15 examines the step-by-step negotiation process and how to prepare for and adjust to the inevitability of continuous incremental bargaining.

The final chapter – Chapter 16 – pulls together the conclusions of the preceding essays and lays out a future agenda for researchers and practitioners in the negotiation field.

I hope the ideas and thoughts in these essays will propel creative thinking and yield the needed research and analysis.

Note

1 Kremenyuk, Victor, ed. (1991). *International Negotiation*. San Francisco: Jossey-Bass.

2
NEGOTIATION IS A CREATIVE EXPERIMENT

"In the long run, all solutions are only experiments."[1] Here, Zartman is referring to the outcomes of the negotiation process, in particular, those concerned with ending civil wars. He is saying that negotiation is an experimental process in and of itself, and as such, it produces potential solutions that are worthy of trying, but not definitively effective. These solutions can be considered to be hypotheses that still need to be tested to see if they really work. Just as much, the negotiation process is an experiment, where different strategies and options are considered in an experimental way. Those strategies that appear reasonable to reduce the conflict or problem, that might persist over the longer term, and that can yield a mutually achieved agreement are worth pursuing and comparing, but are not 100% guaranteed.

Experiments commonly are conducted to support or reject a hypothesis. They look at the cause-and-effect, the "what if," relationship among factors and manipulate some of these factors to determine if they, in fact, yield the expected result. When considering most experiments in the context of the negotiation process, one thinks of bargaining games used to train students or negotiation simulations used to prepare diplomatic analysts or practitioners. But the experimentation that we want to discuss in this essay is not about a game used for training purposes, but of the real-life negotiation process – its intentions and how it operates.

Experiments

Experiments are systematic mechanisms designed to test a hypothesis using scientific methods. They typically start with a hypothesis, which is a proposed explanation for an occurrence or outcome that can have its roots in logic, perception, or previous observations. It is usually stated as an if-then relationship. In the context of negotiations, a hypothesis might be, for example, "If we offer

DOI: 10.4324/9781003314400-2

positive incentives – like official recognition or increased trade – to the other party, then they are more likely to agree to wind down tensions at the border." The hypothesis can usually be stated as testing whether an independent variable, in this case, the presentation of a specific negotiation tactic, strategy, or formula, for example, has an expected effect on a dependent variable, for example, a change in the other party's perspective on the situation and, eventually, on the negotiated outcome.

In preparation for a negotiation, or in the heat of the negotiation process, such hypotheses can be generated by each negotiating team based on their own interests, the power context, and their perception of what the other side might be willing to accept. They can also arise from analyses or dialogues with the other parties which reveal their interests, opportunities, and weaknesses, etc., and what might lead them to change their positions. Examples from earlier negotiations with the same parties or similar situations in other countries can provide hints at what hypotheses could be tested. The negotiating environment, after all, is one in which it is anticipated that parties may change their minds and their future actions based on the dialogue, the offers and counteroffers, and incentives and risks that are presented at the table.

Once the hypothesis is formulated, the experimental testing of the hypothesis begins. Negotiation experiments are not like laboratory experiments that have a control group to be compared with. They are field experiments, conducted in real-world situations, meaning that there are always extraneous factors that can influence the outcome for which you have no control over. Field experiments allow practitioners to examine how manipulation of the independent variable – the new tactic or formula – leads to changes in the dependent variable, the outcome of the experiment. While the results of field experiments suffer from the lack of extraneous or control factors, they do offer a degree of generalizability.

The negotiation experiment is highly complex. While it can start out being an experiment with only two players who are testing one hypothesis each, it can quickly evolve into a multi-hypothesis experiment, even at the bilateral level, with multiple tests being examined simultaneously. Add a few more parties and the playing field of experimentation becomes very large and complex.

In the end, the negotiation process can be characterized as a *grand* field experiment – in fact, multiple overlapping experiments – that start with hypotheses developed by each engaged party about how they might best achieve their desired outcome and motivate behavioral change in the other parties by promoting independent variables – using certain strategies and tactics. Through numerous interactions, it can be seen whether each hypothesis has been validated or not, hopefully as the parties come closer to developing a workable formula for the negotiated outcome.

Historically, the negotiation process is one of the oldest social experiments, short of warfare, where you test different options and strategies to get what you want in a peaceful manner.

Creativity Hypotheses

At the heart of most of these negotiation experiments are creative hypotheses, introducing approaches to problem-solving that may not have been tried or tested previously. The negotiation experiment is one way to use such creative ideas by embedding them in hypotheses that can be tested through the negotiation process and implementation of its outcomes. Negotiation experiments allow practitioners to attempt new and creative ideas and see if they will resolve or manage the conflict or problem at hand.

Mooney and Taylor distinguish between four conceptual approaches, each one providing a different perspective on explaining creativity.[2] One school of thought views creativity primarily as a personality trait, an attribute embodied in the cognitive and emotional style of a person. For this school, the creative person is special and endowed with special gifts. A second school views creativity as a special type of problem-solving search process, a deliberate iterative process that requires time and gestation to reach creative conclusions.[3] For this school, creativity is a process that can be taught. A third school evaluates the environment in which creative thinking occurs, suggesting that a special atmosphere may be responsible for stimulating and sustaining creativity. A fourth school views creativity as the product of behavior and thought, as an output of a creative process. For this essay, we focus our attention on the second school – creativity as a problem-solving process.

Stein offers an operational definition of creativity: Creativity is a process by which persons develop novel outcomes that are acceptable, useful, and satisfying to a given audience.[4] The process is one of hypothesis formulation, hypothesis testing, and communication within an environment that, at best, promotes creativity, and at a minimum, does not inhibit its use. The outcome is usually a new way of perceiving things, a new possibility or opportunity, or a new path or direction to explore. It is always a step-level change from the way things are today. Importantly, Stein's definition does not imply that creativity is the sole province of geniuses; rather, creativity is available to everyone and can be acquired as a skill through training.

Stein's definition is probably the most useful for the study of creativity in negotiation; it is possible to observe, recognize, and categorize creativity in the proposals placed on the table, those that offer a new vision of a future changed reality. The creative process is a problem-solving search process which consciously attempts to break through current limitations and deliberately fills in gaps in thinking.

Stein's integration of the literature describes creative thinking as proceeding through the basic stages of the typical problem-solving process – hypothesis formation, hypothesis testing, and communication of the results. However, Stein insists that creative thinking is more irrational and takes greater leaps of judgment into the unknown than is typical in simple problem-solving behavior. Indeed, Stein describes the heart of the creative process as being driven by three factors: inspiration, intuition, and aesthetic feeling. While these factors can be observed, the processes by which they operate are quite difficult to describe, let alone explain. Other researchers, on the other hand, contend that creativity is truly embedded in the problem-solving paradigm.[5] While unexplainable flashes of insight do occur, creative thinking is primarily a deliberate iterative search process that requires time and gestation to reach creative conclusions. It is a process that can be tracked and explained.

Negotiation Freshness

Impasses in negotiations often require creative and novel proposals to extricate the parties from the quagmire of stalemate. The term "freshness" seems to bear a useful connotation for this impasse-breaking concept that we are trying to understand. A fresh resolution, in the face of impasse, is one that introduces creativity and novelty, either in the offer itself, in the construction of the overall formula, or in the general approach or packaging of the offer. Old offers and approaches clearly have not worked. A novel direction is required – one that is fresh and offers new possibilities. This freshness can be stated in hypotheses that can be tested through negotiation experiments.

There is an element of discovery involved in freshness. Behaviorally, it requires a renewed search for options. The process of discovery results in finding something that may not have been seen before in the same light, something nonobvious.

Strategy Freshness

Freshness in strategy is not to be confused with ripeness for resolution, despite their common organic metaphor.[6] Ripeness for resolution is stimulated by the perception of parties to a conflict of a mutually hurting stalemate and their identification of a way out of this stalemate. It is the recognition of an opportunity for solution. Freshness, on the other hand, describes the novel strategies, proposals, and approaches that introduce new insights and new opportunities for agreement in negotiation that were not previously available or apparent to the parties. Freshness in negotiation strategy development is a function of creativity.

The importance of creativity in resolving impasses has been recognized by negotiation researchers and practitioners. Raiffa refers to creative compensation arrangements as a strategy to develop acceptable formulas in stalemated negotiations.[7] Druckman, Husbands, and Johnston discuss the importance of "frame-breaking changes" at critical turning points in negotiation.[8] These constitute step-level changes in the negotiation life cycle that enable the discussion to take on fresh and novel approaches – to break out of old patterns. From a practitioner's perspective, Benedick identifies the benefits of creative approaches in environmental negotiations.[9] Kidder describes the potential utility of novel proposals in a labor-management stalemate.[10] And Stein refers

14 Negotiation Is a Creative Experiment

to the dramatic and innovative approaches used by President Carter to break the age-old deadlock between Egypt and Israel leading to the 1978 Camp David Accords.[11] Despite this recognition, few researchers have examined the impact of creativity on the negotiation process and outcome systematically and empirically.

Pruitt has directly addressed the issue of creativity in negotiation strategy.[12] He views the introduction of creative techniques as a way of achieving integrative, positive-sum agreements. His typology of five creative approaches to strategy development all require a refocusing of the original negotiation problem, the development of a new and changed reality. These include:

- Broadening the pie: Increasing the size of the resource being allocated.
- Nonspecific compensation: Making payoffs to the other side in some other currency that it finds beneficial.
- Logrolling: Trading off one issue for another.
- Cost cutting: Minimizing costs incurred by one party in accepting what the other side wants.
- Bridging: Satisfying the true interests of both sides.

Freshness may appear in a new offer, in a new approach, or in both. It is possible that an offer may be fresh but the approach is old, or vice versa. From a practical perspective, a fresh offer or approach must be perceived as fresh by all parties in the negotiation. It must be viewed as breaking new ground in a positive way by all sides. Otherwise, if it is viewed as one-sided, it will not serve its purpose, that is, to break the impasse in negotiation. Hare and Naveh show this to be the case in the Camp David Summit.[13] By coding first-hand accounts of the 1978 Camp David talks using Bale's Field Diagrams and Taylor's five levels of creativity, Hare and Naveh identified proposals that could be considered inventive and innovative which served to break the deadlock between the Egyptians and Israelis. Several proposals that rated high on the creativity scale did indeed result in a breakthrough between the parties; other proposals that scored low on the creativity scale did not conclude in agreement. Overall, the authors suggest that creative approaches were effective because they redefined the relationship between the two parties.

Fresh offers or approaches can be the product of multi-party endeavors or unilateral initiatives. Parties who are bargaining in good faith, but who are caught up in stalemated talks, may be willing to work together cooperatively to develop creative ways out of their mutual impasse. A multilateral approach to developing fresh offers presents an opportunity to ensure that all parties feel a sense of ownership over the new directions. On the other hand, one party, by itself, may have that flash of insight required to deduce a fresh proposal or approach. In this case, the other parties must also be convinced that the proposal or approach is truly fresh and novel, providing a new and positive path out of the current quagmire.

Process Freshness

The utility of fresh, creative processes may be critical at three stages of negotiation. A major problem in intractable conflicts is, first, getting the parties to the table. Creativity processes can stimulate a change in attitudes or definitions of the problem enabling the parties to accept negotiation as the primary vehicle for conflict resolution. This adjustment of attitudes or reframing of the conflict is especially important in emotion-laden issues involved in ethnic and national identity conflicts, for example. This is a pre-negotiation phase in which each party, operating independently, may benefit from the use of creative thought processes to move away in a step-level fashion from old ways of thinking about the conflict.

If the parties can be convinced to come to the table, the next phase is for them to come together to present ideas and, possibly, set an agenda for negotiation. This is a bi- or multi-lateral phase in which creative processes can help all the parties develop a new and joint redefinition of the problem. A mutual understanding of the conflict is a first step in establishing a common framework from which the parties can move from impasse to solution. As well, creative processes can aid parties in thinking of new formulas or principles upon which to base a solution.

If an agenda is established for negotiation, then the parties can proceed into a third phase, that of negotiation itself. Here, creative processes can help in the problem-solving process of continual redefinition of the problem as new positions, strategies, demands, and concessions are presented as hypotheses that can be tested through a negotiation experiment. Creative processes can also assist in generating new options for solution.

The Criteria of Freshness

How can a creative process or strategy be distinguished from a noncreative one? Three criteria can be established to define creativity in negotiation:

1. Positive sum: The process or strategy must present an integrative solution that all parties view as increasing their benefits. This attribute focuses on equity and fairness.
2. Problem redefinition: The process or strategy must transform the existing representation of the problem so that old patterns that have resulted in stalemate can be broken. The bargaining space is thereby redefined. This attribute deals with how the proposal changes the negotiation milieu.
3. Break with the past: The process or strategy must present a totally new way of solving the impasse that does not reflect past solutions and experience, but is truly novel and innovative. This attribute focuses on how the proposal employs new and different mechanisms to achieve its ends.

These criteria emphasize the novel, innovative, and mutually beneficial nature of fresh, creative processes, and strategies in negotiation.

Examples

To demonstrate how negotiation can be viewed as a creative experimental phenomenon of fresh strategies and outcomes, three cases of stalemated negotiations are presented in which creative hypotheses, offered in the context of experimentation, appear to have helped untangle the impasse and get the talks on their way again.

Paris Negotiations on Vietnam

The secret, as well as public, negotiations to end the hostilities in Vietnam came to a standstill in October 1971.[14] The North Vietnamese wanted to discredit the effectiveness of the Vietnamization program and were unhappy over the seemingly unshakeable commitment taken by the United States to keep President Nguyen Van Thieu in power in the South. The United States, on the other hand, felt it had received no signs of faithful reciprocity from the North after pursuing a course of sincere concession-making for about one year. In addition, there were serious signs of misperception and mistrust on both sides that cast doubt on intentions and made stalemate more likely.

As Zartman indicates, this impasse in the negotiations necessarily required a change in the ambient reality surrounding the talks. This change took two forms. Along the military dimension, there was a major escalation initiated by Hanoi – the Spring offensive of March 1972 – followed rapidly by the American bombing of Hanoi and Haiphong and the mining of Haiphong harbor. These actions together succeeded in reinforcing the perceptions on both sides that a situation of military stalemate had been achieved and that the only way out of the conflict was a negotiated settlement.

On a political level, US National Security Advisor Henry Kissinger introduced what could be considered a fresh and creative approach to the renewed negotiations, which Szulc views as the real turning point in the negotiation. First, he sought out the Soviets, a third party but committed ally of Hanoi, as a sounding board for new proposals and as a channel to right some old misperceptions. Second, he introduced a major step-level change in US policy – a proposal for a tripartite council to govern the South until elections, to include the existing Saigon government, neutral elements, and the Vietcong. This fresh offer provided the United States with maintenance of the Thieu government, while also providing Hanoi with explicit representation by the Vietcong in the provisional government. Zartman indicates that this proposal was greeted with astonishment and surprise by the Soviets.

Breaking of the impasse and ultimate convergence in this case may be viewed as a function of some basic experimentation with the negotiation environment – some military changes that reminded the other side of strong commitments to one's interests and some political changes that employed elements of freshness. Kissinger was playing a somewhat risky and unusual strategy by using the Soviets as a go-between with Hanoi. Rather than working directly with the other party in the talks, he sought the good offices of a certainly skeptical third party. He also used an element of surprise and innovation in presenting the new tripartite offer.

Both of these strategies satisfy the freshness criteria. They offered a new way to achieve a satisfactory positive sum solution – both sides obtained representation in a future government. They redefined the problem by suggesting an innovative form of joint rule, whereas previously the problem was defined in a zero-sum fashion. Finally, these strategies certainly broke with past approaches – by emphasizing enhanced communications with the enemy's key ally and dropping of the US commitment to Thieu.

Panama Canal Negotiations

Between 1969 and 1972, the negotiations between the United States and Panama over the future status of the Panama Canal that had begun during the Johnson administration in 1964 were at an impasse.[15] Once serious joint discussions ended, the stalemate period was characterized by joint hostile escalations – an escalation of US demands reversing previous concessions made and an escalation of Panamanian threats of violence. Both President Richard Nixon and Commander Omar Torrijos had dug their heels in deep.

Torrijos was the one who stepped forward to introduce a fresh and creative approach for breaking out of this impasse. The new concept that he presented, which changed the ambient reality of the negotiations, was to internationalize the canal issue. Backed by a strong coalition of Latin American states that he had been courting, Torrijos escalated what was essentially a bilateral conflict by giving it a multilateral audience at the United Nations Security Council. In early 1973, he was successful in getting a resolution passed there that urged a new treaty be concluded between the United States and Panama. This resolution would not have been so spectacular if it were not for the one-sided vote that promulgated it. Thirteen members of the council voted in favor of the resolution, the United Kingdom abstained, and the United States cast the sole negative vote.

Torrijos' fresh experimental strategy significantly altered the nature of the audience attentive to the canal negotiations. Rather than having to battle the United States alone, Torrijos' novel strategy shifted the balance of power in the direction of Panama by transforming the nature of the talks into a major North-South conflict issue where the United States was clearly in the minority.

This strategy meets the threefold criteria for creative and fresh approaches. The power asymmetry between Panama and the United States presented an incalculably wide gap, and the internationalization strategy of Torrijos tended to even out this power imbalance. Whereas the United States had previously controlled a zero-sum outcome, there was now a possibility to distribute the benefits more evenly between the two principals. Torrijos' strategy also significantly redefined the problem. What was previously a bilateral problem was now a salient North-South problem in which the United States had to deal in a much more conscious and constrained fashion when making future demands and concessions. Finally, the Torrijos strategy was a major break with past approaches, an experimental hypothesis. He introduced an influential third party into the process – the United Nations – that emphasized the seriousness of the situation and escalated the interest of the United States in resolving the conflict.

Middle East Negotiations: Unending Experimentation

For 70 years, the Israeli-Palestinian conflict has been the breeding ground for many negotiation experiments. They begin with hypotheses about what might work and they have been tested in the real world, but to date none have yielded successful outcomes. Despite their failure to produce a lasting solution, a few of these experiments stand out as interesting tests of creative hypotheses. In each of these experiments over time, the parties targeted different negotiation factors to see if that would produce better results.

Camp David Accords (1978)

The principal negotiation hypotheses behind the Camp David experiment were *process-based*. First, if a leading Arab state would reach out to Israel seeking to normalize relations that would push Israel to accept the offer. Second, if a third-party mediation context was designed that engaged Israel and a major Arab state, like Egypt, that could purportedly speak on behalf of the Palestinians – where the Palestinians would not have to participate directly – then Israel would likely agree. It would also take Egypt out of the conflict equation, moving the situation much further toward stabilization. Anwar Sadat's initiative to address the Israeli parliament in Jerusalem in November 1977 was a trigger suggesting Egypt's sincere interest in altering its contentious relationship with Israel. The Israelis picked up on this opportunity as anticipated. As soon as he became US president in early 1977, Jimmy Carter pushed many diplomatic attempts to rejuvenate the Geneva Middle East peace talks that had broken off in 1973; the desire for a mediated approach between Egypt and Israel that covered both the Palestinian issues and Egypt-Israel relations was of great interest to the United States. The two-part agreement that emerged from the Camp David talks in September 1978 covered a Middle East framework that resulted in an autonomous self-governing authority in the West Bank and Gaza Strip, as well as partial withdrawal of Israeli military from those territories. The second framework normalized relations between Egypt and Israel in return for the Sinai peninsula being restored to Egyptian control.

Oslo Accords (1993 and 1995)

The hypothesis motivating the negotiation experiment of the Oslo Accords was focused on the *process* and the *actors*. It was expected that a mediated process involving the directly conflicting parties could yield an agreement that could be successfully implemented. It was hypothesized that mutual recognition of the other side would break the long-held diplomatic taboos that had prevented positive movement since the Camp David Accords were signed. The Norwegians served as mediators who brought the Israelis and Palestinians to the table – initially as a Track Two effort, without government officials involved. Through Letters of Mutual Recognition, each side accepted the other – the Israelis accepted the Palestinian Liberation Organization (PLO) as the representative of the Palestinians, and the PLO renounced terrorism and recognized Israel's right to exist. An interim declaration of principles established a Palestinian Authority with provisions for limited self-government and a partial withdrawal of Israeli troops from Gaza and Jericho, among many other provisions. The United States provided support in implementing these accords, but the situation broke down a few years later with the onset of renewed conflict.

Abraham Accords (2020)

The main negotiation hypothesis backing up this negotiation experiment to agree to the Abraham Accords was primarily that *actors matter*. A secondary hypothesis was that each actor could be sold on the agreement with Israel if it was also promised some "mutually enticing opportunities."[16] If agreements can be forged between Israel and several Arab states – even if not with the Palestinians directly – it was hypothesized that the Middle East conflict will subside and, eventually, the Israelis and Palestinians might be coaxed to a peace agreement. By engaging with four Arab states in the Middle East – though not the frontline states in the Arab-Israeli conflict – the United States was able to convince them of the benefits of normalizing their relations with Israel. While normalization of relations with Israel was the primary feature of the agreements, there were side deals: for the United Arab Emirates, it was a halt to Israeli annexation plans of West Bank territories and promotion of active economic relations; for Bahrain, it was activation of trade and tourism initiatives; for Sudan, it was the offer of more US economic assistance; and for Morocco, it was US recognition of Moroccan sovereignty over the Western Sahara. By the end of 2020, each of these four Arab countries and Israel agreed to sign these agreements for normalization, with the hope of stabilizing the region over the longer term.

Directions for Future Research and Support for Practice

Creative experimentation in negotiation deserves attention by both the research and practitioner communities. As demonstrated in this essay, creative hypotheses can be an important element in explaining the dynamics of flexibility and impasse resolution, as well as a skill that can be trained in a practical sense. Several research directions can advance the study of the role and impact of creative approaches on the negotiation process and outcome.

Case Studies

Additional case studies of negotiation deadlocks that have been resolved through the use of creative solutions will serve to illustrate and describe how these techniques have been applied in the past. Interviews with and memoirs of the principal parties in a negotiation where creative approaches were experimented with could be the primary data sources. These case studies should describe the impasse situation, attempts to resolve the conflict — both creative and non-creative — and the short- and long-term effects of these proposals. A common framework will help to analyze these cases comparatively.

Correlates of Creativity

A more systematic, comparative assessment of creativity in negotiation is warranted. Such a study would examine empirically whether strategies classified as being creative are indeed more effective in resolving negotiation impasses than other types of strategies. It would identify which of the creative strategies are most effective under certain circumstances and it would assess the situational and processual correlates of creative strategies. First, an inventory of historical negotiation stalemates would need to be generated within a particular issue area, such as arms control or the environment. Second, criteria against which creative approaches can be identified and distinguished from other approaches need to be developed and data gathered on each case in the inventory. This would include characteristics of the impasse itself, descriptive attributes of the approach, how it was generated and implemented, and its relative effectiveness in terms of breaking the impasse. Third, additional situational and process factors should be collected as these are hypothesized to stimulate or inhibit the impact of creative approaches. Data sources can include richly descriptive accounts of the negotiations, memoirs, and interviews with the principals. Finally, correlational analyses can be applied to determine the factors that covary with, stimulate, or inhibit the use and effectiveness of creative strategies.

Simulation Experiments

Experimental simulation games can be designed to test the effect of applying creativity heuristics in impasse situations. Under controlled conditions, the utility of alternate creative techniques can be introduced into a deadlocked negotiation scenario to determine their direction and degree of impact on achieving positive-sum integrative solutions. Several activities, more directly in support of improved negotiation practice, should also be considered.

Stimulating Freshness through Practitioner Training

Stein indicates that the research literature is sufficiently rich in its understanding of creative persons that we are capable now, and confident, in recommending techniques that will help stimulate creativity in others.[17] We understand many of the personality and cognitive factors that yield creative thinking. He, as well as others, in fact, provide detailed descriptions and empirical evaluations of techniques appropriate for motivating individual and group creativity under a variety of circumstances. Many of these techniques may be appropriate to stimulating and experimenting with freshness in stalemated negotiations.

There are four basic conditions that must be satisfied to stimulate creativity. They include working within an atmosphere that facilitates free-wheeling and stream of consciousness thinking; developing a large quantity of focused ideas; building upon ideas that have been previously identified; and deferring evaluation of those ideas that are proposed, so that individuals are not inhibited and all ideas are viewed initially as acceptable.

Together these criteria provide the opportunity for individuals to perform creatively. Certainly, not all negotiators are innate creative personalities, but they can be taught. Training of negotiators in the use of creativity would include recognition of opportunities to be creative, the development of environments that facilitate the application of creative approaches, and the design and implementation of creative strategies.

There are many techniques used to stimulate creativity, which are more or less appropriate depending upon the circumstance and issue. These heuristics can be classified into three categories where they have been found useful in stimulating creative thinking. All three categories, described below, are meaningful from the point of view of diagnosing the impasse environment and developing fresh offers and approaches that can be tested in negotiation situations.

Problem Understanding and Structuring

The creativity heuristics in this category are particularly useful in performing diagnoses of the negotiation environment – the current and anticipated positions, interests, and strategies of negotiating parties.

- Analogies: It is often easier to place new information into proper context and assess its importance if it can be compared to other situations and circumstances by analogy.
- Roleplaying: This technique helps by putting the negotiator into the shoes of the other party to facilitate better understanding of their intentions, motivation, and interests.
- Gaming: This technique is a more active version of roleplaying in that the negotiator can assess, through behavioral simulation, how different parties might "play out" their roles within a given scenario.
- Flowcharting: This technique offers the negotiator a structured way to display facts – in a timeline, on a map, or as inputs and outputs of a process – to better understand the underlying structure of the impasse.

- Association Matrix: This technique also helps the negotiator understand the impasse situation better by structuring his perceptions of it. A matrix is developed that compares all of the events that have and may yet occur within a given timeframe. The events are listed on both axes of the matrix. The cells are then filled in by the negotiator to identify whether there was a positive, negative, or null influence of each event on the others in a pairwise fashion.
- Link Analysis: This technique sorts evidence in a structured and revealing way to uncover nonobvious linkages and relationships between entities and events. It can be used by negotiators to understand the nature of the impasse and the juxtapositions of interests and positions of the various stakeholders.

Hypothesis Generation

This grouping of creativity heuristics is targeted at generating meaningful alternatives for impasse-breaking strategies.

- Brainstorming: This is a group technique to generate new ideas and explore various solution options in which there is strong emphasis on not evaluating, criticizing, or judging these ideas which might tend to inhibit creative thought.
- Attribute Listing: This technique involves the identification of the major attributes of a desired negotiation outcome. The negotiator elaborates on all of the possible values that each attribute can take on and thereby considers new alternatives.
- Morphological Analysis: This technique involves dividing a problem into its component parts and then subdividing each of these further. By looking at each of these basic dimensions in combination, the negotiator can assess systematically many alternatives for action, some which can be easily dismissed, some that will be obvious, and others that will be nonobvious and intriguing.
- If-Then Chains: In this technique, negotiators develop a decision tree that elaborates all possible actions – both within and outside their control – and their likely consequences downstream.
- Alternate Hypotheses: Using this technique, the negotiator generates alternate hypotheses and explanations of the current impasse. If the alternate hypotheses are tested and disproven, the primary hypothesis is thereby strengthened.

Hypothesis Testing through Experimentation

These creativity heuristics help the negotiator test, evaluate, and conduct tradeoffs of alternative hypotheses and strategies.

- Categorization: Using this heuristic, the negotiator creates a category system in which fragments of information are placed over time. It can help in identifying possible patterns and trends.

- Extrapolation: This technique extends and projects the predicted consequences if events are slowed down, sped up, or kept at the same rate.
- Tradeoffs: This technique evaluates alternative hypotheses against a set of established criteria. Hypotheses can then be prioritized in terms of likelihood based upon satisfaction of these criteria.
- Outcome Utilities: Multiple decision options can be evaluated by comparing their likely downstream consequences.

Negotiation Support Tools that Stimulate Creativity

Some tools can be provided to negotiators, outside of a training program, that might help to stimulate creativity. Raiffa believes that decision support systems, such as decision analysis, can facilitate creative thinking.[18] Such tools can help negotiators generate and evaluate options in a systematic way, oftentimes freeing them from past ways of thinking.

Roles for Mediation and Third Parties

Many creativity techniques, and the development of a facilitating environment for the presentation of creative proposals, can be promoted by mediators or other third parties. While the principals may not be able to offer fresh suggestions, it is often extremely appropriate for a third party to do so.

Conclusions

The world is continually beset by a host of intractable conflicts. Many age-old impasses are never resolved, while new stalemates join the ranks. These conflicts range the gamut in terms of issue and intensity: the Arab-Israeli conflict stands out here. Creative experiments may be viable options to resolve these conflicts. Systematic research on the effectiveness of creative strategies, as well as practitioner training to identify appropriate opportunities for the use of these approaches, are sorely needed.

Notes

1. Zartman, I. W., ed. (1995). *Elusive Peace: Negotiating an End to Civil Wars*. Washington, DC: The Brookings Institution: 24.
2. Mooney, R. L. (1963). "A Conceptual Model for Integrating Four Approaches to the Identification of Creative Talent," in C. W. Taylor and F. Barron, editors, *Scientific Creativity: Its Recognition and Development*. New York: John Wiley & Sons; Taylor, C. (1988). "Various Approaches to and Definitions of Creativity," in R. Sternberg, ed., *The Nature of Creativity*. Cambridge: Cambridge University Press.
3. Tardif, T. and R. Sternberg (1988). "What Do We Know About Creativity?" in R. Sternberg, ed., *The Nature of Creativity*. Cambridge: Cambridge University Press; Weisberg, R. (1988). "Problem Solving and Creativity," in R. Sternberg, ed., *The Nature of Creativity*. Cambridge: Cambridge University Press.

4. Stein, M. I. (1974). *Stimulating Creativity: Individual Procedures*. New York: Academic Press.
5. Tardif and Sternberg (1988), op.cit.; Weisberg (1988), op.cit.
6. Zartman, I. W. (1986). "Ripening Conflict, Ripe Moment, Formula, and Mediation," in *Perspectives on Negotiation: Four Case Studies and Interpretations*. Washington, DC: Center for the Study of Foreign Affairs, Foreign Service Institute, U.S. Department of State.
7. Raiffa, H. (1991). "Contributions of Applied Systems Analysis to International Negotiation," in V. Kremenyuk, ed., *International Negotiation: Analysis. Approaches. Issues*. San Francisco, CA: Jossey-Bass Publishers.
8. Druckman, D., J. Husbands, and K. Johnston (1991). "Turning Points in the INF Negotiations," *Negotiation Journal* (January).
9. Benedick, R. (1991). "Lessons for Practitioners," Presentation at the conference on International Environmental Negotiation at the International Institute for Applied Systems Analysis, Processes of International Negotiation Project, Laxenburg, Austria.
10. Kidder, L. (1987). "Breaking a Stalemate with a Creative Alternative," *Negotiation Journal* (April).
11. Stein, J. (1989). "Prenegotiation in the Arab-Israeli Conflict: The Paradoxes of Success and Failure," in J. Stein, ed., *Getting to the Table*. Baltimore, MD: Johns Hopkins University Press.
12. Pruitt, D. (1987). "Creative Approaches to Negotiation," in D. Sandole and I. Sandole-Staroste, eds., *Conflict Management and Problem Solving: Interpersonal to International Applications*. London: Frances Pinter Publishers.
13. Hare, A. P. and D. Naveh (1985). "Creative Problem Solving: Camp David Summit, 1978," *Small Group Behavior* 16,2: 123–138.
14. Zartman, I. W. (1983b). "Reality, Image, and Detail: The Paris Negotiations, 1969-1973," in I. W. Zartman, editor, *The 50% Solution*. New Haven, CT: Yale University Press; Szulc, T. (1974). "How Kissinger Did It: Behind the Vietnam Cease-Fire Agreement," *Foreign Policy* 15 (Summer).
15. Habeeb, W. M. and I. W. Zartman (1986). "The Panama Canal Negotiations." Washington, DC: Foreign Policy Institute, School of Advanced International Studies, The Johns Hopkins University.
16. Zartman, I. William (2000). "Ripeness: The Hurting Stalemate and Beyond," in Paul C. Stern and Daniel Druckman, editors, *International Conflict Resolution After the Cold War*. Washington, DC: National Research Council.
17. Stein (1974), op.cit.
18. Raiffa, H. (1982). *The Art and Science of Negotiation*. Cambridge, MA: Belknap Press.

3
ENGINEERING NEGOTIATION SITUATIONS FOR IMPROVED OUTCOMES

Negotiators can adjust and engineer the context in which their talks take place with the hope of making them more productive and successful. The principal questions for negotiators are what to do, when, and how. To "engineer" the situation implies skillful planning, shaping, and modification of the circumstances to produce a desired result. A genetic biologist, for example, might engineer genetic material to yield a vaccine with new properties. Scientists on the Space Shuttle might engineer the atmospheric and gravitational conditions in an experiment to test their impact on crystal formation. In this sense, it also may be possible in a very practical way, to carefully engineer the international negotiation situation so that it is more likely to possess the conditions and prerequisites that will produce improved outcomes. Engineering invents useful products and processes based upon scientific principles and requires a joint understanding of the science *and* the needs of consumers. So too, negotiators may be able to play active roles in engineering their environment for success, if more targeted research is conducted on situational factors that shape and mold facilitative conditions.

Certainly, we are concerned here with engineering *human* processes, not physical principles. But the analogy is still relevant. Experienced international negotiators have always sought to modify and manipulate negotiation situations, structures, and strategies to maximize their interests in bargaining and reach mutually acceptable agreements. Their efforts to change the negotiation conditions to their benefit typically are based on their practical skill, intuition, instinct, and experience. Foreign Minister Holst of Norway, describing the talks leading to the Oslo breakthrough in the Israeli-Palestinian conflict, suggested that the determining factors responsible for the parties overcoming their long-term impasse were primarily situational.[1] The private venue, the secrecy surrounding the talks, keeping the negotiations out of the limelight of publicity, and the growing personal relationships among the participants were, in his mind,

DOI: 10.4324/9781003314400-3

the critical situational catalysts which were carefully engineered to produce the breakthrough. But such efforts are not always successful and these techniques are not always portable to other negotiations or negotiators.

A more scientific and systematic approach can be taken. Relevant, though conceptual, findings in the existing body of research literature can provide the basis for further analyses that seek to identify influential situational factors under realistic international conditions. This includes the need to analyze the effects of multiple situational factors simultaneously. On the basis of such research, scientific cues for negotiators can be defined, indicating the appropriate factors which, if modified and shaped by the negotiators under a variety of circumstances, are likely to make the negotiation environment more conducive to successful outcomes. Effective negotiating, in this sense, is not only having proper strategies, being persuasive, or being a good problem-solver; it also implies being a good engineer and modifier of the situation – making sure that the playing field is laid out in the most beneficial way.

What we are missing to date is sufficient research to establish a scientific foundation for this engineering approach. Investigators have a good understanding of both basic research findings that exist and the needs of practical negotiators. The challenge is to conduct more systematic research using realistic conditions that can provide the basis for applied guidance to negotiation practitioners on how they might engineer negotiation situations to improve outcomes.

This essay examines two specific ways of operationalizing this engineering approach to negotiations. In the first part, we seek to uncover the complex packages of situational factors in negotiation that tend to induce flexible bargaining behavior, that is, decisions to compromise or problem-solve. Preliminary findings already suggest that it is possible to identify systematically such packages of situational factors over which negotiators have control or can manipulate.[2]

In the second part, we seek to identify how particular types of intervention – using creative reasoning approaches and, perhaps, third party engagement – can be used to improve the likelihood of successful negotiation outcomes. When negotiations are at an impasse, creative ideas are essential to restarting the process, but often this catalyst must be introduced into the situation by third parties. Here we analyze the empirical impact of such new ways of thinking on engineering the negotiation process and outcome.

Further research can test these hypotheses under controlled, but realistic circumstances. This research approach enables the experimenter, like the negotiator, to manipulate various situational factors. The results will suggest the conditions under which specific attempts to engineer the situation will be more prone to succeed.

Engineering the Situation for Bargaining Flexibility

Position change in negotiation is influenced by the way bargainers react to a variety of factors in the situation as well as the broader context in which talks are embedded. Results of many experiments make evident the importance of situational variables in driving the bargaining process toward or away from satisfactory settlements.[3] Examples of important situational variables are the type of pre-negotiation planning (strategizing or studying the issues), the extent to which the bargainer is accountable to team members or constituents, concession rates of the other parties, the presence or absence of constituents or other interested parties during bargaining, time pressures induced by deadlines, whether salient coordinating solutions exist, and the attractiveness of best alternatives to negotiated agreements (BATNAs). Unfortunately, relationships between these variables and bargaining behavior have been analyzed, by and large, from data collected from students engaged in relatively simple bargaining games. Much less is known about the influence of these variables on bargaining flexibility in such complex settings as international negotiation.

If negotiators can engineer these situational factors, it may improve bargainer flexibility. Druckman describes an investigation of the effects of many situational variables on decisions to make compromises in a simulated international negotiation concerned with international regulation of industrial emissions.[4] Sixteen situational factors that were found to be important in earlier experiments were embedded in the scenario at different stages through which the simulated negotiation unfolded. Each stage consisted of a description of the situation confronting the role-playing diplomat. Following each stage, participants were asked how far they were willing to move from their initial assigned positions on an issue, their desired outcome, and the likely outcome. Questions about tactics they would use and their perceptions of the situation were also included. Their responses were analyzed statistically for the combined impact of the situational variables at each stage.

The results showed that bargainers were less willing to compromise and were more competitive when operating within the set of situational factors that induced inflexibility. However, bargainers showed the expected shift from inflexible to flexible in the final stage when the situation was reengineered to produce flexible responses. In addition, using a paired comparisons exercise, particular aspects of the engineered situation could be ranked in terms of their relative impact on flexibility. Thus, it was possible to identify specific situational factors which, if engineered to be present or absent in a particular negotiation, would likely yield greater flexibility on the part of the negotiators.

Further research can use interactive simulations to examine the impact on negotiating flexibility of a variety of situational factors that reflect realistic international negotiation conditions. These situational factors can include, for example, conditions where the negotiator is a delegate (not the primary representative of his/her country), pre-negotiation planning that consists of studying the issues, familiarity with the opponent and amiable relations with them, holding the talks in a peripheral location and in an informal format, talks where only partial agreements are sought, situations where there is a power differential among the parties, the introduction of innovative leadership in the talks, negotiations where there is only light media coverage, instituting a firm deadline, and including third party intervention. Ultimately, the experiments should seek to compare the effects of these contrasting situations on process measures of convergence during negotiation and outcome measures of the types of agreements reached. Are these situational factors flexibility-inducing, inflexibility-inducing, or a mixed outcome?

Several other situational factors that could be tested include: (a) providing detailed information about each nation's budget, private sector pressure on the government negotiators, and administration policy orientations; (b) inserting an active mediator in each stage of the inflexibility scenarios; (c) mixing the scenarios by creating an endgame that is either conducive or non-conducive to agreement following earlier stages geared in the opposite direction; (d) producing coalition dynamics by creating blocs of nations aligned on one or more issues; and (e) reducing the number of variables embedded in each stage by highlighting only those variables shown to have relatively strong impacts in earlier experiments.

Creative Reasoning as Negotiation Engineering

An all-too-common frustration of peaceful attempts to resolve conflicts is the sudden occurrence of stalemate. At best, when this happens, bargaining eventually resumes due to a change in the situation or the efforts of a principal or third party. At worst, the conflict persists or intensifies. We want to understand if preliminary experimental results that identified and tested particular cognitive approaches, in particular, creative reasoning, can indeed help bargainers overcome impasses and, possibly, avoid them altogether.[5] Specifically, we want to examine the impacts of creative processes on the ability of deadlocked parties to reach agreement in negotiations and to evaluate the extent to which creative reasoning can reengineer the bargaining process by producing greater flexibility among the parties.

New cognitive orientations to the bargaining situation, represented by creative reasoning, offer the opportunity for novel solutions and breakthroughs which are needed in bargaining processes that have come to an impasse. It is often the parties' perceptions of risky and unfair outcomes that result in deadlock; creative reasoning by both parties can result in a significant reframing of these assessments to unleash new possibilities for successful solution. If such creative approaches can be introduced, taught or embedded into the bargaining process, bargainers could possess the mechanism to overcome and avert deadlocks and resolve conflicts efficiently.

How effective are such techniques in helping to get intractable negotiations "unstuck"? Can they really help conflicting parties think about their problems in novel ways, paving a new pathway to the negotiation table? And how can negotiators engineer the process to introduce creative reasoning as an active mechanism to adjust the perceptions of all parties and reach agreement in bargaining?

Creative reasoning is defined as the process by which novel outcomes are developed that are viewed as acceptable, useful, and satisfying to a given audience.[6]

The process is characterized as a problem-solving search to break through current limitations and deliberately fill gaps in thinking. Creative reasoning addresses difficult long-standing problems by finding novel ways of reframing and redefining the issues.[7] The outcome is usually a new way of perceiving things, a new possibility or opportunity, or a new path or direction to explore. It is always a step-level change from the way things are today. By focusing on creative thought processes, we can evaluate a highly portable skill and set of procedures that negotiators and mediators can learn and apply to engineer many situations when they approach impasses.

Future research can think of creativity as a process, one in which a particular cognitive reasoning process leads negotiators on new paths to search for mutually acceptable solutions. A promising creativity heuristic that is likely to be important in engineering the negotiation process is *analogical reasoning,* an inferential process by which a resemblance, similarity, or correspondence is perceived between two or more things. When using analogies, the problem is restated in terms of something very familiar. By comparison and through different lenses, new ideas and options may be generated.

How can analogical reasoning be introduced into the negotiation situation to transform a bargaining impasse? Traditionally, bargainers conduct problem solving by delving into the details through study and analysis of the issues, positions, demands, and offers. An analogical approach, on the other hand, can help negotiators move away from the given problem area, which may be emotion-laden and seen as intractable. Having greater separation from the conflict, they can reframe the problem and seek solutions with reference to other similar experiences. This digression from the problem-at-hand is what is hypothesized to bring new ideas and new opportunities to the table. Several psychological researchers have produced experimental results that suggest the value of introducing such analogical processes.[8]

Spector conducted a study that addresses the problem of how to *induce* creative thinking.[9] It addresses our concept of *engineering the negotiation situation* head-on by focusing on a particular problem-solving approach which, if introduced into an impasse situation, can help to restart negotiations. Thirty-six international graduate students participated in an experiment by playing negotiator roles in a scenario patterned after the impasse in 1989 between Slovakia and Hungary over building a joint hydroelectric project on the Danube River. In the experimental condition, half the subjects were trained in using analogical reasoning to solve problems; in the control condition, the other half of subjects were trained to use a traditional "study and analysis" form of problem solving. Both conditions proceeded through three rounds of unilateral planning and bilateral negotiations, seeking to overcome and resolve the impasse.

The results demonstrate clearly a statistically significant difference in the ability to reach agreement between the creativity condition (reached more successful agreements) and the control condition (mostly failed in reaching agreement) (chi-square, $p<.05$). The use of analogical reasoning during pre-negotiation preparation appears to have had a positive effect on reaching mutually acceptable agreements that overcome stalemates, while pre-negotiation preparatory approaches of study and analysis were less successful in achieving joint outcomes when the parties were at an impasse. Moreover, the creativity subjects behaved in a more flexible manner, being more apt to change their perception of the "best solution" from round to round than the control group.

Subjects in the creativity condition generated a large number of varied analogies during the unilateral problem-solving phase, were able to expand upon them when interacting with their partner, and then employed them in the bilateral negotiations. For example, some looked at the dam problem through the lens of systems analysis, biological and natural functions, childhood and familial experiences, business relationships, political conflicts, and social/economic interactions. Subjects were able, with surprisingly little instruction, to digress from the problem presented to them in the scenario by using analogical reasoning. A sampling of the diversity of analogies developed by the subjects is presented in Table 3.1. It suggests how a complex problem – or impasse – facing negotiators can be thought of in new ways to develop new paths toward solution.

Subjects who were prolific analogizers appear to have been able to go on their exploratory digression from the problem and to return with novel solutions and tradeoffs that facilitated impasse resolution. It is also interesting to note that the subjects in the creativity condition perceived their bilateral negotiation task to be of significantly greater difficulty than the subjects in the study condition. Analogical reasoning adds cognitive complexity to the negotiation task – another reason for the perception of greater difficulty. While using analogies may add value to the search for commonly acceptable solutions, it can make it a more stressful and demanding activity.

The results from this pilot negotiation experiment help to shed some light and new insights on the effects of creativity engineering. The use of creativity heuristics can yield negotiation processes that are capable of overcoming established impasses. However, the solutions that result are not necessarily more creative or superior than those generated by more traditional means. It appears that creativity heuristics engender a unique process that is more flexible, with the capacity for greater adjustment and alignment to accommodate new visions of a desired end-goal. And the harder one works at generating creativity heuristics, the more likely that it will yield success. The generation of more analogies produces the greater likelihood of a negotiated agreement. While analogical reasoning was not a particularly difficult skill to learn and put into practice immediately, it had some drawbacks, especially in making the negotiation interaction appear to be much more demanding and stressful than to those subjects in the study condition.

Although analogical reasoning appears to have some promise in stimulating the resolution of a negotiation impasse, we need to probe deeper into the process by which such creative activity impacts on negotiator perceptions and behaviors to understand the mechanisms that produce the effects. The generation

TABLE 3.1 Sampling of Analogies Used in the Slovakia–Hungary Hydroelectric Project Experiment.

Direct analogies: A connection is made to another field of knowledge.

- The dam is like the heart of the human body. Water comes in and flows out in phases, like blood in the human heart. The dam is like the human circulatory system, with blood vessels growing anew and taking over the role of others.
- The dam dispute is like a couple that is getting a divorce. Properties must be divided, plans must be changed, and holidays must be canceled. Both parties have claims on the other and hold the other responsible. Often both parties lose or perceive that they have lost.
- The dam dispute is like a society driven by market forces versus one driven by social caring programs. How can the caring be distributed – through market forces and prices or through social negotiation? What would happen if the dam were up for sale?
- Hungary and Slovakia are like two orphaned teenagers – insecure, poor, suspicious, passionate, and desperate. They need adults – parents or wise and calm grandparents – that both sides respect to help them out of this mess.
- The situation is like that of a company whose managing director has died. Two rival executives each have new responsibilities and are in competition for the post of Chief Executive Officer (CEO). How do they manage the resources of the company now? How do they find face-saving solutions?

Symbolic analogies: A connection is made based on an image that comes to mind.

- The water flowing through the dam reminds me of sea fisheries. If we catch too much fish now, there will not be enough for the future. But if we do not catch any fish now, we get hungry. All countries try to catch lots of fish, but there needs to be some rules to balance current and future needs.
- The dam dispute is like two children fighting over a toy. One truly wants the toy; the other does not want it but wants to prevent the first one from having it.
- The dam dispute makes me think of a person with one leg moving and the other one stuck in place – one part can function well but, with the other one, can work even better.
- The dam dispute reminds me of my neighbor who rakes the leaves on his side of the fence only, though the leaves on both sides are from his trees. As well, I never help him with the dandelions in his lawn that are seeded from my property.

Personal analogies: A connection is made through identifying or empathizing with the problem.
If I were the dam:

- I would feel torn between my two suitors: one loves me, but the other hates me.
- I would not cause problems for countries.
- I would feel like the meat inside a sandwich. I do not want to be used as an excuse for a territorial dispute or potential war.

Fantasy analogies: A connection is made through fantasizing or wishing how the problem might be formulated.

- I wish that the flow of the river could generate energy just by flowing, just as electricity generates heat when flowing through a radiator or as the wind generates energy when passing by a windmill.
- I wish that the river could satisfy all needs, that it could remain in its own natural flow to support flora and fauna but also satisfy new human needs.

Source: Bertram I. Spector (1995). "Creativity Heuristics for Impasse Resolution: Reframing Intractable Negotiations," *The Annals of the American Academy of Political and Social Science* 542: 81–99 (November). Copyright © 1995 (The American Academy of Political and Social Science. DOI: 10.1177/0002716295542001006).

of analogies facilitated an excursion away from the details of the problem at impasse. Novel ideas were generated and explored that might not have been found otherwise. In the course of the experiments, it was observed that the use of analogies enhanced the social relationship between the bargainers, allowing them to understand each other better and build confidence and trust. The sharing of analogies also engendered humor and introduced some playfulness into the negotiation interaction. These are all elements of the process by which creative reasoning intervenes on negotiation activity. The nature of this process needs to be examined further to evaluate what it is about creativity heuristics that make them effective vehicles to resolve impasses.

Further experimentation can also examine the value of substituting third party mediators or facilitators for the negotiators as the channel for introducing creative problem-solving approaches. This might be a more pragmatic approach for engineering the negotiation situation. The goal of this research would be to determine if introducing a third party into the negotiation mix could yield more effective results. The mediator can help the subjects use analogical reasoning processes to think in novel ways about the problem and possible solutions. Different types of analogies can be used: direct (the problem is placed in the context of another totally different field), fantasy (the problem is stated in terms of how you wish it to be), personal (one attempts to put oneself into the problem), and symbolic (images of the problem are used as starting points to explore different options). Subject proficiency in using analogical reasoning is obviously important in terms of the fidelity of the results. Subjects in the creativity condition need to receive training and go through a practice session using these techniques before the negotiation simulation; even after just a brief training effort, subjects in the pilot test were able to generate very imaginative analogies within the context of the impasse scenario.

Next Steps

Finally, from a very practical perspective, there remains the question of how such negotiation engineering tools can be delivered to practical international negotiators so that they will become integrated into their everyday planning, strategizing, and execution of negotiation activities. At least three avenues present themselves for realistic transfer of these techniques.

- In addition to formal diplomatic practice, more attention needs to be paid to training what is known about the negotiation process and about negotiation engineering tools at diplomatic academies and international relations institutes.
- There needs to be more communication channels between negotiation researchers and scholars and negotiation practitioners to facilitate dialogue. This will enable practitioners to communicate their needs and priorities and for scholars to evaluate and adjust their analytical tools and innovative processes.

- Demonstration of a concept can be a powerful tool to influence and persuade. Whenever possible, practical negotiators should extend invitations to negotiation scholars and researchers to work together in national delegations to actual negotiations. The experience of working together on a common negotiation problem is sure to present opportunities for both the researcher and practitioner to learn about the needs and techniques of the other side. It will also provide a real venue to demonstrate the value and shortcomings of existing negotiation support approaches. By seeing these techniques in action, practitioners will be able to judge for themselves how to apply these approaches in the future and researchers will be able to assess how much further they need to revise and refine the negotiation support techniques they have already designed.

Notes

1 Holst, J. J. (1993). "Reflections on the Making of a Tenuous Peace, or the Transformation of Images of the Middle East Conflict." Presentation to the School of International and Public Affairs, Columbia University, New York, NY.
2 Druckman, Daniel (1993). "The Situational Levers of Negotiating Flexibility." *Journal of Conflict Resolution* 37: 236–276.
3 Pruitt, Dean and M. Kimmel (1977). "Twenty Years of Experimental Gaming: Critique, Synthesis, and Suggestions for the Future." *Annual Review of Psychology* 28: 363–392; Pruitt, Dean (1981) *Negotiation Behavior*. New York: Academic Press.
4 Druckman (1993), op.cit.
5 Spector, Bertram (1993). "Creativity in Negotiation: Directions for Future Research," Laxenburg, Austria: IIASA Working Paper WP-93-4 (January). Also published in Dutch in *Negotiation Magazine* V,4: 153–162 (December 1992); Spector, Bertram (1995). "Creativity Heuristics for Impasse Resolution: Reframing Intractable Negotiations," *The Annals of the American Academy of Political and Social Science* 542: 81–99 (November).
6 Stein, Morris (1974). *Stimulating Creativity*. New York: Academic Press.
7 Weisberg, R. (1988). "Problem Solving and Creativity," in R. Sternberg, ed., *The Nature of Creativity*. Cambridge: Cambridge University Press.
8 Bouchard, T. (1972). "A Comparison of Two Group Brainstorming Procedures." *Journal of Applied Psychology* 56: 418–421; Dreistadt, R. (1969). "The Use of Analogies and Incubation in Obtaining Insights in Creative Problem Solving." *Journal of Psychology* 71: 159–175; Gick, M. and K. Holyoak (1983) "Schema Induction and Analogical Transfer." *Cognitive Psychology* 15: 1–38.
9 Spector, Bertram (1995), op.cit.

4
THE PSYCHOLOGY OF NEGOTIATION

The human factor cannot be ignored when trying to explain negotiation process dynamics and outcomes. Intuitive recognition of the importance of personality, perception, and persuasion as crucial driving forces in international negotiation is sprinkled throughout the literature, from the earliest writings. For example, the need to cultivate particular personal virtues to deal with princes, and the passions that move negotiators were clearly identified in eighteenth century European treatises.[1] Moral and intellectual qualities, as well as assorted human frailties, were considered to play an "immense" role in the diplomacy of the Congress of Vienna.[2] Intensive one-on-one communications and signaling between labor and management negotiators were observed as mechanisms that release bargainers from institutional controls and allow them to react in relation to their inner personal perceptions, expectations, and personalities.[3] Stonewalling and deadlock in the Vietnam peace negotiations were positively related, according to one United States diplomat, to the degree of human comfort and amenities afforded negotiators.[4] However, progress in negotiation is likely to proceed more seriously and expeditiously if the perquisites of diplomacy are reduced and personal motivation is shifted to the timely resolution of conflict rather than the hedonistic temptations that diplomats find in places like Paris or Geneva.

Psychological predictors of negotiation processes and outcomes have been examined as well in the research literature in the context of a wide range of theoretical and experimental frameworks.[5] Such research, in addition to intuitive judgment and first-hand observation of negotiation dynamics by practitioners, suggests that psychological characteristics are important motivating forces in achieving outcomes.

Starting from this literature, this essay describes an empirically based study that was designed to examine the roles of personality, perception, and persuasion

DOI: 10.4324/9781003314400-4

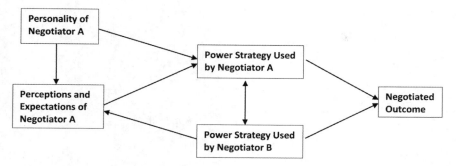

FIGURE 4.1 Psychological Model of Two-Person Negotiations (from the perspective of Negotiator A).

in negotiation. A psychological model of negotiation was formulated, an experimental vehicle was developed to simulate distributive bargaining, and the resulting empirical data were analyzed via the model to determine the degree of impact of micro-level factors in negotiation phenomena. The findings confirm the potency of psychological explanations of the bargaining process and outcome.

Psychological Impacts on Negotiation

Figure 4.1 depicts a simple psychological model for dyadic negotiations. The model plots the determinants of the bargaining process from the perspective of one side in a two-person bargaining situation. Negotiator personalities affect perceptions and expectations of the situation, the desire to compromise, the use of bargaining strategies, and the achievement of objectives. Perceptions of the other bargainer's intentions, motives, and goals also impact upon the give-and-take of the negotiation process. Finally, transactions in bargaining situations are viewed as persuasive power episodes that modify competing bargaining positions and goals so that satisfactory and acceptable outcomes are possible.

The Negotiation Simulation

The author developed a simple negotiation game with the objective of studying the impact of power, personality, and perception on the negotiation process and outcomes.[6] The "Camp Game" presents a problematic situation to two negotiators that can produce either a distributive or integrative solution. While providing a particular context for negotiation, the scenario of the Camp Game was designed to reduce role-playing effects. The players negotiate as themselves, in a scenario that all can understand and that requires very little in terms of situation, background, and role identification. The objective was to reduce the influence of role and context over personality.

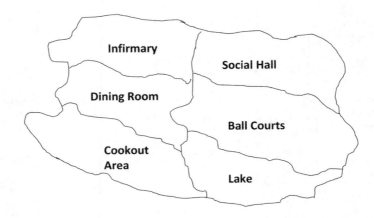

FIGURE 4.2 Map for the Camp Game.

The premise of the Camp Game is very simple. The scenario concerns a series of bargaining encounters between two persons who are told they each paid exactly one-half of the total price for a campsite and its facilities. The campgrounds consist of six territories, each equal in size: an infirmary, social hall, dining room, ball courts, cookout area, and lake. Figure 4.2 displays the map of the camp. Each player desires to operate a separate camp on the grounds with as many of the necessary facilities as possible. Neither has enough money left to build new facilities. So, each player's task is to negotiate with the other an acceptable distribution of the available six facilities.

Players' positions are subjectively defined by those territories they themselves prefer to obtain. The explicit end-goal for each player is to arrive at a final distribution of all six territories with their co-player, and to try to make this final distribution as close as possible to their own bargaining position. The way the simulation is designed, the bargaining process and outcome are determined by player motives, utilities, expectations, and behavioral transactions.

The bargaining proceeds in structured offer-counteroffer transactions. Each bargainer responds to the previous offer of the other player. Each offer and subsequent counteroffer form a round of play; the bargaining can continue for several rounds so each player can exercise a bargaining strategy to influence the other. The negotiation sequence proceeds until all territories are distributed or the experimenter-imposed time limit (two hours) is reached. All bargaining is conducted through written messages; "behavior" in the simulation consists of verbal statements and behavior potentials.

Several characteristics of this game distinguish it from the often-used Prisoners' Dilemma game and make it more appropriate to the analysis of psychological impacts.[7]

- The Camp Game simulates a substantive, business-like distributive negotiation. The intent is to provoke subject interest, motivation, and involvement.

- The simulation was developed in a context somewhat familiar to graduate and undergraduate college subjects. The intent here was to enable the participants to behave naturally and react in accordance with their own personal dispositions. Subjects were not given roles to play; they were encouraged to act as themselves.
- The familiar, non-technical, and non-role-playing scenario helped to activate self-motivation. All subjects volunteered, came on their own time, were not graded, and received no monetary reward, and yet most were willing to spend more than two hours participating in the bargaining sessions.
- To ensure uninhibited, behavioral expression of personality, without excessive experimenter-imposed roles, bias, or incentives, the Camp Game allowed subjects to choose their bargaining tactics from among a wide range of powerful and persuasive acts. Each tactic could be modified to suit the personal style of the subjects and players were also encouraged to devise their own tactics.
- The game was founded on mixed-motive goals. The objectives of each player were to compete to maximize individual interests, as well as to cooperate to maximize joint gain in a final agreement.
- Bargaining goals were set by each participant based on personal interests and subject to change throughout the session. Bargainers were initially dealt equivalent resources and situations so that neither was placed in offensive or defensive positions in relation to the other.

Hypotheses

A set of hypotheses was tested that focus on psychological impacts in negotiation and based on propositions in the literature.

Hypothesis 1: Negotiators with significantly different personality characteristics and perceptions of the situation are likely to choose different bargaining tactics and strategies.[8]

Hypothesis 1A: Trusting strategies are likely to be chosen by negotiators who have high needs for achievement. Exploitative strategies are likely to be chosen by negotiators who have high needs for power. Suspicious strategies are likely to be chosen by negotiators who have high needs for affiliation.[9]

Hypothesis 1B: Negotiators who perceive low threat from the adversary are likely to choose cooperative and trustworthy strategies. Negotiators who perceive high threat from the adversary are likely to choose exploitative strategies.[10]

Hypothesis 2: Adversarial bargainers in two-party negotiations who have complementary personality characteristics are likely to negotiate acceptable outcomes. Noncomplementary negotiator personalities are likely to be highly defensive, rigid, and unyielding, resulting in deadlocked outcomes.[11]

Hypothesis 3: The use of persuasive bargaining strategies that are motivated by power tactics is likely to modify positions and produce acceptable negotiated outcomes over time.[12]

Experimental Measurement

Strategies

For each move, negotiators recorded their preferences on a position sheet and strategy sheet. On the position sheet, the bargainer described their current personally acceptable minimum bargaining position – their present image of their own goals, and their expectations of the opponent's position.[13] On the strategy sheet, bargainers recorded their messages and signals to their opponent and responded to the last move. Here, subjects can operationalize and communicate powerful and persuasive strategies to convince the opponent to modify its position and accept the terms of one's own bargaining goals. The six basic power tactics described to the subjects are:

- *Commitment:* Convince your co-player you have committed yourself to get a certain territory no matter what.
- *Exchange:* Give your co-player a territory and suggest that they give you a territory you want in return.
- *Force:* Attempt to take the territory you want by force.
- *Obligation:* Convince your co-player they are obligated to give you a certain territory you want.
- *Promise:* Promise to give a territory to your co-player if they give you the territory you want.
- *Threat:* Threaten to use force on your co-player's territory if they do not give you the territory you want.

Each tactic involves the characteristics of intention, volition, and contingency, and thus are potentially persuasive vehicles to modify conflicting positions and achieve convergence. To make the simulation more realistic and to enable the occurrence of bluffs if desired, commitments, obligations, promises, and threats are considered to be merely statements of intent, that is, the bargainer need not follow through with the predicted contingency. Exchange and force tactics, however, are deeds and considered to go into effect immediately when they are chosen; they may not be bluffed.

Statistical analysis of the bargaining tactics employed by each negotiator uncovered several patterns of behavior that we have labeled "bargaining strategies." Q-technique factor analysis of the subjects on their behavioral tactics uncovered four major dimensions that explain 83.06% of the total variance. Each

TABLE 4.1 Bargaining Strategies.

Strategy	Distinguishing tactic	Percent usage
Creative Cooperative Type	Promise to Share	13.5%
Active Cooperative Type	Exchange	13.5%
Passive Cooperative Type	Promise to Exchange	30.8%
Active Hostile Type	Force	30.8%
Unclassified	Ambiguous	11.4%

dimension is interpreted as a bargaining strategy. These strategies are characterized as coherent plans, be they consciously or unconsciously devised, to persuade or coerce the other side and achieve a solution. A consistent and intercorrelated set of tactics to influence the other bargainer's values and position appears to be the most efficient means of achieving a favorable outcome.

The four bargaining strategies that were identified can be distinguished by the predominant use of a certain bargaining tactic. Three of the strategies denote cooperative patterns, and one, a conflictual pattern. Table 4.1 lists the strategies and the tactics that describe them.

Bargainers who employed the *creative cooperative strategy* used their own initiative in devising a cooperative means to solving the bargaining dilemma. Typically, they promised their adversary that they would be willing to share certain areas of the campground conditional upon the other's acceptance. The *active-passive distinction* of the other two cooperative strategies is made in relation to the attributes of exchange and promise tactics. By using exchange tactics, bargainers immediately relinquish property to their partner, while promises offer a territory only if the partner relinquishes one first. Thus, the former actively concedes territories, while the latter makes concessions contingent on the occurrence of other events controlled by the adversary. The *active hostile strategy* is characterized by the use of unilateral coercive measures, namely force. In addition, a small number of bargainers did not appear to use any consistent or identifiable strategy and are listed as unclassified.

Each subject's factor loadings on the four dimensions serve as data values for these variables. Thus, four orthogonal interval scale variables, one for each strategy, were created based on these loading coefficients. They can be interpreted as the degree of correlation between each subject and each dimension. As values approach ±1.0, the subject's strategy choice is best (or least) described by the factor; as values approach zero, the subject's behavior becomes independent of the factor.

Personality

The results of a large segment of the experimental literature point to the study of personality needs and motives as important determinants of bargaining behavior. The personality variables in our simulation game were derived from subject's responses to the Stein Self-Description Questionnaire (SDQ), which was administered a week or two prior to the simulation. Unlike many single-trait personality tests, the Stein SDQ measures the hierarchical structure of multiple needs to enable integrative interpretations of the total configuration of personality.[14] The validity and reliability of the Stein SDQ have been the object of several experimental, cross-cultural, and assessment studies.[15] The test is extremely simple to administer to large groups at a single sitting and has been designed for research purposes to enable easy coding.

Each subject was asked to rank order descriptions of the twenty manifest needs in the questionnaire (see Table 4.2) in relation to how well they thought the needs described themself. Manifest needs are those which are expressed in the social world and thus have potentially overt impacts as inhibitors or facilitators of real action taken by a person.[16] Twenty ordinal scales were created, one for each need.

Subject's responses to the Stein SDQ were compared to each other using the Spearman's rank-order correlation coefficient. Subjects whose need rankings were highly ($r > .25$) similar were paired to play in the bargaining simulation so as to control for the effects of highly dissimilar interacting personalities. Terhune (1970) argues that like-pairing enables motivational effects on behavior to be more clearly detectable.

Perceptions

Perceptual variables were derived from a seven-point semantic differential instrument that tapped subject perceptions of the opponent's last move along evaluation, potency, stability, aggressiveness, and competitiveness dimensions.[17] Moreover, bargainer's perceptions of conflicts of interest with their opponent were calculated during each negotiation round by measuring the intersection of each player's actual goals with their expectations of their opponent's goals.

Controls

Certain experimental controls were included to minimize any factors that might bias the players' attitudes or behavior and thereby interfere with the free operation of personality and perception. First, care was taken in the instruction booklet, and briefing and practice sessions not to bias the players' predispositions toward their counterpart. For instance, each pair consists of "co-players" rather than "partners" or "opponents," terms that possess positive and negative connotations. Bargainers were not directed toward particular strategies or territories. As noted earlier, special attention was taken not to evoke exclusively competitive or cooperative objectives in the game. Suggestive labels or instructions were eliminated.[18]

Second, since we are testing for the effects of personality on behavior, the players had to be provided with a full range of behavioral options to allow them unrestricted opportunities to manifest their personality characteristics. In addition to the six basic negotiation tactics that were presented to the subjects ahead

TABLE 4.2 Definitions of Murray's Manifest Needs as Employed in Stein's Self-Description Questionnaire.

Need	Definition
Abasement	I passively submit to external forces. I accept injury, blame, criticism, and punishment. I surrender. I am resigned to fate. I admit my inferiorities, errors, wrong-doings, or defeats. I blame myself.
Achievement	I accomplish difficult things. I try to overcome obstacles and to achieve a high standard. I compete with others and try to surpass them. I am ambitious and aspiring.
Affiliation	I like to be with and enjoy cooperating with other people. I like to please and win the affection of others whom I like. I like to be with friends and am loyal to them. I love and trust others.
Aggression	I overcome opposition forcefully. I fight and attack. In my talk I belittle, censure, or ridicule others. I am argumentative. I am severe with others.
Autonomy	I resist coercion and restrictions. I avoid or leave activities in which others try to dominate me. I am independent and free to act according to impulse. I defy convention.
Blamavoidance	I avoid situations in which I might be blamed for my actions. I avoid situations in which I might lose the love of others. I am apprehensive, inhibited, and fearful about hurting others. I try to be inoffensive. I am concerned about the opinions of others.
Counteraction	Should I fail in something I return to master it. I overcome, my weaknesses and repress my fears. I do things to prove I can do them. I am determined, I maintain my self-respect on a high level.
Defendance	I defend myself against criticism, blame, and attack. I conceal or justify my mistakes and failures. I refuse to admit my inferiorities and weaknesses.
Deference	I admire and support people who are superior to me. I believe in conforming to the wishes of my superiors. I conform to custom. I am obliging. I admire, give respect, and revere others.
Dominance	I control my environment. I influence others. I am forceful, masterful, assertive, and authoritative. I am confident in my relations with others.
Exhibition	I try to make an impression on others. In a group, I am seen and heard. I entertain others, attract attention to myself, and enjoy an audience. I try to excite, amaze, shock, and amuse others.
Harmavoidance	I avoid pain, physical injury, and illness. I stay away from dangerous situations. I am cautious and hesitant about being in situations where I might encounter harm.
Infavoidance	I avoid situations which might be humiliating or embarrassing to me. I am inclined to avoid action because I fear failure. I get nervous and embarrassed – before and during an event. I am easily ashamed or mortified after the event.
Nurturance	I am a sympathetic person. I enjoy helping helpless people. I am inclined to support, protect, and comfort others. I avoid hurting others.
Order	I like to put things in order. To be neat, clean, tidy, and precise are very important to me. I like to arrange and organize things.
Play	I do things for fun and without any further purpose enjoy play and relaxation from stress. I like to laugh and joke about things. I am easy-going, lighthearted, and merry.

(Continued)

TABLE 4.2 Definitions of Murray's Manifest Needs as Employed in Stein's Self-Description Questionnaire. (*Continued*)

Need	Definition
Rejection	I am very critical and discriminating in the choice of friends. I stay away from people whom I dislike. I am indifferent to, avoid, or reject people who are inferior to me; I am inclined to be snobbish. I tend to be disgusted and bored with other people.
Sentience	I seek and enjoy sensuous impressions. I have and enjoy aesthetic feelings.
Sex	I like to establish relationships with the opposite sex. I am not afraid of my sexual feelings. I enjoy feelings of love and of being attracted to the opposite sex.
Succorance	I am drawn to people who can sympathize with me. I seek out people who can advise and guide me and who give me emotional support. I seek affection and tenderness from others.

Source: Morris I. Stein, "Booklet on the Self-Description Questionnaire," Unpublished manuscript, undated.

of the simulation (see above), the game rules were designed to allow negotiators to develop additional creative approaches and new strategy possibilities.

Third, familiarity between subjects was considered a major factor to be controlled for. Past experience with or attitudes toward one's co-player might bias the use of particular strategies or influence one's psychological environment. To control for these effects, interaction took the form of written messages rather than face-to-face communications. Co-players were assigned to different rooms and did not know the identity of whom they were bargaining with.

Since participation in the experiment was voluntary, the self-selection process could introduce additional bias in the sampling procedure that might result in an experimental group that is unrepresentative of the population. It has been hypothesized that only particular types of people volunteer to be subjects for experimental research. Since this potential bias is conceived as a personality difference between volunteers and non-volunteers, and personality motives are among the major variables tapped, the compositional nature of our resultant sample was taken into account and generalizations made on the basis of this understanding.[19] A total of 45 volunteers from three undergraduate political science courses participated in the final trials of the Camp Game. In all, twenty-six games were played; several subjects played two games although with different co-players each time.

Results

Psychological Dynamics of Strategy Choice

Creative Cooperative Strategies

The path analytic results in Figure 4.3 indicate that the greater the bargainer's need for succorance (p= .272), but the lower their need for affiliation (p= -.296), the more likely their choice of creative cooperative (promise to share) strategies.[20]

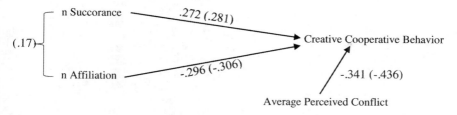

FIGURE 4.3 Final Path Model: Creative Cooperative Behavior[21].

Moreover, the exercise of this strategy is more probable if the negotiator's perception of conflict with their counterpart is low (p= -.341).

How can we interpret these linkages? It appears that creative cooperative strategies are motivated by self-oriented personality needs for emotional support, approval, and respect rather than needs promoting cooperation and friendship. Moreover, the choice of these highly cooperative strategies is likely if the perception of conflict is low.

It seems unusual that the desire for friendship – establishing close and trusting social relations – is particularly singled out as having a negative impact on creative cooperative strategies. Sharing appears to be a friendly gesture, after all! But the personality type that would choose a sharing strategy is not looking for friendship. Rather, they are seeking the respect and praise of others for their initiative and creativity. A negotiator who exercises this sharing strategy seeks the approval of others for their cooperative acts solely to satisfy their self-oriented ego needs to be considered a "good person," not to make or keep friends. Creative cooperation might indeed foster friendliness, good feeling, and acceptable agreements, but the motivation that lies behind this strategy is more concerned with satisfying self-oriented needs than gratifying other-oriented needs through developing trust and friendship.

Perceptions of low conflict in the negotiations are also likely to motivate the choice of creative cooperative strategies. Sharing demands mutual acceptance of a departure from the norm of private ownership of the campgrounds. In high threat situations especially, the initiator of a sharing scheme might fear non-reciprocation and failure of their bargaining strategy. Thus, we find that sharing strategies tend to be initiated when overall threats are considered to be low.

Active Cooperative Strategies

What personality types choose active cooperative (exchange) strategies? The higher a bargainer's need for abasement (p= .322) and the lower their need for harm avoidance (p= -.394), the more likely their use of this strategy (see Figure 4.4). A third need, n Sentience, has a weaker though significant direct effect (p= .205). Not surprisingly, as the perception of conflict with the other negotiator decreases, the use of active cooperative strategies increases (p= -.230).

44 Psychology of Negotiation

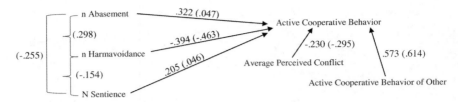

FIGURE 4.4 Final Path Model: Active Cooperative Behavior.

The strongest path impacting on a negotiator's choice is their opponent's use of this strategy (p=.573).

How can these psychodynamics be explained? Active cooperative strategies extend immediate rewards – in this case, properties of the campgrounds – to the adversary, free of any explicit limiting conditions. It is hoped that reciprocation in kind will follow, but that rides purely on the initiator's faith and trust in their opponent's good will. Although this appears to be a highly altruistic and trusting strategy, its motivating dynamics are somewhat nonobvious. Surprisingly, active cooperation is chosen by negotiators who have a masochistic desire to concede and surrender under low conflict conditions! Exchange is not pursued for altruistic motives. Rather, negotiators who choose this strategy are attempting to satisfy their needs by submitting to others and exposing themselves to harm and danger!

But, at the same time, these negotiators must assume that giving territories to the other party will result in reciprocal acts. As indicated by the negative relation between the need for harm avoidance and use of active cooperation strategies, such negotiators are willing to take on the risk of giving away a territory. They don't know if they will get something in return, but they are hoping they will.

Those who exercise this strategy, at least in its initial stage, appear to eliminate from their repertoire of behaviors all possible mechanisms of control over their environment. They surrender to the whims and possible domination of their opponents by actively conceding campground property to them without the guarantee of receiving any benefit in return. Moreover, it was observed that exercisers of this strategy demanded little from their opponents. This combination of high concessions and low demands spells potential disaster for these strategists. They are taking a chance and hoping that the other party will view their initial offer positively and react in a similar fashion.

The fewer territories left as the negotiation proceeds, the worse one's payoff will likely be in the final negotiated outcome. Since there is a possibility that concessions will not be reciprocated, the exercise of this strategy is extremely risky, and leaves the initiator in a potentially helpless and defeated position. At the same time, the finding that this strategy tends to be chosen during low conflict situations suggests that its users are willing to take the risk and, possibly, feel good about their offer to the other side.

Finally, the opponent's use of active cooperative strategies appears to have a strong effect on inducing reciprocation. When one negotiator begins to exchange territories, the other is inclined to follow suit in imitative fashion. Thus, the faith in reciprocation inherent in this strategy appears to be borne out in the experimental sessions. This strategy may indeed be successful in redistributing camp territories and arriving at outcomes. However, the psychological motives in the preceding discussion suggest that the person who exercises this strategy may not be pursuing conciliation or favorable agreements at all by their actions. Rather, they reciprocate in equivalent fashion not out of convention, because it is the established bargaining norm; their true motivation is to give in to the other party who might be viewed as stronger or more powerful.

Passive Cooperative Strategies

The path model presented in Figure 4.5 indicates that several personality needs motivate the choice of passive cooperative (promise) strategies. The need for exhibition is a major determinant (p= .371); bargainers who desire to impress, excite, and amuse others find this strategy satisfying. The association of playfulness, and seduction with this strategy is reinforced by the strength of the causal path between the need for sex and the choice of promise tactics (p= .349). Consistent with this constellation of need motivation, both the achievement (p= -.297) and autonomy (p= -.322) motives are negatively related to the use of passive cooperation. The non-serious, playful orientation of this strategy limits the aesthetic and sentient satisfaction that can be derived from choosing it (p= -.272). Finally, a direct path causally relates the negotiator's perception of a cooperative other to the use of passive cooperative strategies (p= .285).

This strategy is characterized by the use of promises – offering the adversary a reward condition upon their compliance with your demands. Thus, this

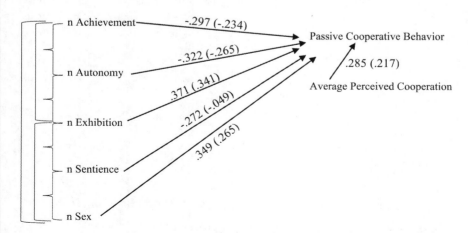

FIGURE 4.5 Final Path Model: Passive Cooperative Behavior.

strategy employs a typical form of power, where conditional verbal statements attempt to change the target's image of their ambient reality to bring about a convergence of positions. Because this strategy involves the possibility of actions to be pursued in the future, it opens the door to bluffing and deception. That is, although a negotiator may promise a camp property to the adversary in exchange for something they desire, the negotiator may never intend or fulfill their promise, regardless of what the adversary does. By bluffing, negotiators can obtain what they want if the other side complies, without incurring immediate costs themselves. However, a negotiator must beware of establishing a reputation of untrustworthiness.

Bargainers who are passive cooperative strategists are motivated by needs for play, seduction, cleverness, and exhibitionism. The bluffing option provides negotiators with the ability to surprise their opponent, present them with the unexpected, be clever, and outwit them. But it is not an achievement-oriented strategy. Bluffing may lower credibility and result in future responses of non-compliance. Thus, it is rejected by highly achievement-oriented persons as potentially unreliable and risky. Highly autonomous negotiators also reject passive cooperative strategies. Once the promise offer is made, the initiator defers to their counterpart to react – to comply or not – leaving them passive over the outcome and dependent on their opponent's decision. Finally, if the opponent is perceived as cooperative and inclined to concessions and compliance, a negotiator is likely to attempt a passive cooperative strategy. A cooperative and compliant opponent is more likely to fall for a bluffed promise than an aggressive one who poses a threat of noncompliance and may initiate retaliatory tactics.

Active Hostile Strategies

The motivational base of active hostile (force) strategies is much different than the three other strategies. No significant paths link the choice of this strategy with personality factors (see Figure 4.6). However, the opponent's use of this strategy is strongly and positively related to one's imitative choice of the same

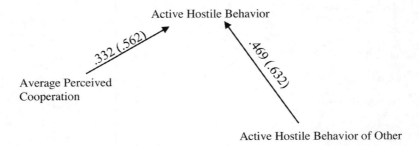

FIGURE 4.6 Final Path Model: Active Hostile Behavior.

behavior (p= .469). Perceived cooperation of the other also motivates the use of force tactics (p= .332).

How can these findings be explained? Active hostile strategies appear to be motivated by expectations that the other side will fall into line and yield to coercive fait accompli. Force tactics are used in an exploitative fashion – to take advantage of those perceived to be cooperative and conciliatory. This strategist is also motivated by the maxim that force must be met by counterforce. Here again we witness a lock-in phenomenon where the initiation of a unilateral policy of coercion is responded to in kind.

A forceful retaliatory effort maintains a negotiator's credibility as an active and potent bargainer. Appeasement of an aggressive opponent might merely encourage them to further aggressive measures. Faced with the possibility of losing all access to desired camp territories due to coercive acts, a negotiator may feel they must defend their interests by pursuing a like-minded active hostile strategy.

Personality Mix of Bargaining Adversaries

The complex flow of explicit communications and tacit signaling between two negotiators helps motivate the essential process of value and position change, and thus, the ability to achieve a convergence of interests and agreement. Negotiation analysts assume that the ease with which this interaction process progresses is highly dependent on the subtle mixture of protagonist personalities.[22] In two-person bargaining situations, the other side can serve as a catalyst, facilitator, or impediment. Whichever one the bargainer is of these three depends on the personality mix of the bargainers around the table, whether they are complementary or conflictual. Highly dissimilar and noncomplementary personality types, for instance, are likely to become highly defensive in dealing with each other and hold rigid and unyielding bargaining positions. The probable negotiation outcome resulting from such a personality mixture is standstill and deadlock.[23] Thus, negotiation dynamics and the possibility of reaching favorable outcomes can be facilitated by taking into account the personality mix of bargaining adversaries.

We examined this issue using data from the experimental negotiation sessions. First, each negotiator was categorized on the basis of personality similarity with their opponent. The degree of personality similarity within each dyad was measured by calculating the Spearman's rank-order correlation on the Stein SDQ need rankings for both dyad members. Coefficients above .45 were judged to be highly similar, between .25 and .44 moderately similar, and below .24 highly dissimilar.

Table 4.3 compares pairing similarity and strategy. Bargainers in each pairing category can be analyzed to determine significant differences in strategy choice. The results indicate a distinct impact of personality pairing on bargaining patterns, but also offers a new perspective on how this impact alters the choice of strategies.

TABLE 4.3 The Effects of Personality Pairing on Bargaining Behavior Types (in %).

Personality pairing → Bargaining behavior types ↓	High similarity (N = 14)	Moderate similarity (N = 18)	High dissimilarity (N = 14)	Missing data (N = 6)
Creative Cooperative	7.1	5.5	21.4	33.3
Active Cooperative	28.6	5.5	7.1	16.7
Passive Cooperative	14.3	44.5	35.8	16.7
Active Hostile	35.7	39.0	21.4	16.7
Other	14.3	5.5	14.3	16.6
TOTAL	100.0	100.0	100.0	100.0

Pairs composed of like personalities act less defensively; and this frees them to act in a more competitive, aggressive, and self-maximizing manner. They tend to use more coercive strategies. Dissimilar personality pairs, on the other hand, being more defensive in their behavior toward each other, tend to be more cautious and cooperatively oriented in order not to incur aggressive reactions.

The logic of these findings runs against the grain of previously held assumptions. Negotiations conducted by dissimilar personalities are likely to yield cautious, but friendly, proceedings with frequent resort to persuasive rather than coercive tactics. Complementary personalities, on the other hand, are likely to turn negotiations into aggressive, hostile, and self-seeking interchanges rather than pursuing joint maximizing efforts.

Negotiation as Learning

A review of approximately fifty after-action reports that were written by game participants reveals some interesting propositions about how any negotiation process works and reinforces the idea of negotiation as a group learning process. While these reports are limited in terms of systematic analysis, interesting generalizations from the practical gaming experience can be derived. Some of these findings and propositions are presented below.

Ripeness and Breakthrough

Ripe moments did not occur often in the Camp Game; the context did not naturally promote the occurrence of hurting stalemates. However, deadlines and frustration about lack of progress in the negotiation did produce situations that could be categorized as breakthroughs, which in some cases led to agreement.

> *Breakthroughs are more likely when both sides develop an understanding of what the other side wants from the talks and can more accurately anticipate the other's needs and demands. Without such ability to anticipate the other, breakthroughs do not generally occur.*

Formula-Detail and Strategies

Many of the teams used the campground map effectively to prioritize their own interests, develop formulas, and communicate them to the other team. The presentation of formulas by each party (often as trial balloons) appeared to promote a mutual understanding of the other's needs, helping each side anticipate the needs of the other and present clear options for compromise and agreement. Without a reciprocal sharing of formulas and overall goals, negotiations took on a random and unproductive quality.

> *Very little learning of the other's goals or strategies is accomplished when the negotiation process takes the form of demand-concession transactions. However, teams appear to be able to learn much more about the other's goals and strategies if negotiations take the form of a formula-detail process.*

> *When both sides devise clear formulas and share them with the other side early in the negotiation, it is possible to proceed quickly to the negotiation of details. When only one party develops a formula or when neither does, the negotiation process often becomes illogical, inconsistent, contradictory, and random.*

> *Formulas that are contextual, thematic, and integrative (for example, to develop a tennis camp or a sailing camp) appear to be more sustainable and likely to lead to agreement than those formulas which merely divide or prioritize the camp territories. Non-thematic formulas are quickly dropped and those negotiation processes revert to demand-concession bargaining.*

Development of a clear and thematic formula appears to provide negotiation teams with a greater understanding and vision of their own objectives. It provides unity, meaning, and value to the team and motivation to the negotiation process as a whole.

Learning and Strategies

Pre-negotiation preparations and inter-session caucuses were extremely important to share information and impressions among the team members and to devise the strategies for the next round. They essentially helped team members assess what they themselves wanted out of the negotiations, but contributed less about what the other side wanted.

> *Internal team caucuses are negotiations by themselves, requiring the need for learning and adjustment among team members.*

Tit-for-tat strategies were evident in many of the negotiations.

> *Teams often become disheartened if they do not see clear and rapid reciprocation of their strategies.*

Adaptive learning about the other team, when it happened, tended to yield creative strategies, based on solutions not yet rejected in previous rounds of negotiation.

> *Negotiation between teams over the rounds can be characterized as an adaptive learning process, revealing details about the other side's goals, interests, and strategies. If learning takes place about the other party's wants and needs, early high expectations of one's own outcomes are often dropped or modified.*

> *The negotiation process, by itself, can engender a belief that solutions should be attainable that satisfy all sides. Once entered into, there is a general commitment to using negotiation processes to identify a mutually acceptable outcome; parties do not resort to alternate processes.*

Teams sought to find out about the other side's needs and their expectations, but were often not successful. Communications were usually unclear and incomplete — intentionally and unintentionally — making the negotiation process extremely inefficient and often resulting in missed opportunities for convergence. Learning on the part of team members was rarely linear. Misplaced expectations, wrong assumptions, and a general lack of information provided insufficient cues to learn about the other parties' needs, goals, and interests, prolonging the negotiations.

A broad interpretation of these many cases and rounds of the Camp Game suggests strongly that while the participants are "learning by doing," the negotiation process they are operating within is clearly a learning process too. Interests, objectives, and perceptions are adjusted as more is discovered about the other side. Even if the learning is not explicit, negotiators can find out about the other side incrementally by analyzing and inferring motive and intent to strategies and statements. Adjustments are made to expectations and strategies are adapted as responses to the other side's actions and behaviors, moving the parties from their initial positions, interests, and strategies to new ones, sometimes leading to a convergence of interests and outcomes.

Discussion

By means of statistical analysis, in this case, causal path analysis, data derived from the negotiation experiments were examined to uncover the specific motivational elements at work in this redistributive negotiating scenario. The analysis serves to test the model's validity as a method of understanding and predicting negotiation dynamics. The results indicate that each bargaining strategy is motivated by different sets of psychological and behavioral predictors; a unique psychological profile can be elaborated for users of each bargaining strategy.

Furthermore, the empirical findings show that the reasons why particular strategies are chosen cannot be explained by simple and obvious answers.

The reasons are sometimes surprising and complex, but at the same time, extremely revealing of the latent motives that drive the choice of particular strategies. The degree of complementarity of the bargaining adversary personalities also is shown to have an important impact on the choice of strategies.

Contrary to the assumptions of the initial model in Figure 4.1, negotiation outcomes are found to rest more heavily on personality and perceptual predictors than on the bargaining strategies that are exercised. This experimental finding suggests the need to revise the psychological negotiation model. A proposed revision is presented in the concluding remarks below.

Figure 4.7 summarizes the psychodynamics of bargaining strategy choice that were uncovered in the experimental analysis. As our original psychological model suggested, the decision to use a particular bargaining strategy to achieve one's goals is highly determined by inner personal dynamics such as the negotiator's personality, perceptions of the situation, and use of persuasive power. The analytical conclusions attest to the fact that if we come to the bargaining table knowing something about our counterpart – what motivates them, what their basic needs are, how they view the negotiation situation, and what they expect us to do – we will be in an improved position to predict their choice of strategy and prepared to deal with them and reach an early and favorable agreement. To the extent possible, the pre-negotiation period should include time for analysis of one's negotiating counterparts – their personality factors, motives, perceptions of the situation, expectations of others, etc. Some data can be derived from those who know the other parties or have negotiated with them in the past. Additional information might be available from their writings, media reports, and past activities and statements.

Moreover, attention should be paid to the personality mixture of negotiators. This is an element that can be controlled and manipulated directly and effectively by each bargaining side prior to arriving at the bargaining table. Care must be taken in choosing the active bargaining agent, not only from the perspective of who can present and defend your position the best, but on the basis of how they might interact with and appear to the other side's negotiating agent on a personal level.

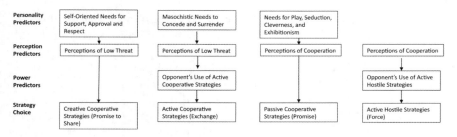

FIGURE 4.7 Psychological Impacts on the Choice of Bargaining Strategy

So far, we have examined the psychodynamics of strategy choice. Now, we turn to the dynamics of bargaining outcomes. We made the assumption in our initial psychological model that the interaction of bargaining strategies and the underlying power tactics that motivate them are likely to be good predictors of the negotiation outcome. How bargainers act during the negotiation process to influence each other's values, positions, and goals is likely to affect the individual and joint payoffs. The "goodness" of payoff in the case of the Camp Game can be measured by an outcome ratio operationalized as the number of desired territories possessed by a player divided by the total number of territories desired in the last round of bargaining.

However, using the same causal path analytical technique as before, our results indicate that bargaining strategies are basically unrelated to the degree of payoff received in the bargaining outcome. The strategies used by each negotiator to persuade the other had insignificant effects on how well each fared in the end!

This finding might be an artifact of those bargainers in the experimental sessions who did not have time to complete their negotiation interactions and achieve a stable outcome prior to the two-hour limit. As well, the college bargainers in the experiments were unsophisticated in the use of power tactics and may not have employed them in the most productive fashion.

However, assuming that our data are valid, can we find alternate explanations to predict bargaining payoffs? An examination of the major correlates of bargaining payoffs in the experiments suggest that adequate projections of how well negotiators may fare can be derived from understanding the personalities and expectations of the bargainers.

Our analysis uncovered the profile of a successful bargainer in the context of the experimental negotiation situation. A negotiator attains high final payoffs in an agreement if they are achievement-oriented, but not overly aggressive or hostile (n Aggression, Pearson $r= -.28$). Their appearance to the opponent is also crucial. The more conciliatory and friendly they appear to be, the better they will fare in the outcome (perceived cooperation, $r= .32$). Moreover, high payoffs for a negotiator are associated with their adversary's personality characteristics as well. If your opponent is impulsive (n Autonomy, $r= .25$), fears social and potentially harmful situations (n Harmavoidance, $r= .28$), and possesses a low sense of efficacy and self-worth (n Counteraction, $r= -.30$), you are likely to fulfill your own bargaining goals and achieve a high payoff. Such an opponent is either too uninterested, avoidant, or timid to counteract a strong drive to individual goal maximization.

As a result of these findings and the preliminary disconfirmation of the model's assumptions about the power determinants of negotiation outcomes, a revised model can be constructed. This revision restructures the model to reflect a more complete psychodynamic explanation of the negotiation process and outcome. Not only are bargaining strategies predicted by psychological causes, but negotiation outcomes are as well (see Figure 4.8).

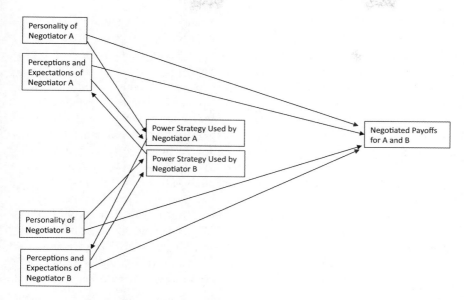

FIGURE 4.8 Revised Psychological Model of Two-Person Negotiations.

If our findings are correct and the revised model is a good schematic of negotiation dynamics, then we are confronted with a radical conclusion. We can predict how well one can fare in negotiations prior to the negotiation process! In large part, the outcome depends not on the persuasive effects of power strategies, but on the personalities and expectation of the negotiators and the dynamics of the mixture of their personalities and expectations. This is not to say that power and persuasion have no effect at all on the payoff one can achieve. In some cases, the highly credible employment of power strategies may be extremely useful in moving parties closer to agreement. But our general finding, in the context of hypothetical distributive negotiations, is that power played a minor role in determining the degree of payoff each negotiator received.

Conclusions

How have the hypotheses proposed at the outset of this study fared in the analysis? Hypothesis 1 certainly has been reinforced: negotiators who have significantly different personality profiles and situational expectations are likely to employ very different behavioral bargaining strategies. Each distinct behavior style is activated by a decidedly different set of motivational elements.

The more highly specified Hypotheses 1A and 1B were not substantiated by the experimental results. Surprisingly, none of the bargaining strategies are significantly motivated by high needs to achieve goals (n Achievement), influence others (n Dominance or n Power), overcome the other's demands (n Counteraction), oppose the adversary in a forceful manner (n Aggression), or defend oneself against aggression (n Defendance). Conceptually, these are needs that should relate strongly to important aspects in the negotiation process. However, empirical evidence was summoned on behalf of several nonobvious, though crucial, personality need configurations instead.

As for the impact of expectations on bargaining behavior (Hypothesis 1B), low threat perceptions are important predictors of cooperative, as well as conflictual, strategies. In the former case, cooperative reciprocity appears to be the motivating factor. In the latter instance, exploitation of a weak other seems to activate hostile responses. While these results can be explained logically with benefit of hindsight, prior knowledge that a negotiator perceives low threat can lead to a prediction of cooperative, as well as hostile behavior.

The inverse of Hypothesis 2 was produced by the experimental results. Rather than complementary personalities transacting toward acceptable and cooperative outcomes, they were found to employ risky, fait accompli strategies. They tend to be active and rash in their tactical commitments. Non-similar pairs tend to be more cautious and defensive, and use contingent, verbal means of persuasion. This second type does not necessarily iterate toward more deadlocked outcomes than the first type.

Finally, Hypothesis 3 was not substantiated. Although power tactics were found to be crucial in motivating particular types of behavioral responses, they could not predict outcomes. Instead, personality and perceptual variables were identified as outcome predictors. Bargainers obtain higher payoffs if they are motivated by aggressive needs, are perceived to have friendly intentions, and have adversaries who are excessively impulsive, escapist, and inefficacious.

We have explored many of the behavioral and psychological dynamics of negotiation within the experimental context of a hypothetical business situation. Many of the findings have important implications for practicing negotiators in the international arena in terms of planning strategy, predicting the other's likely strategy, and predicting the likely payoff using particular strategies. It would be an invalid exercise to generalize all of our specific results to all types of negotiations. But the findings do attest to the general fact that psychological factors can be potent predictors of the bargaining process and outcome. Further experimentation using vehicles such as the Camp Game is required to reinforce and validate our findings.

Notes

1 DeFelice, F. (1976). "Negotiations, or the Art of Negotiating," in I. W. Zartman, editor, *The 50% Solution*. New York: Doubleday Anchor; DeCallieres, Francois (1963). *On the Manner of Negotiating With Princes*. Notre Dame, IN: University of Notre Dame Press.
2 Nicolson, Harold (1946). *The Congress of Vienna*. New York: Harcourt and Brace; Nicolson, Harold (1964). *Diplomacy*. New York: Oxford.
3 Douglas, Ann (1957). "The Peaceful Settlement of Industrial and Intergroup Disputes." *Journal of Conflict Resolution* 1.

4 Cooper, Chester L. (1975). "The Iron Law of Negotiations." *Foreign Policy* 19, Summer.
5 Aquilar, F. and M. Galluccio (2008). *Psychological Processes in International Negotiations: Theoretical and Practical Perspectives*. New York: Springer; De Dreu, Carsten, Bianca Beersma, Wolfgang Steinel, and Gerben van Kleef (2007). "The Psychology of Negotiation: Principles and Basic Processes," in A. W. Kruglanski and E. T. Higgins, editors, *Social Psychology: Handbook of Basic Principles* (2nd edition). New York: Guilford Press; Druckman, Daniel, editor (1977). *Negotiations: Social Psychological Perspectives*. Beverly Hills, CA: Sage; Pruitt, Dean G. and Peter J. Carnevale (1993). *Negotiation in Social Conflict*. Pacific Grove, CA: Brooks Cole; Rubin, Jeffrey Z. and Bert Brown (1975). *The Social Psychology of Bargaining and Negotiation*. New York: Academic Press; and many others.
6 Spector, Bertram I. (1975). "The Effects of Personality, Perception and Power on the Bargaining Process and Outcome." Ph.D. Dissertation, New York University.
7 Terhune, K. (1968). "Motives, Situation, and Interpersonal Conflict Within Prisoner's Dilemma." *Journal of Personality and Social Psychology Monograph Supplement* 8. No. 3, Part 2; Scodel, A., J. Minas, P. Ratoosh, and M. Lipetz (1959). "Some Descriptive Aspects of Two-Person Non-Zero-Sum Games, I." *Journal of Conflict Resolution* 3; Minas, J., A. Scodel, P. Marlowe, and H. Rawson (1960). "Some Descriptive Aspects of Two-Person Non-Zero-Sum Games, II." *Journal of Conflict Resolution* 4; Rapoport, Anatol and A. Chammah (1965). *Prisoner's Dilemma: A Study in Conflict and Cooperation*. Ann Arbor, MI: University of Michigan Press; Shaw, Jerry and Christen Thorslund (1975). "Varying Patterns of Reward Cooperation." *Journal of Conflict Resolution* 19, March; Marlowe, D. and Kenneth J. Gergen (1969). "Personality and Social Interaction." In G. Lindzey and E. Aronson, editors, *Handbook of Social Psychology*. Second Edition, Vol. 3. Reading, MA: Addison-Wesley Publishing Co.; Maxwell, G. and D. Schmitt (1968). "Are 'Trivial' Games the Most Interesting Psychologically?" *Behavioral Science* 13; Vinacke, W. Edgar (1969). "Variables in Experimental Games: Toward a Field Theory." *Psychological Bulletin* 71.
8 Vinacke (1969), op.cit.; Terhune, K. (1970). "The Effects of Personality in Cooperation and Conflict." In Paul Swingle, editor, *The Structure of Conflict*. New York: Academic Press.
9 Terhune (1968), op.cit.; Terhune (1970), op.cit.
10 Deutsch, Morton (1960). "Trust, Trustworthiness, and the F Scale." *Journal of Abnormal and Social Psychology* 61.
11 Terhune (1970), op.cit.
12 Zartman, I. William (1976). "The Analysis of Negotiation." *The 50% Solution*, in I. William Zartman, editor. New York: Doubleday Anchor Books.
13 Iklé, Fred C. and Nathan Leites (1962). "Political Negotiations as a Process of Modifying Utilities," *Journal of Conflict Resolution* 6.
14 Stein, Morris I. (1963). "Explorations in Typology." In R. W. White, editor, *The Study of Lives*. New York: Atherton Press.
15 Stein, Morris I. and John Neulinger (1968). "A Typology of Self-Descriptions." In M. M. Katz, et al., editors, *The Role and Methodology of Classification in Psychiatry and Psychopathology*. Washington, DC: Government Printing Office, Public Health Service Publication No. 1584; Stein, Morris I. (1971). "Ecology of Typology." Paper presented at the Association of American Medical Colleges Conference on Personality Measurement in Medical Education, Des Plaines, IL; Spector, Bertram and Joseph H. Moskowitz (1975). "Risk and Styles of Political Dissent Within the Executive Branch: Some Social Psychological and Personality Correlates." Unpublished manuscript, CACI, Inc.
16 This list of manifest needs was initially developed by psychologist Henry Murray; see Murray, Henry A. (1938). *Explorations in Personality*. New York: John Wiley and Sons, Inc.

17 Madron, Thomas W. (1969). *Small Group Methods and the Study of Politics*. Evanston, IL: Northwestern University Press.
18 Baldwin, John D. (1969). "Influences Detrimental to Simulation Gaming." *American Behavioral Scientist* 12, July–August.
19 Neulinger and Stein (1971), op.cit. Compared to a much larger and heterogeneous test group, the personality characteristics of the majority of subjects participating in the game were more conformist, counteractive, achievement, and dominance-oriented, and thus may respond in more hostile formations than a "normal" group (see Spector 1975, op.cit.).
20 These and all path coefficients that are presented are statistically significant at the .05 level or below. The method employed for deleting insignificant paths – or "theory trimming" – is discussed in Kerlinger, Fred N. and Elazar J. Pedhazur (1973). *Multiple Regression in Behavior Research*. New York: Holt, Rinehart, and Winston, Inc. The signs on path coefficients linked to SDQ needs are reflected to ease interpretation.
21 Standardized path coefficients (betas) are shown next to each path arrow in Figures 4.3, 4.4, 4.5, and 4.6. Coefficients in parentheses are Pearson r correlations. To aid in interpretation, the signs on all coefficients linking personality needs to other variables have been reflected. N = 49 excluding dummy players.
22 Neirenberg, Gerald (1973). *Fundamentals of Negotiating*. New York: Hawthorn Books.
23 Terhune (1970), op.cit.

5
THE NEGOTIABILITY OF NATIONS

Negotiation is a behavioral process among parties to solve a problem, settle a conflict, or achieve a common goal. As with any process, sometimes it is easy and sometimes it hard to accomplish. The course that this process takes depends largely on many contextual factors, not least of which are the characteristics of the other parties in the negotiation and the chemistry of those characteristics with the negotiator's own. Key elements that describe "who" one is negotiating with, such as the ease or difficulty of negotiations, their capacity to negotiate, and party trustworthiness can be assessed and their confluence described as a country's *negotiability* quotient.

Negotiability, as defined here, does not focus on individual personalities of negotiators. Rather, it is a way to monitor how a nation negotiates and the extent it can be trusted to execute the agreed provisions. Simply, it focuses on a country's *ability to negotiate and its reliability to implement negotiated agreements* – a country's capacity to negotiate effectively and in good faith. Negotiability monitors aspects of a nation's negotiation prowess. By understanding the other party's negotiability, one can better understand what makes the other side tick and whether they are or will be a good partner in the negotiation. This measure can incorporate, for example, a nation's understanding and capacity to conduct negotiations, the ease or difficulty by which it does so, and its commitment and trustworthiness in following through on agreements made, among others.

I distinguish a *nation's* negotiability from whether an *issue* is "negotiable." For an issue to be negotiable, there needs to be some agreement among parties that how the issue is dealt with is open for discussion and adjustment. An issue is negotiable if parties are willing to consider new ways to understand it, address it, or resolve it. But when talking about a nation's negotiability, we are focusing instead on how open, closed, prepared, and committed a country is to engage in the process of negotiating. It is a way of thinking about and understanding a nation's entry into a

DOI: 10.4324/9781003314400-5

negotiation setting that can help the other parties to prepare and work with each other in the most productive way.

Negotiators typically prepare for upcoming talks during the pre-negotiation phase. They analyze the issues being considered, their own interests, what they are seeking to get out of the negotiation, the power relationship among parties, and the implications of different provisions and potential outcomes, among many other factors.

One consideration that is perhaps the most important to analyze at this early phase is how the other side is likely to behave in the negotiation setting. Trying to understand the other side's negotiating style is typically a subjective matter. How negotiators from particular countries operate, interact, bargain, and make decisions may be understood by other negotiators who have engaged with them in the past via anecdotes, or worse, stereotypes. Sometimes, there are news reports about the negotiators or opinion pieces that they have written that can provide some insight into their modus operandi.

Cultural factors can also play an important role in how a nation's negotiators operate; intercultural negotiations can be affected by divergences in values, beliefs, manners, and approaches to the process which can shape actions.[1] Scholarly research of how culture affects negotiation behavior is still limited by broad presumptions of cultural approaches based on a relatively small number of cases. There are few clear and measurable ways to assess cultural inclinations, especially at the international negotiating table. All of these factors – among many others – are usually considered in the pre-negotiation stage to prepare for effective talks.

An Example of Negotiation Styles

Practitioners and researchers try to develop narratives of national negotiation styles. For example, North Korea is often portrayed as conducting its negotiating behaviors in such a way as to gain leverage and power based on its understanding that it is almost always negotiating from a position of weakness.[2] They practice crisis diplomacy and brinksmanship: making unconditional demands for unilateral concessions, bluffing, threatening, stalling, or setting deadlines. Their style is to engineer the environment to pressure the stronger parties to concede. As part of their strategy, the North Koreans typically do not agree to anything until the entire package of issues is finalized. By refusing to make incremental concessions along the way, they maintain whatever leverage they have until the final agreement is reached. Their style is seen as being tough, rough, rugged, and contentious, but cautious. They do not accept any preconditions.

A negotiation style narrative is usually based on past experience bargaining with diplomats from those countries. It is largely subjective and qualitative, and likely to vary based on impressions at the time and the nature of the issues being negotiated. Like cultural explanations of negotiation behavior, these narratives are not subject to corroboration and not likely to provide a strong basis for future negotiation encounters.

Measuring Negotiability

Rather than rely on cultural concepts or style narratives, perhaps there is a more objective, reliable, and multidimensional way to assess and measure a nation's likely negotiation behavior. According to Shefska, bargaining over the sale of used automobiles is subject to negotiability measurement.[3] A buyer can refer to a negotiability database of used vehicles to assess if the seller is likely to be willing to bargain on the listed selling price. This negotiability quotient is based on three factors: the supply of similar vehicles locally, the amount of time the seller has listed the vehicle for sale, and how close it is to the end of the month. The higher the index, the more willing the seller is likely to be to haggle about the price, but the lower the index, the more unwilling the seller will be. Measuring the negotiability of nations in preparation for an international bargaining session is a bit more complicated.

How can a nation's negotiability be monitored and measured to help practitioners prepare? When measuring national negotiability, the focus needs to be at the country level across a variety of dimensions that considers how the country is prepared to negotiate and eventually implement the agreement if the negotiation is successful. Currently, there are no clear quantitative indices that specifically assess a country's negotiation behavior or reliability, but there are existing measures that can serve as proxies for what we are looking for. Negotiability can be considered to include several key dimensions and indices (see Table 5.1).

TABLE 5.1 Dimensions and Measures of Negotiability.

Dimensions	Potential measures
Legitimacy and Authority. Is the government of the country viewed as a legitimate government? Does it possess the authority to rule?	• Voice and accountability index (World Bank Governance Indicators)
Rule of Law. Does the country govern based on the rule of law or through corrupt networks or authoritarian dictates? Can one believe the actions taken by government in a negotiation setting to be reliable and based on the country's system of laws and regulations?	• Rule of law index (World Bank Governance Indicators)
Government Effectiveness. Is the government viewed as effectively governing the country?	• Government effectiveness index (World Bank Governance Indicators)
Capacity and Resources. Does the government have proven capacity to make decisions and implement policy at the domestic and international levels?	• Gross domestic product per capita (World Bank Open Data)
International Confidence. Does the international community view the country as politically stable and a reasonable place to invest in? Is corruption seen as being under control?	• Foreign direct investments as a percent of GDP (World Bank Open Data) • Political stability index (World Bank Governance Indicators) • Control of corruption index (World Bank Governance Indicators)

60 Negotiability of Nations

These five dimensions capture key aspects of a nation's capacity to negotiate and implement negotiated agreements. They assess the extent to which:

- The government is viewed as legitimate and stable.
- The government is founded on the rule of law and not on undemocratic and unpredictable decrees and, so, is relatively predictable.
- The government has the ability and authority to follow-through on its decisions.
- The government has the wherewithal to conduct negotiations and implement policy.
- The government is seen as a valid and reliable partner by other countries.

In this study, the measures that we draw upon to capture these dimensions are well-established indices, but they are not specifically focused on a nation's negotiation behavior. We offer them as potential measures and believe they suggest the general directions of the dimensions which can be meaningful to practitioners and to researchers. Further research could offer additional paths for monitoring these negotiability dimensions.

Trial Measurements

For this study, only a few countries were selected for testing that would likely yield very different results for the negotiability quotient. Australia, France and the United States were expected to score fairly high, while Iran, Sudan and North Korea would score poorly, and Indonesia would be somewhere in between (see Figure 5.1). For simplicity's sake, we only use the World Bank Governance Indicators to measure four out of the five negotiability dimensions.

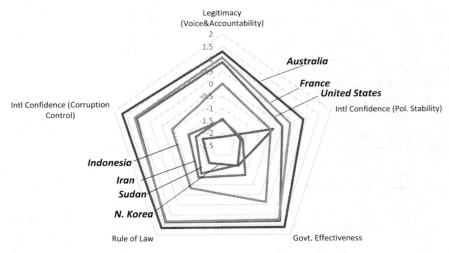

FIGURE 5.1 Negotiability Dimensions for Seven Countries.

Our assumptions are proven correct. Australia, France, and the United States score in the upper one-third on all dimensions. Iran, Sudan, and North Korea score in the lower one-third on all dimensions. And Indonesia is in the middle. This suggests that the three higher scoring countries have high legitimacy, rule of law, government effectiveness, and international confidence, while the three lowest scoring countries are at the other end of the spectrum.

A negotiator could look at this data and conclude that the top three countries are likely to be more valid partners in international negotiation sessions, while the lowest three countries would be more unreliable negotiators, untrustworthy, and probably unlikely to follow-through on any agreement.

Practitioner Considerations

When negotiators are entering the pre-negotiation planning phase, they need to assess many factors. A critical set that is also very hard to monitor relates to who they will be negotiating with – are they trained and capable, are they trustworthy, can their words be believed, and are they reliable partners? These concerns – all related to a nation's negotiability quotient – are difficult to measure.

Practitioners often turn to cultural factors to better understand the other parties at the negotiating table. Culture is a very important consideration in influencing negotiation behavior and explaining it. But trying to measure culture is a highly subjective endeavor. The negotiability quotient presented in this essay is more objective, can be measured quantitatively over time, and incorporates several factors that relate in some way to cultural identities.

You can measure a specific nation's negotiability, but international negotiations involve interactions between two or more countries. The mixture of negotiability among all the involved countries, including your own, is what matters. How the nation's characteristics mix and match will dictate how easily the talks will proceed. Practitioners should compare their negotiability profile with the profiles of the others at the table to get the best picture of how the negotiations are likely to advance.

A country's negotiability can change over time; it is not a static feature. As a result, the dimensions that are monitored should be reviewed on a longitudinal basis and data that is used to assess current negotiability ratings should be kept up to date. In addition, some aspects of negotiability may change across issue areas over time. For example, how a nation reacts to issues and provisions that arise in a security negotiation may be very different from how it behaves in a trade or environmental negotiation. It would make sense, as a result, to see if there are adjusted data that can be monitored that focus on the negotiation issue at hand.

Conclusions

Negotiability measurement and analysis is an essential feature of pre-negotiation planning that should be mandatory for all practitioners. It is also a good and practical alternative to cultural explanations of negotiation behavior.

Future research should consider different formulations of the negotiability quotient for nations – using alternate indices or measures that capture the negotiability dimensions. Research can also assess whether different dimensions are relevant for different issues and sectors that may be the focus of negotiation. As well, research can further examine how negotiability correlates with success factors in negotiation – if certain negotiability features promote success in achieving agreements that are favorable to a country's goals.

Notes

1 Cohen, Raymond (1997). *Negotiating Across Cultures*. Washington, DC: United States Institute of Peace Press; Faure, Guy Olivier, and Jeffrey Rubin (1993). *Culture and Negotiation*. Newbury Park, CA: SAGE.
2 Carlin, Robert (2019). "Negotiating with North Korea," February 19. Stimson Center. At: https://www.38north.org/2019/02/rcarlin021919/#:~:text=As%20a%20general%20rule%2C%20North%20Korean%20negotiators%20proceed,carve%20out%20room%20for%20flexibility%20down%20the%20line; Snyder, Scott (2000). "Negotiating on the Edge: Patterns in North Korea's Diplomatic Style." *World Affairs* 163, 1: 3–17.
3 Shefska, Zach (2020). "How is Negotiability Score Calculated?" At: https://help.yaamember.com/hc/en-us/articles/360056761413-How-is-Negotiability-Score-calculated-.

6
INCOMPLETE INTERNATIONAL NEGOTIATIONS
Adding Implementation Formulas

International negotiations that result in an agreement are typically viewed as successful, but this is actually only an interim or processual achievement. Certainly, negotiating agreements is a difficult process, especially when resolving long-lasting conflicts, initiating security pacts, or generating paths toward economic cooperation. But if one or more parties do not follow through on implementing their negotiated commitments, the ultimate outcome of the overall process can be seen as a failure.

The assumption at the end of most negotiation processes is that the agreed provisions will be implemented by all parties so that the negotiated results will have the desired impact. Success needs to be measured and determined not by words (that is, the negotiated agreement), but by deeds (how that agreement is implemented).

Most research on international negotiations has converged on three interlinked processes: *pre-negotiation* efforts – how the parties get to the table, *negotiation* efforts – how the parties present their interests to one another and reach a deal, and *post-agreement negotiation* efforts – how the parties modify the negotiated provisions over time to adjust to changing conditions. One critical subprocess in this chain that has often been overlooked and is not included in many international negotiations is concerned with what happens immediately after an agreement is negotiated to ensure that the provisions are faithfully executed.[1] Is the implementation of negotiated provisions to be left totally to the anticipated good intentions of the engaged parties? It would make sense to extend the negotiation phase that achieved agreement on the technical and substantive provisions of the agreement to include an additional subprocess that hashes out an action plan that prescribes how the technical provisions will be implemented and the rules that the parties must comply with to ensure the negotiated agreement is faithfully put into effect.

This essay examines not why negotiation *processes* fail, but why negotiated *agreements* fail when they are not implemented as expected. Can the negotiation process be adjusted to avert the potential for negative results as a result of unimplemented provisions? We examine options to activate explicit and inclusive negotiation efforts focused on how agreed provisions can be implemented effectively by all engaged parties. The resulting implementation strategy must be included as a mandatory feature of the overall negotiated outcome, not one left to chance.

Based on research about failed implementation, we can design more rigorous and targeted approaches to establish "implementation negotiations" as an embedded process in international talks that seek to end a wide range of conflict and/or problem-solving situations. First, we review research findings about negotiated agreements that then fail to get implemented. Then, we turn to studies that examine why implementation of negotiated agreements is so often a problem, especially for agreements that end civil wars. Next, we lay out a detailed approach to incorporate negotiations about implementation strategies that can be appended to the overall negotiation process. Lastly, a practical structure for this special type of negotiation will be presented.

Research on Agreement Implementation

Much research has addressed why the negotiation process sometimes fails – why conflict parties that have agreed to negotiate cannot find a solution and then break off talks with no agreement while the conflict continues.[2] Usually this happens after talks have been under way, the parties' interests in an agreed solution have been presented, and options to resolve the conflict have been exchanged and discussed. But after all of this, at least one side still considers the status quo more desirable than accepting a compromise or an outcome that the other side wants.

Zartman considers another scenario – where a negotiation process might produce a partial success, but consciously stops before reaching a complete peace agreement, what he calls a "partial peace." He examines peace agreements that result in a ceasefire, but do not resolve all the issues at the core of the conflict.[3] Ceasefire agreements typically address only a very limited number of issues – primarily stopping the armed violence – and leave more difficult issues for some future negotiation. These partial agreements may include only certain parties to the conflict, leaving out those that might not be ready to make compromises, but could easily turn into spoilers. Such agreements may be sufficient for the time being, but are usually not durable. Because important issues and actors may remain outside the negotiated agreement, such partial negotiations might yield a temporary ceasefire, but could be difficult or impossible to sustain due to an absence of trust and confidence in the other parties.

What we are interested in examining here is different. In many cases, negotiating parties persevere and nail down an agreement that all say they can live with. Each agrees to the provisions of the agreement and commits to implementing their end so that the problem or conflict that initiated the negotiation process can be fitfully resolved. But for some reason, the negotiated agreement is not implemented as anticipated. The expected follow-through by the engaged parties to fulfill the negotiated provisions does not happen, leaving the conflict situation still in play. Since the negotiations have ended, that leaves the field wide open for the initiating conflict to reemerge. Why does this happen even after what appears to be faithfully conducted negotiations and agreement? Walters suggests this is a frequent occurrence.[4] Successfully negotiated agreements to end civil wars, for example, were not implemented in Laos, China, the Philippines, Angola, Afghanistan, Chad, Uganda, Somalia, Liberia, and Rwanda between 1940 and 1992.

One reason that negotiated agreements fail to get implemented is that not enough thought by the conflict parties was directed toward figuring out an action plan for implementation at the time the agreement was reached. The parties may have dialogued extensively, and developed and bargained over formulas that would resolve the technical issues that were at the heart of their disagreements. An agreement laying out how they would resolve their differences may have been put into words and signed by all parties, but they may not have worked out a detailed plan of action that would turn those words into concrete implementable initiatives.

Some data exists on the extent to which implementation planning is included in peace negotiations. The Language of Peace database that includes the texts of 979 interstate and intrastate peace agreements signed between 1942 and 2020 indicates that 71% of agreements overall include some provisions related to how the agreements will be implemented, but they are typically not comprehensive.[5] These mechanisms include monitoring bodies (45%), observers (11%), procedures to follow in case of violations (11%), implementation timelines (29%), and general implementation provisions (47%).

Another collection of interstate and intrastate peace agreements – The Peace Agreements Database – contains 1,915 texts signed between 1990 and 2021 that are related to more than 150 different peace processes.[6] This database finds that 38% of the texts include enforcement mechanisms, 29% include provisions for an international mission to enforce the agreement, 43% include the United Nations or another international actor as signatory to the agreement, and only 1% includes a provision for parties to hold a referendum domestically to approve the agreement.

These findings suggest that the inclusion of implementation provisions in the negotiations of peace agreements is not at the top of the list for engaged parties or mediators. It does happen some of the time, but it is not considered a mandatory feature of these peace negotiations. Somehow, in most cases, the engaged parties are expected to live up to their commitments, but there are only limited pre-thought plans for how they will do this or how the agreement will be enforced.

Note that these databases only include agreements on interstate and intrastate peace treaties, not negotiated agreements concerning the environment, trade, economics, security, business, legal, scientific, or cultural issues, among others.

There has been very little research conducted on how these other agreements have been implemented and whether implementation provisions were included in their negotiation processes. There is no reason why there should not be a concerted effort to incorporate such implementation negotiation efforts in all types of international negotiations. After all, why leave implementation to chance after all the difficult work to achieve agreement to solve the conflict or problem? If done right, always including negotiations about the implementation of agreement provisions as part of the overall issue-related negotiation stands to make the entire negotiation process more effective and impactful.

Even if some attempts have been made to include implementation plans into negotiated agreements, they are often stymied in their initial steps. One of the first implementation problems that internationally negotiated agreements might face is a ratification battle domestically in the legislature and/or executive branch, only after which detailed implementation of specific provisions can proceed. Ratification does not guarantee compliance with the provisions of the agreement, but it does indicate a willingness and intent to comply. The need to ratify opens up multiple domestic negotiations among supporters and opponents of the agreement – essentially restarting multi-actor negotiations once again, but now at a national level, with many new interests and issues on the table. As a result, these multiple processes, in each of the engaged actors to the original agreement, can take a long time to complete and could very well activate spoiler factions that prevent domestic ratification and implementation.

In the United States, there is a long list of unratified international agreements that have been signed at the negotiating table, but not ratified or implemented by the United States to date.[7] These include 37 agreements that were negotiated between 1948 and 2016, including International Labor Organization conventions, the Vienna Convention on the Law of Treaties, the Maritime Boundary Agreement between the United States and Cuba, the Convention on the Elimination of All Forms of Discrimination against Women, the Convention on Biological Diversity, the UN Convention on the Law of the Sea, and many more.

Focusing on 94 international environmental agreements (between 1921 and 1989) in particular, Spector and Korula found several factors that play a significant role in effecting domestic ratification speed.[8] Over the entire period, the average length of time to ratify these agreements was 5.8 years, but by the 1980s the average time was closer to 3 years. Issue complexity in the agreement is a major contributing factor to the delay – from 4.75 years on average for single issue agreements to 7.2 years on average for multi-issue agreements. Higher GDP countries ratified the treaties faster than lower GDP countries. Nations where public concern was focused on international environmental problems ratified the treaties faster than countries where the public was more concerned about local environmental issues. If ratification of negotiated agreements takes such a long time, that typically puts the rest of the negotiated provisions on hold, while state parties to the agreement may begin to become wary of the intentions of other signatories.

Implementation of Agreements Ending Civil Wars

Most in depth research on how and why negotiated agreements are implemented (or not) has been conducted in relation to peace agreements that end civil wars. As described earlier, the negotiation of these intrastate peace agreements has included implementation provisions to some degree. However, in intrastate contexts, the fragility and factionalization of a country, its institutions, and its population make implementation a tenuous activity, highly subject to failure, especially if the rules of implementation are not defined along with the conflict management/resolution provisions themselves. There are many important lessons that can be learned from how these intrastate conflict implementation negotiations have been carried out, as well as the assessment of their relative success.

A study of 23 cases where comprehensive civil war peace agreements were negotiated and signed found that less than half of these agreements were actually implemented by the parties.[9] The parties failed to fulfill their commitments. Another study examines the implementation of 34 intrastate peace agreements signed between 1989 and 2012.[10] Only 49% of these 34 agreements were fully implemented within 10 years of the signing or earlier. A total of 38% experienced some, but incomplete, implementation, whereas 13% were not implemented at all. Of these agreements, 76% included particular provisions for internal or third-party verification and reporting of compliance with the agreement over the course of 10 years – among many other ceasefire, conflict management, and political reform provisions. However, only 59% of these verification provisions were actually implemented.

When Implementation Fails

Peace agreements that end civil wars often are missing the detailed implementation mechanisms that are necessary to turn words into deeds. What are some of the reasons that can explain why so many peace agreements to end civil wars are not implemented?

Missing Incentives and Fear of Cheating

From a motivational perspective, there are often no negative incentives or legal sanctions if actors fail to comply with their commitments. As a result, there is a constant fear by each side of cheating by the other. If third parties are engaged, they often have only minimal leverage over the active participants. To follow-through on the agreement, financial support from the outside is usually required, but may not be forthcoming.[11]

Low State Capacity

The level of state capacity is another factor that can contribute to implementation failure, especially after a civil war. If capacity is high, implementation success can be strongly predicted, but as state capacity weakens, third party interventions become more important for successful implementation. Research shows that if capacity is very low, even extensive third-party efforts are not likely to be sufficient to ensure effective implementation of negotiated agreements.[12]

Different Teams Negotiating and Implementing

The team negotiating the substantive agreement is often not the same team that implements the agreement domestically in each of the signatory countries.[13] As a result, there is often a lack of coordination, push back, or worse, deadlock, in the implementation process.

Changing Power Relationships and Context

The implementation environment can transform quickly, resulting in a change of power relationships. The actors engaged in implementing the agreement continually compare the risks and vulnerabilities for themselves and others of carrying out the negotiated provisions. If there is power asymmetry among the parties or if one side perceives that it has an advantage, then implementation is likely to lag or fail. This would be the case if spoiler factions emerge and they believe it is in their interest to undo the negotiated agreement. But in situations of power symmetry and where all the parties perceive a mutual vulnerability, they are all more likely to implement the provisions. Sometimes, this requires an opening for continual ad hoc bargaining among the actors during the implementation period to compare changing perceptions of the situation.[14]

Uncertainties in Power-sharing Provisions

Power-sharing provisions in the negotiated agreement are often considered to be essential to effective implementation. But research shows that the implementation of power-sharing provisions has varying impacts depending on how authority is allocated. If the provisions deal with military or territorial power-sharing, the concessions that have to be made by all sides are costly and slow-moving, but the data show that implementation has a positive effect on maintaining the peace. If the provisions address political power-sharing, the results are often seen quickly, but there is no impact on a lasting peace.[15]

Drivers of Compliance

On the other hand, what factors encourage signatories to keep their commitments related to peace agreements? A study by Werner and Yuen suggests that negotiated agreements that last – where commitments are maintained and the provisions are implemented – do so if they increase the *costs of defection*, enhance *monitoring and enforcement* by third parties, and *reward cooperation*.[16] These motivators need to be elements of the negotiated agreement, which must specify not only who gets what and when, but how these provisions will be enforced. These enforcement features encourage trust among the actors and discourage noncompliance with agreed-upon terms. Actors certainly take risks that the other side will not live up to its commitments, especially when negotiating peace agreements to civil wars. And because the context is typically fragile and apt to change over time, uncertainty can grow resulting in lagged implementation. But persistent third-party pressure, including their imposition of threats if provisions are not implemented as agreed, can be a critical element in countering this uncertainty. If third-parties lose interest or reduce pressure on the agreement's actors, the agreement can fall apart.

One of Werner and Yuen's most important insights is that negotiated agreements which are vulnerable to high risks and uncertainty should embed some flexibility within the agreement to *adjust the provisions over time* to keep the terms up-to-date and in play. The possibility for re-negotiation or post-agreement negotiation to modify the provisions can reduce fears that actors may have that a changed environment over the longer term might not lean in their favor.

Mislin et al. concur that post-agreement behavior is largely determined by *economic motives*.[17] The parties to the agreement know that promises made are not always promises kept. A perception of the other side's trustworthiness can help negotiations arrive at a positive conclusion; an agreement can be struck. But skepticism about whether the other side will honor its negotiated commitments can persist into the implementation period. This unease can be reduced by structuring an economic cost-benefit equation, with positive and negative incentives, into the agreement or into a contingent agreement that addresses post-deal implementation – with rewards or punishments if the negotiated provisions are fulfilled or not.

Implementation Strategies that Can Be Negotiated to Enhance Execution

What works best at making civil war peace agreements stick are *trust-enhancing mechanisms*.[18] Even after an agreement has been negotiated between parties that have been in conflict over their common country, there is usually a lot of questioning over whether the other side can be trusted to implement the provisions. That is why outside guarantors must be packaged within the negotiated agreement – typically international third parties – to conduct monitoring and verification of the actions of all parties to demonstrate that there is no cheating. Beyond the monitoring task, these guarantors can also be assigned the more proactive jobs of creating buffer zones, forging external military alliances, generating trade and economic relationships as a reward for faithful implementation, and withholding resources as negative incentives for cheating behaviors. The third party promises to step in if there is a problem. Walter refers to this strategy as creating a context of "credible commitment" by all signatories to the peace agreement. It needs to be incorporated in the agreement when negotiated, rather than left to some future opportunity.

In line with Walter's conclusion, an analysis of agreements between 1946 and 1997 found that the durability of civil war peace agreements is improved if an *international peacekeeping mission* is included as a negotiated provision.[19] This international presence reduces uncertainty among the parties based on their monitoring and verification, and raises the costs of breaking the agreement, in which international assistance and military support can be removed. The international mission can also prevent accidental violations and promote continued dialogue among the parties that builds confidence.

But there is no cookie-cutter approach for designing effective implementation strategies. They need to be formulated based on the context, the level of distrust, and the degree of difficulty faced by the parties. There must be a focus on confidence building among the parties, and that can include international involvement in the implementation process, allocation of sufficient resources, and the option of coercive reactions if there is defection from the implementation plan.[20] This can include United Nations, great power, or regional power engagement working in coordination with one another, and prioritizing and sequencing the implementation of the many provisions of the agreement.

Analyzing a database of 51 civil war settlements, long term implementation was found to be more successful when the conflict actors agreed – in the negotiated text – to submit military information to international third parties, allowing the internationals to actively monitor and verify the agreement's implementation process.[21] This, in addition to the inclusion of power-sharing provisions between the conflict parties in the agreement, helped to address information uncertainty and the other's intentions.

These findings are reinforced by other studies. "Monitoring and oversight mechanisms" (MOMs) are found to be very effective in ensuring the successful implementation of civil war peace agreements.[22] MOMs can take the form of a committee, commission or board that monitors and oversees implementation of the agreement and determines compliance. In addition to monitoring, verifying and reporting on party compliance with agreement provisions, MOMs can provide a forum for continuing negotiations when adjustments are needed, provide parties with early warning about potential pitfalls in the future, and offer opportunities to include civil society groups in the peace implementation process. Analysis shows that MOMs need to be incorporated in the negotiated agreement and be able to operate from the very start of the implementation process. They benefit if they have clear lines of accountability to the conflict parties and long-term commitments to operate.

The *inclusion of civil society* in the negotiated provisions to conduct monitoring and verification of conflict party actions is another approach that has been shown to be a positive element that strengthens agreement implementation.[23] Civil society organizations bring local knowledge, access to communities, and useful skills if further mediation is needed to facilitate implementation of the negotiated provisions. They can be included by and report to the MOMs, while getting financial support from the MOMs directly.

Another mechanism that has been employed to facilitate agreement implementation in civil war peace agreements is to mandate in the negotiated agreement that signatories generate *constitutional amendments* with direct citizen engagement within a year of signing.[24] This was done in the 2016 Colombian Comprehensive Peace Agreement. It resulted in an environment where implementation was viewed as more legitimate and the parties were viewed as credible and compliant with the agreement. Another study shows that 79% of civil wars that ended with a negotiated agreement developed new post-conflict constitutions because they were mandated by the agreement, and this served to legitimize and institutionalize the agreement's reforms and made them subject to law enforcement.[25]

Establishing rules and procedures for *sequencing and timing* implementation in the negotiated agreement is also often critical to overcoming factionalism.[26] By setting up a timeline to introduce and execute provisions of the agreement – often in parallel with one another – blocking coalitions and spoiler factions can be prevented because all parties can see that all the agreed provisions are in fact proceeding, even if some take longer to achieve results than others.

Based on this research, it appears that negotiating and embedding these types of implementation strategies into the negotiated agreement adds value to the technical and substantive solution that was arrived at. They offer the mechanisms that can make or break the outcome of the negotiations. But as discussed in Chapter 2, the negotiation process and its outcomes are, after all, only experiments. Negotiators try out ideas, plans, and formulas that they think will satisfy their interests and the interests of the other parties, thus honing in on the outcomes that all parties are searching for. But they are never sure how the solutions will play out, given ever-changing contexts. So, negotiators experiment with the utility and viability of the conflict-focused negotiated provisions. When negotiators append these negotiated provisions with concrete implementation strategies to execute these provisions, it can add an extra layer of confidence that the technical solutions that were negotiated will indeed be applied and achieve their goals.

A Way Forward: Negotiating Implementation Formulas

If successfully negotiated agreements fail to get implemented due to insufficient, ignored, mishandled, or delayed action to carry out the agreement's provisions, it could be a signal that one important element of the negotiation process was missing – how the agreed provisions would be implemented. After the technical provisions were hashed out among the parties, there could have been a final set of negotiation sessions to itemize a detailed implementation formula that all could agree on. This implementation formula would – as much as possible – seek to ensure that the parties have a plan and know what to do to transform the words in the agreement document into tangible deeds that will have their intended effect. This negotiated implementation formula could serve as a plan to transform a successfully negotiated agreement into actions that will have an impact on the problem and/or conflict that initiated the negotiation in the first place.

A formula that specifies how the negotiating parties agree to resolve their problem/conflict is at the heart of most negotiations. It delves into the issues under discussion and provides actionable proposals on how those issues can be resolved that all can agree to. Once such a formula that tackles the contentious issues is negotiated and decided, most negotiations conclude with an agreement that outlines this formula and the process is deemed a success. But one additional set of negotiations to operationalize the implementation of this formula would bring the process one step closer toward ensuring that the agreement is executed faithfully and as intended. While it cannot guarantee implementation, a negotiated implementation formula would provide additional confidence that the engaged parties will live up to their commitments as expected. One can envision such an implementation formula as a plan of action that is tied directly to the negotiated provisions that were agreed to by the parties to resolve the problem or conflict issues that initiated the negotiations.

As an operational plan of action, the implementation formula needs to address several specific questions at a minimum:

- Will a committee of engaged parties and/or third parties be established to administer the implementation process?
- When does implementation begin?
- Who will do what, when, and in coordination with whom?
- What is the timeline and sequencing for provision implementation?
- Who is assigned to monitor and verify that these implementation actions are indeed accomplished?
- How often will monitoring and verification reporting be provided to the parties?
- Is domestic ratification required by the parties to finalize the agreement? Can implementation of provisions proceed whether the agreement is ratified or not?
- What happens if parties fail to implement provisions as agreed to? Are rewards and punishments specified for parties if they appropriately follow-through (or not) on their negotiated commitments?
- If adjustments are required in the post-agreement period, who is assigned to initiate additional dialogue, coordination, negotiation, or mediation?
- Is there a role for third parties to push the implementation forward?
- Are civil society, businesses, and the media given roles to support implementation?
- Where will the needed resources (technical and financial) come from to support the implementation?

The itemization of how negotiated provisions should be implemented using these and any additional questions seems to be a critically essential element of any formal agreement. The negotiation of these implementation issues should become mandatory for any important agreement – especially one where there is a power asymmetry among the parties that can produce a crisis of trust and confidence that the other party will actually follow-through on their commitments. When the parties to an agreement wield differing levels of power and influence, the weaker parties can genuinely believe that there is a major risk in implementing the negotiated compromise due to the threat of potential cheating that would put them in a very precarious spot.

The main reason for negotiating an implementation formula as part of the overall negotiated agreement is to generate more certainty that the provisions will be executed. But having an agreed implementation plan will also provide the engaged actors a greater sense of trust and confidence that the other parties will do as they agreed, thereby reducing the risk that one side's compromise will not be taken advantage of by the other side.

Certainly, the elements that are included in an implementation formula need to be aligned contextually to the situation and the sector or issue area that the agreement addresses. Agreements that end civil wars, end interstate wars, initiate new trade provisions, or commence climate change initiatives, for example – because of their very different provisions – are likely to require different types of implementation actions by the parties in different sequences and timelines. These differences do not minimize the need for an implementation formula, but may require variations in the way the negotiated provisions are planned and executed.

Generally, negotiators should be strongly motivated to conduct such implementation negotiations once the basic agreement has been reached. Why not add a bit more certainty that all of their efforts will yield the results they intended, rather than having the agreement fall flat if not implemented? When parties initially sit down at the table and develop the overall negotiating agenda, implementation planning should be included on the list of issues to consider – if they get that far. Making such implementation negotiations mandatory will push the agreements reached one step closer to achieving their intended impacts and produce more negotiation processes that are truly successful.

Notes

1 Walter, Barbara F. (2002b). "Re-Conceptualizing Conflict Resolution as a Three-Stage Process," *International Negotiation* 7, 3: 299–311.
2 Faure, Guy-Olivier, editor (2012). *Unfinished Business: Why International Negotiations Fail.* Athens, GA: University of Georgia Press.
3 Zartman, I. William (2021). "Gray Peace: Is Part of a Peace Sufficient?" *International Negotiation* 26, 3: 359–365.
4 Walter, Barbara F. (2002a). *Committing to Peace: The Successful Settlement of Civil Wars.* Princeton, NJ: Princeton University Press.
5 Language of Peace (2021). *Language of Peace Database.* At: languageofpeace.org.
6 University of Edinburgh (2021). *Peace Agreements Database (PA-X, Version 5).* At: peaceagreements.org.
7 US Department of State (2019). "Treaties Pending in the Senate, October 22, 2019." At: https://www.state.gov/treaties-pending-in-the-senate/.
8 Spector, Bertram and Anna Korula (1993). "Problems of Ratifying International Environmental Agreements," *Global Environmental Change* 3, 4 (December): 369–381.

9 Walter (2002a), op.cit.
10 Joshi, Madhav, Jason Michael Quinn and Patrick M Regan (2015). "Annualized implementation data on comprehensive peace accords, 1989–2012," *Journal of Peace Research* 52, 4: 551–562.
11 Stedman, Stephen (2002). "Policy Implications," in Stephen Stedman, Donald Rothchild and Elizabeth Cousens, editors, *Ending Civil Wars: The Implementation of Peace Agreements*. Boulder, CO: Lynne Rienner; Walter (2002b), op.cit.; Shinn, James and James Dobbins (2011). *Afghan Peace Talks: A Primer*. Santa Monica, CA: RAND Corporation.
12 DeRouen Jr., Karl, Mark J. Ferguson, Samuel Norton, Young Hwan Park, Jenna Lea and Ashley Streat-Bartlett (2010). "Civil war peace agreement implementation and state capacity," *Journal of Peace Research* 47, 3: 333–346.
13 Program on Negotiation (2020). "Putting Your Negotiated Agreement Into Action." At: https://www.pon.harvard.edu/daily/negotiation-skills-daily/we-have-a-deal-now-what-do-we-do-three-negotiation-tips-on-implementing-your-negotiated-agreement/.
14 Bekoe, Dorina A. (2005). "Mutual Vulnerability and the Implementation of Peace Agreements: Examples from Mozambique, Angola and Liberia," *International Journal of Peace Studies* 10, 2: 43–68.
15 Jarstad, Anna K. and Desiree Nilsson (2008). "From Words to Deeds: The Implementation of Power-Sharing Pacts in Peace Accords," *Conflict Management and Peace Science* 25, 3: 206–223.
16 Werner, Suzanne and Amy Yuen (2005). "Making and Keeping Peace," *International Organization* 59, 2: 261–292.
17 Mislin, A. A., et al. (2011). "After the Deal: Talk, trust building and the implementation of negotiated agreements." *Organizational Behavior and Human Decision Processes* 115, 1: 55–68.
18 Walter, Barbara F. (1997). "The Critical Barrier to Civil War Settlement," *International Organization* 51, 3: 335–364.
19 Fortna, Virginia Page (2003). "Scraps of Paper? Agreements and the Durability of Peace," *International Organization* 57 (Spring): 337–372.
20 Stedman (2002), op.cit.
21 Mattes, Michaela and Burcu Savun (2010). "Information, Agreement Design, and the Durability of Civil War Settlements," *American Journal of Political Science* 54, 2: 511–524.
22 Verjee, Aly (2020). *After the Agreement: Why the Oversight of Peace Deals Succeeds or Fails*. Washington, DC: US Institute of Peace.
23 Ross, Nick (2017). "Civil Society's Role in Monitoring and Verifying Peace Agreements: Seven Lessons from International Experiences" Geneva: Inclusive Peace & Transition Initiative (The Graduate Institute of International and Development Studies).
24 Güiza-Gómez, Diana Isabel and Rodrigo Uprimny-Yepes (2021). "Legitimizing and enshrining peace commitments: Inclusivity and constitution-building in the Colombian peace process," in Jorge Luis Fabra-Zamora, Andrés Molina-Ochoa, Nancy C. Doubleday, editors, *The Colombian Peace Agreement: A Multidisciplinary Assessment*. London: Routledge.
25 Nathan, Laurie (2019). *The Ties That Bind: Peace Negotiations, Credible Commitment and Constitutional Reform*. Basel: Swisspeace.
26 Lynch, Catherine (2005). "Implementing the Northern Ireland Peace Settlement: Factionalism and Implementation Design," *Irish Studies in International Affairs* 16: 209–234.

7
WHAT MATTERS WHEN IMPLEMENTING NEGOTIATED AGREEMENTS?

The 26th Conference of the Parties (COP) of the UN Framework Convention on Climate Change, held in Glasgow in November 2021, was similar in certain respects to earlier international meetings on environmental issues – a North-South divide on many issues seemed to drive debate. Despite differences, by the end of the conference, the Glasgow Climate Pact was adopted by all countries. Reflecting on the Pact, the World Wildlife Fund global lead on climate, Manuel Pulgar-Vidal, said "We must acknowledge that progress was made. There are now new opportunities for countries to deliver on what they know must be done to avoid a climate catastrophe. But unless they sharply pivot to implementation and show substantial results, they will continue to have their credibility challenged."[1] What he is saying is that the key to success of this latest installment in environmental negotiation efforts is whether the parties can actually implement the agreed provisions. Time will tell.

This essay studies the problem of implementing negotiated agreements. What are the key factors that push provisions forward or put obstacles in their way during the post-negotiation period? Is power asymmetry the primary factor determining implementation or are there others? In particular, as the first step on the road to implementation, what is the likelihood that the negotiated agreement will be ratified and accepted at the national level? We examine this problem through an analysis of international environmental agreements.

North-South Divide

In June 1992, a predecessor environmental negotiation conference was held in Rio de Janeiro – the United Nations Conference on Environment and Development (UNCED), also known as the Earth Summit. A major result of UNCED was "Agenda 21," an innovative action program that called for investments in new

DOI: 10.4324/9781003314400-7

sustainable development strategies. Just as the Glasgow talks resulted in skepticism about countries' ability to muster the political will to implement and deliver on agreed provisions of the negotiation, so too, post-negotiation implementation of the UNCED results 30 years ago yielded skepticism and disappointing results.

Despite UNCED's achievements in initiating several additional environmental agreements on climate change, biological diversity, and forest management, the UNCED negotiations experienced an intense power struggle between the developing and industrialized countries to achieve what appeared to be mutually exclusive goals of economic development and environmental protection.[2] The cross-sectoral objective of sustainable development, while intended as an integrative target between the rich and poor nations, was largely paid lip service to when placed in competition with parochial national interests.

Put simply, many countries in the developing South sought to emphasize their own long-term goals for economic development; in many cases, this meant bypassing sound environmental standards and aggravating already deteriorating environmental conditions. They viewed climate change as a problem created by the North, where the South was the primary victim. The South was largely focused on getting commitments by the North to substantial technical and financial transfers that would help the South deal with the problem of emissions and address the consequences of climate change, while enabling countries to pursue their development goals.[3]

At the same time, there were countries in the industrialized North committed to stabilizing emissions and taking some responsibility for environmental damage. But there were also many countries concerned about the economic consequences they would face if they agreed to more aggressive environmental standards. Also, many in the North did not want to appear to succumb to "blackmail" by Southern countries who could maintain or increase their emissions unless economic transfers were forthcoming.[4]

While an agreement was finally hammered out at the UNCED meeting, it was a product of tradeoffs between the rich and the poor, one that was deeply rooted in very unequal power resources. Does this divide among countries during the negotiations also impact the subsequent implementation of the negotiated agreement?

Power Asymmetry and Alternate Explanations

The bulk of powerful economic and technological resources – financial assets, environmentally sound technology, and skilled manpower, etc. – are possessed by the North, while other strengths – the force of numbers, the potential for generating blocking coalitions, etc. – are often found with the South. If power, in fact, only emanates from the possession of raw resources, the initial expectations of inequality and asymmetry in power positions would be well founded. However, the more compelling behavioral definition of power implies that all national actors can use certain strategies and tactics to advance their interests, thereby actualizing power through exercising their political will. The resource-poor are not necessarily weak if they can pursue their interests skillfully through the use of promises, warnings, threats, and commitments.[5]

Although resource wealth does not translate necessarily into power in a relationship between nations, it can influence the way the parties themselves conceive of their dispute and interactions. When the parties frame their conflict in terms of power and power asymmetry, their dispute can assume a zero-sum character and become difficult to reconcile; it can influence flexibility and the extent to which the disputes are in fact negotiable.[6] Even perceived power differentials can elevate the specters of unfair advantage, competition, and self-interest over the pursuit of superordinate goals and the need for interdependent action which are required to resolve many sustainable development problems at global and regional levels.

Using a power-based explanation of the North-South conflict on sustainable development, the stereotypic scenario emulates the following pattern: Resource-anchored perceptions of power asymmetry produce fears and beliefs on the part of the resource-poor that they are engaged on an uneven playing field, that the negotiation process is unjust, and that their only recourse is to confront the North in negotiations. This often takes the form of inflexible positions and the building of blocking coalitions to oppose new environmental agreements. After a negotiation, this confrontation can continue to be manifested as an inability, refusal, or delay in implementing negotiated accords. The South overcompensates for its apparent weakness by energizing its political will through the behavioral exercise of this confrontational power.

Is the North-South confrontation framed simply and solely in terms of resource-wealth, resource-poverty, and strategic power as suggested in this scenario? Our contention is that it is not. Other factors can explain the confrontation convincingly. Alternate hypotheses that deflect the impact of resource-based power and emphasize the roles of other determinants of conflict, such as differing issue priorities, political commitments, or political incapacities, can provide cogent explanations for conflict. After all, single factor explanations of such complex issues as the North-South conflict are likely to be inadequate; multidimensional explanations must be sought.

Beyond improved explanations and the analytical rigor of testing alternate hypotheses, there could be significant payoff for practical applications. These alternate explanations can help the conflicting parties reframe their image of the conflict in a more negotiable way, which is amenable to integrative positive sum solutions. If the North-South conflict, for example, can be explained in terms other than an intractable power struggle and these results are transmitted to policymakers and negotiators, the door may be opened to a more constructive approach to practical problem solving, free of the rigid bonds often imposed by asymmetrical power relationships. For example, positional conflicts between North and South might be more simply explained by the low priorities that some countries attach to particular sustainable development issues than by differences in power. Some countries may experience so many problems in trying to implement environmental policies domestically that their failure is assured; but their failure is much more a function of domestic political incapacity than an absence of international power. As well, power asymmetry may be less significant in explaining North-South conflicts than the differences in vigor with which political action is taken by some developing and industrialized countries to deal with environment-development issues.

None of this is to imply that perceptions of power asymmetry are inconsequential; to the contrary. Perceptions of power asymmetry are conceived as being the catalyst for much of the current intractability of environmental negotiations and other issues of common concern between North and South.[7] Our examination does not seek to ignore the impact of power differences, but to neutralize it analytically by providing other plausible explanations that the parties to the conflict might latch onto instead. Power explanations carry a value-laden and inflammatory message to the perceived weaker party. By explaining the confrontation in terms that are more benign, perhaps the existing negotiation roadblocks set up by parties who are convinced of the power asymmetry argument can be dismantled and more flexible approaches taken to resolve the conflict.

This essay analyzes empirically the differences between North and South on sustainable development issues to evaluate the usefulness of such alternate hypotheses.[8] We look in particular at one public manifestation of North-South conflict – the delay in or non-ratification of international environmental accords by developing countries. We seek to explain, in other than power terms, the reasoning for the significant difference in North-South behavior on this subject. We hope that our examination facilitates not only analytical explanations, but can influence future practice as well. If the relationship between North and South on these critical issues can be desensitized, that is, if the conflict can be defined in a more benevolent, positive sum way as a result of the analysis, the parties might be coaxed into reframing their differences in a truly resolvable and less contentious manner.

Drivers of Agreement Ratification

The factors that drive the post-agreement negotiation process, and in particular, the national ratification process, in the aftermath of international negotiation successes may be different from those that motivated the initiating negotiations.[9] Actors, venue, issues, interests, tactics, and audiences are different, and in many cases, probably more irascible in the domestic setting than in the international context. The irony is that the difficulties experienced in implementation persist despite the precedent of cooperation and the cooperative framework for future action that was established by the initiating agreement.

Usually, the first stage in the post-agreement process – national ratification or acceptance – presages the upcoming problems, including delays, improper implementation guidelines and rule-making, and inadequate enforcement and verification.[10] Based on a sample of 33 global environmental treaties catalogued by the United Nations Environment Program between 1921 and 1989, Spector and Korula found that the time required for national ratification averaged 5.8 years. Ratification of accident liability treaties were among the shortest, averaging at 2.8 years, and industry regulatory treaties were at the other end of the range, averaging at 10.1 years! No matter how the data were categorized, the length of time required for national acceptance of negotiated agreements is very long, suggesting major problems in the implementation phase.

In preparation for the April 1993 Lucerne Environment for Europe Ministerial Conference sponsored by the United Nations Economic Commission for Europe (UN/ECE), the Swiss Federal Office of Environment, Forests and Landscape sent a questionnaire to 46 ECE countries to elicit their reasons for limited or non-participation in seven major international environmental agreements affecting all countries in the European region.[11] Thirty-one responses were received and several patterns emerged, the most striking being the differences in response between the newly independent states of Central and Eastern Europe and the rest of the ECE countries, in a way mirroring the developing-developed country differences on a global scale. In general, the Central and Eastern European countries indicated (1) low national priorities and relevance of these conventions given their current national interests, and (2) high domestic incapacity to implement convention provisions properly. They cite a lack of knowledge of the issues, a lack of administrative infrastructure to adhere to the conventions and enforce participation, a lack of appropriate domestic legislation, the negative financial impacts of participating, and a lack of the needed technologies. These same issues of priorities, problems, and implementation actions were also elevated as important factors influencing post-agreement ratification behavior on a global basis by Spector and Korula.[12]

Three alternate hypotheses emerge from these findings. The basic power asymmetry explanation begins the list: that perceived power differences are at the root cause of the North-South conflict and these differences extend to the post-negotiation phase.

Hypothesis$_0$ (Power Explanation): North-South differences in ratification of global environmental agreements are a function of perceived differences in power. The greater the perceived asymmetry in power, the greater the differential in ratification rate.

As stated earlier, our study seeks to find other significant factors that can explain the difference in ratification rates equally well. If these significant factors are introduced as intervening variables in the relationship between North-South and ratification outcomes, it is hypothesized that the difference in ratification rate will diminish.

Alternate Hypothesis$_1$ (National Priority Explanation): North-South differences in ratification of global environmental accords are influenced by the saliency to a country of the particular environmental issues addressed by the accords. By controlling for countries with high national priorities on a given issue, it can be seen analytically that North-South ratification rates will tend to equalize.

Alternate Hypothesis$_2$ (Political Action Explanation): North-South differences in ratification rates can be attributed to differences in the intensity with which countries act to alleviate environmental problems, sector by sector. By controlling for those countries that take concrete and targeted actions, differences in the ratification rate will disappear.

Alternate Hypothesis$_3$ (Capacity Explanation): The ability or incapacity of a nation to implement environmental policy domestically can be influential in affecting ratification rates. By controlling for those countries with high domestic incapacity, ratification rate differentials will dissipate.

Methodology

A country-by-country data base was developed from various sources to examine these hypotheses. Data were collected for 146 countries. The dependent variable, *the percent of global environmental treaties ratified by sector* for each country, was calculated.[13] These data include a total of 124 international legal instruments and agreements in the environmental field from 1921 to 1990 that were listed in the UN Environment Program (UNEP) catalog of treaties. Regional agreements were not included in our calculation so that there would be an equal opportunity for all countries to have ratified all treaties, resulting in a final set of 37 agreements. The sectors for which treaty ratification data were available are: conservation and living resources, atmospheric pollution and ozone, marine environment and pollution, hazardous substances, nuclear safety, and the working environment, as well as several broad and cross-sectoral environmental agreements.

The independent variable, the *developmental level* for each country, was collected from the United Nations Development Program's Human Development Report 1991.[14] Least developed and developing countries were aggregated and numbered 115; industrialized countries numbered 31. This variable was used as a proxy for perceived power asymmetry: designation of developmental level by the UNDP assigns each country the status of resource-rich or resource-poor, which by definition, proffers perceived power differential. The statistical significance of the relationship between developmental level and ratification rate across all countries in the sample was tested first (H_0). Then, control or intervening variables were introduced into this same relationship to test if each one, taken separately, would significantly change the strength of the relationship (H_1, H_2, and H_3).

The control or intervening variables were coded from UNCED Secretariat-developed summaries of the National Reports submitted by most countries and regional organizations prior to the Rio meeting.[15] The full reports, which are of varying quality and detail, describe the priorities, current and future activities, and problems that each party experienced domestically sector-by-sector in the environmental area. The Secretariat produced three volumes that translated, where necessary, and extracted systematically this type of information from each report.[16] All summaries were examined by two coders independently, the information categorized, and coder disagreements resolved. Four basic variables were generated from this data for each country and each environmental sector: *national priority for the sector* (ranging from no stated priority to multiple statements of priority), *current domestic activity to resolve problems* in the environmental sector (ranging from no activity, to studies, to legislation and regulations put into effect, to physical changes in the effected infrastructure), *future domestic activity* (planned activities categorized along the same continuum as current activity), and *problem categories* (factors that prevented governments from initiating activities to resolve sectoral problems, including political, administrative, legislative, financial, and technical difficulties). The particular types of problems encountered by each country were also coded sector-by-sector. National priority was assumed if a country stated an interest in an environmental sector, indicating that the issue was on its national agenda. Current and future actions reflect real attempts to deal in a positive way with implementing environmental policies at a domestic level. We conceived of the problems factor as reflecting a behavioral power incapacity: what could not be accomplished or what could not be influenced at a domestic level to improve the environmental sector. It identifies the weakness of each country to pursue and succeed in initiating certain desired policy actions.

The priorities, current and future activities, and problems variables were used as the control or intervening factors in H_1, H_2, and H_3, respectively. The database was subdivided by these variables: only those countries that indicated a national priority (that is, having at least one stated priority), concrete current or planned actions (that is, activities that go beyond mere study and analysis efforts), and high levels of domestic incapacity (that is, multiple problems acknowledged) in a particular environmental sector, were included in the analysis of H_1, H_2, and H_3. Operationally, the subset of countries that met these criteria, each taken independently, were examined to determine if a difference in developmental level (representing power resource differentials) would still yield significant differences in ratification rate. Essentially, the design attempts to create analytically homogeneous groupings of countries based on these control factors and hypothesizes that within these groupings the power-motivated difference in ratification rates will be neutralized due to the effect of the control factor.

Analysis and Discussion

Each of the hypotheses was tested in turn. T-tests were used to evaluate the significance of differences in means of the dependent variable (ratification rate) across the two developmental groupings (developing and industrialized countries).

TABLE 7.1 Differences in Ratification Rates for All Nations and Those with Stated Environmental Priorities.

		All Nations		Nations with Stated Priority	
Treaty Type	Country Type	Mean % Ratified	N	Mean % Ratified	N
General Treaties	Developing	45.8	79★	43.7	19★
	Industrial	72.4	29	95.9	8
Conservation/ Biodiversity	Developing	41.6	107★	42.0	77★
	Industrial	69.2	31	70.3	24
Atmosphere	Developing	62.8	111★	67.2	72★
	Industrial	93.6	31	94.1	28
Marine Pollution	Developing	32.3	80★	34.8	51★
	Industrial	49.6	30	53.9	19
Nuclear Safety	Developing	25.3	86★	★★★	
	Industrial	46.0	30		
Toxic Waste	Developing	36.2	78★	35.5	59★
	Industrial	58.9	30	59.4	23
Work Environment	Developing	27.6	33★★	★★★	
	Industrial	39.5	25		

★ T-test, p<.0001; ★★ T-test, p<.025; ★★★ Insufficient data

Ratification and Perceived Power Differentials (H₀)

Table 7.1 compares ratification patterns between North and South sector-by-sector. The results in the All Nations column demonstrate highly significant differences between North and South on ratification rates when all nations in the sample are included. H_0 is confirmed by these findings; the divide between North and South on power resources makes a difference.

The ratification histories for global environmental treaties sector-by-sector are consistent: the average percentage for treaty acceptance is always lower for developing than for industrialized countries and this difference is statistically significant. Overall, general treaties, conservation/biodiversity, and atmospheric treaties are most frequently ratified, while marine pollution, nuclear safety, toxic waste, and work environment accords are generally ratified less frequently.[17]

Ratification and National Priorities (H₁)

On average, most countries claim that most environmental sectors are of relatively high priority on their respective national agendas, with very little difference between North and South. As indicated in Table 7.2, North and South find conservation/biodiversity, atmosphere, marine pollution, and toxic waste issues of extremely high priority. Except on atmospheric issues, the extent of interest in these environmental sectors is amazingly similar for developing and

TABLE 7.2 National Priorities by Sector (% of Countries Stating High Priorities).

Sector	Developing	Industrialized
General	16	6
Atmosphere	65	90
Conservation/Biodiversity	72	77
Marine Pollution	54	64
Nuclear	2	10
Toxic Waste	76	74
Work Environment	3	0

industrialized countries. Much lower priorities are accorded by both blocs to nuclear, work environment, and general issue areas.

H_1 predicts that the significant difference in ratification rates between North and South found above will disappear when we control for national priorities; that is, there should be no conflict between North and South for those countries that are truly committed to resolve environmental problems. However, the findings in the right-hand columns of Table 7.1 do not bear out this hypothesis; significant differences between North and South persist even when the analysis is conducted on the subset of countries with a stated priority for environmental issues.

Thus, the distinction between North and South cannot be simply explained by a general lack of interest and disregard by Southern states of environmental issues. Except for the marine pollution and work environment sectors where the data were insufficient to perform the statistical test, the distinction between North and South on ratification remains significant and even intensifies. What this means is that even if a developing country has a stated policy interest in an environmental sector, the rate of ratification is still consistently lower than for an interested industrialized country.

Ratification and National Activities (H_2)

Do countries that are proactive in correcting environmental problems or constraining future deterioration domestically, regardless of their developmental status, ratify international environmental agreements in a similar fashion on average? Is the activity factor a more salient explanatory variable of ratification rate than the North–South power differential? See Table 7.3. When we examine only the subset of countries that indicates they have acted in a concrete fashion to improve the environment through legislation, regulations or physical changes to infrastructure, there still remain significant differences between the North and South in terms of agreement ratification rate across environmental sectors. In general, the ratification rate is highest for atmospheric treaties and lowest for marine pollution agreements.

TABLE 7.3 Differences in Ratification Rate for Countries that have Performed Current Concrete Activities by Sector.

		Only Nations with Current Concrete Activities	
Treaty Type	Country Type	Mean % Ratified	N
General	Developing	46.3	28★★★
	Industrial	76.9	13
Atmosphere	Developing	75.6	38★★
	Industrial	94.5	18
Conservation/	Developing	44.2	65★
Biodiversity	Industrial	72.3	17
Marine	Developing	36.9	22★★★
Pollution	Industrial	54.2	12
Toxic Waste	Developing	37.4	31★★
	Industrial	62.6	16

Note: There was insufficient data to test nuclear and work environment treaties.

★ T-test, $p<.0001$;   ★★ T-test, $p<.001$;   ★★★ T-test, $p<.01$

When the analysis turns to planned activities for future implementation, one difference between North and South begins to fade (see Table 7.4). While significant differences in ratification rates still exist for general, atmospheric, conservation/biodiversity, and toxic waste agreements, the difference between North and South on marine pollution accords weakens when we look at the

TABLE 7.4 Differences in Ratification Rate for Countries with Any Planned Activities by Sector.

		Only Nations with Planned Activities	
Treaty Type	Country Type	Mean % Ratified	N
General	Developing	46.2	41★
	Industrial	75.4	23
Atmosphere	Developing	62.4	47★
	Industrial	94.8	19
Conservation/	Developing	42.4	61★
Biodiversity	Industrial	72.9	20
Toxic Waste	Developing	38.8	41★★
	Industrial	61.1	18
Marine	Developing	35.6	33[NS]
Pollution	Industrial	47.2	9

Note: There was insufficient data to test nuclear and work environment treaties. While there is a difference in means between North and South on percentage of marine pollution treaties ratified, it is not statistically significant.

★ T-test, $p<.0001$;   ★★ T-test, $p<.01$; NS Not statistically significant.

TABLE 7.5 Percent of Activities Pursued Across All Sectors.

Actions	Current Actions Developing	Current Actions Industrial	Future Plans Developing	Future Plans Industrial
Study	28.5	26.8	68.5	64.2
Legislation/Regulation	27.7	25.7	11.0	12.2
Physical Changes	11.1	15.2	7.9	10.1
Multiple Actions	32.7	32.3	12.6	13.5

Developing Country $N = 115$; Industrialized Country $N = 31$

subset of countries that have planned future activities to combat these environmental issues. While the findings are not statistically significant, H_2 is partially supported. Having planned activities in this sector, regardless of developmental status, reduces the ratification differential between North and South when compared with the other sectors.

Countries that are planning to do something to combat domestic marine pollution problems appear to have more in common than not. The power differences across countries, inherent in their developmental status, play a much reduced role in terms of producing confrontational outcomes. Instead, their shared goal of combatting environmental deterioration appears to engender a common cause among both Northern and Southern countries to ratify international treaties on these issues.

These findings are emphasized when examining the next level of detail. Table 7.5 presents the percentage of each activity type engaged in by developing and industrialized countries. The distributions across country type track very closely. As one might expect, there are greater differences between current activity patterns and future plans, with fewer major commitments other than studying the sectoral issues being projected. The most frequent activities are conducting studies and enacting legislation and regulations. The least frequent are the activities that yield some physical change in the infrastructure to reduce an environmental problem; these usually require extensive financial resources and/or new technologies.

Ratification and Domestic Incapacity (H_3)

H_3 considers the impact of problems encountered in initiating environmental solutions – conceived as domestic incapacity – on ratification rates. If a country perceives it will have major difficulties in implementing an agreement, it may not even attempt to pursue it, thus falling into the nonratification camp. Table 7.6 demonstrates empirically that there is a significant relationship between national incapacity and developmental level.

86 Implementing Negotiated Agreements

TABLE 7.6 Domestic Incapacity and Developmental Level (% of Countries).

	Domestic Incapacity	
Developmental Level	Problems	No Problems
Developing	83	17
Industrial	39	61

Chi-square, $p<.0001$

Eighty-three percent of developing countries perceive themselves to be behaviorally incapacitated in the post-agreement period, as opposed to only 39% of the North. Given this predominant self-assessment by developing countries of domestic incapacity, one would expect that this is a potent factor in producing nonratification of environmental treaties.

Table 7.7 confirms that many of the differences between Northern and Southern countries on ratification rate are reduced to statistical insignificance when one limits the analysis to the subset of countries with high domestic incapacity. Except for significant differences for general, atmospheric, and nuclear agreements, countries that experience high domestic incapacity in implementing

TABLE 7.7 Differences in Ratification Rate for Countries with High Levels of Incapacity.

		Only Nations with High Levels of Incapacity	
Treaty Type	Country Type	Mean % Ratified	N
General	Developing	42.0	49★
	Industrial	85.9	7
Conservation/	Developing	41.4	68[NS]
Biodiversity	Industrial	53.0	7
Atmosphere	Developing	62.9	71★★★
	Industrial	85.9	7
Marine	Developing	32.3	50[NS]
Pollution	Industrial	41.7	6
Nuclear	Developing	22.6	54★★
	Industrial	42.7	7
Toxic Waste	Developing	35.0	50[NS]
	Industrial	57.0	7
Work	Developing	25.6	20[NS]
Environment	Industrial	40.5	6

Note: While there are differences in means between North and South on the percentage of conservation, marine pollution, toxic waste and work environment treaties ratified, these differences are statistically insignificant.
★ T-test, $p<.0001$; ★★ T-test, $p<.001$; ★★★ T-test, $p<.01$; NS: Not statistically significant

TABLE 7.8 Sources of Domestic Incapacity (in %).

Problem Type	Developing	Industrial
Political	1.4	2.8
Administrative	11.6	8.3
Legislative	4.7	5.5
Financial	19.5	30.6
Technological	6.1	13.9
Other	5.4	2.8
Multiple Problems	51.3	36.1

environmental policy, whether in the North or South, appear to ratify accords, on average, at a more similar rate. Incapacity is an equalizer, a common factor possessed by both Northern and Southern countries, that influences ratification behavior equivalently and has a stronger effect on that behavior than the possession of power resources.

At the next level of granularity, it is possible to assess the most frequent sources of domestic incapacity. Table 7.8 presents the most frequently mentioned problems experienced by countries across all environmental sectors. Developing countries perceive cost and administrative incapacity to be the major barriers to enacting domestic environmental policy. Industrialized countries also are concerned about the cost of environmental activities as well as the technological retrofitting that is required.

Finally, is there any recognizable pattern as to when these problems arise in the post-agreement period? See Table 7.9. Most problems are related to the national ratification and acceptance process (48% for the South and 55% for the North). Political and financial difficulties often come to the forefront as sticking points in the domestic negotiations to accept new international agreements. Enforcement problems are the second largest category (41% for the South and 36% for the North). Here, administrative and technical incapacities hamper the ability of countries to implement agreements and gain the acceptance of key stakeholders. Rule-making problems are the smallest category (11% for the South and 9% for the North). In this case, the design of new legislation and rules apparently sets up only minor barriers to implementation of new policy. Interestingly, the degree to which the North and South view these areas as problems across each post-agreement phase is strikingly similar.

TABLE 7.9 Percent of Stated Problems by Post-Agreement Phase.

	Domestic Negotiation/ Ratification	Rule-Making	Enforcement
Developing	48	11	41
Industrial	55	9	36

Conclusions

How countries frame a conflict often colors their responses. The conclusions of this analysis suggest that when developing and industrialized countries frame their differences over environmental issues in terms of power differentials a confrontational outcome is likely. However, were these nations to frame their differences along less sensitive and inflammatory lines, for example, in terms of their common domestic incapacities to implement change policies, that confrontational aspect is likely to recede. Perhaps then, if power-based conflicts are reframed by policymakers to consider their common plights, regardless of power resources available, many North-South problems – including the sluggish ratification of international environmental accords – will become more negotiable. Sustainable development questions could be framed not as power struggles that naturally yield deadlock and impasse, but as problems of incapacity on both sides, deriving from incompatible but potent domestic stakeholders, financial drains, and enforcement complications.

In the case of ratification, such a new outlook might engender more flexible attitudes and tradeoffs in which technical and financial assistance would be more forthcoming from the industrialized countries to overcome Southern incapacities; in return, the developing countries could place national ratification higher on their agendas.

This study suggests that domestic incapacity humbles rather equally. Independent of the power resources possessed, most countries experience problems in changing their systems in accordance with international commitments. When those countries that experience the greatest problems are compared, whether resource-rich or -poor, the impact of their power-based differences becomes less pronounced and their confrontational stance is reduced; their responses to ratification are relatively homogeneous.

In an entirely different context, Sherif sought to explain the transition from conflict to cooperation.[18] Based on a series of famous field experiments, dubbed the "Robbers' Cave Experiments," he concluded that a powerful catalyst of this transition was the introduction of a catastrophic problem, a crisis. Cooperation was generated when each side realized that it could manage to survive the crisis only with the full assistance of its sworn enemy. The problem scenario induced cooperation by interjecting a superordinate goal, one that all sides must participate in achieving. In our study, similar priorities and similar degrees of directed political activity did not provide the same sense of common purpose that problems and incapacity produced. However, shared adversity leveled the playing field and bound former confrontational parties together.

What are the messages for practitioners involved in future sustainable development negotiations? Both North and South need to reframe and redefine the way they perceive their differences: power differences divide, but other shared attributes might serve to bind. But when resource discrepancies are as prominent as they are in the relations between North and South, how can the parties reorient themselves? As there is a role for scientific epistemic communities in defining technical environmental issues for political actors and a role for nongovernmental organizations in assisting national implementation of international commitments, so there is a role for an epistemic community of political, economic and social scientists. This new community can help policymakers reframe their differences in light of shared characteristics – the ones that bind rather than divide. These behavioral scientists are especially skillful at building multivariate models that can highlight and prioritize a range of explanatory factors. The communication of their results to policymakers can produce new visions of the context within which interdependent issues will be addressed. By generating and testing alternative explanations, ones that divert attention from prominent conflict theories to integrative cooperative theories, an important conflict reduction function can be served.

Notes

1 Volcovici, Valerie, Kate Abnett and William James (2021). "U.N. climate agreement clinched after late drama over coal," *Reuters*, November 14. At: https://www.reuters.com/business/cop/un-climate-negotiators-go-into-overtime-save-15-celsius-goal-2021-11-13/.
2 Spector, Bertram I., Gunnar Sjöstedt and I. William Zartman, editors (1994). *Negotiating International Regimes: Lessons Learned from the United Nations Conference on Environment and Development (UNCED)*. London: Graham & Trotman.
3 Paterson, Matthew and Michael Grubb (1992). "The International Politics of Climate Change." *International Affairs* 68, 2: 293–310.
4 Ibid.
5 See Zartman, I. W. and Jeffrey Rubin, editors (2000). *Power and Negotiation*. Ann Arbor: University of Michigan Press, for analyses of several negotiation cases in which resource imbalance between negotiating parties did not yield the anticipated imposed outcome. The negotiated outcomes, usually favoring the weaker party, are attributed to the behavioral exercise of power instead of possession of more resources. In addition, see Fisher, Roger (1983). "Negotiating Power: Getting and Using Influence," *American Behavioral Scientist* 27, 2: 149–166 (November/December); Habeeb, William M. (1988). *Power and Tactics in International Negotiation: How Weak Nations Bargain with Strong Nations*. Baltimore, MD: The Johns Hopkins University Press; and Jonsson, Christer (1981). "Bargaining Power: Notes on an Elusive Concept," *Cooperation and Conflict* XVI: 249–257, who discuss various ways of conceptualizing power and power relationships in negotiation settings.
6 Rubin, Jeffrey and I. W. Zartman (1992). "Review of the Experimental Research on Power." Laxenburg, Austria: International Institute for Applied Systems Analysis.
7 Zartman, I. William, editor (1987). *Positive Sum: Improving North-South Negotiations*. New Brunswick, NJ: Transaction.
8 The author wishes to thank Anna Korula, Mary Geraty, and Rodica Hera for their assistance in data collection. The following organizations supported various aspects of the research: the United States Institute of Peace (under Grant Award No. USIP-124-92S), the Swedish Council for Planning and Cooperation of Research (under Contract No. 920087, A8-5/154), and the Processes of International Negotiation (PIN) Project at the International Institute for Applied Systems Analysis, Laxenburg, Austria. The results expressed herein do not necessarily represent the views or opinions of these institutions.

9. Spector, Bertram I. (1993). "Post-Agreement Negotiation: Conflict Resolution Processes in the Aftermath of Successful Negotiations," Potomac, Maryland: Center for Negotiation Analysis. Working Paper Series (September).
10. Spector, Bertram I. and Anna Korula (1993). "Problems of Ratifying International Environmental Agreements: Overcoming Initial Obstacles in the Post-Agreement Negotiation Process," *Global Environmental Change* 17,4: 369–381 (December).
11. Swiss Federal Office (1993). "Results of the Questionnaire Regarding Seven Environmental Conventions: Participation and Implementation." Bern: Federal Office of Environment, Forests and Landscape, international Affairs Division, March 25.
12. Spector and Korula (1993), op.cit.
13. Sand, Peter, editor (1992). *The Effectiveness of International Environmental Agreements: A Survey of Existing Legal Instruments.* Cambridge: Grotius Publications Ltd.
14. United Nations Development Program (1991). *Human Development Report.* New York: Oxford University Press.
15. United Nations Conference on Environment and Development (1992, 1993). *Nations of the Earth Report, National Reports Summaries,* Volumes 1–3. Geneva: UNCED.
16. Many problems plague the validity of these National Reports. Comparatively, they are inconsistent concerning content and degree of detail, but the summaries tend to equalize these differences. The information that is provided in the reports, moreover, tends to be self-serving, putting governmental policies, activities, and problems in the best possible light to the rest of the world. At the same time, these summaries offer the only central and current source of data on key domestic variables related to implementation of international environmental accords. Acknowledging these difficulties, we made the assumption that only the most positive national environmental portraits were represented, but that a conservative interpretation of country comparisons could still offer insightful behavioral patterns.
17. These results generally conform with the findings in Spector and Korula (1993, op.cit.) in which atmospheric treaties were ratified fastest and marine pollution accords the slowest.
18. Sherif, Muzafer (1967). *Social Interaction: Process and Products.* Chicago: Aldine.

8
DECISION SUPPORT SYSTEMS
Getting Negotiators to Use Them

For the past 26 years, I have been the Editor-in-Chief of an academic journal, *International Negotiation: A Journal of Theory and Practice*. We publish articles by researchers that analyze the international negotiation process to better understand and explain how it works – what leads to successful outcomes and what are the obstacles. But often, the intention of this research is not purely academic or historical; a major goal is to support improvements in practical future negotiation efforts.

Negotiation practitioners always want to enhance their ability to reach agreement and get the best outcomes, and there is much they can learn from analytical research. But there is minimal dialogue and coordination between the analytical and practitioner communities, resulting in little progress toward analytically infused negotiation planning and strategies. This essay examines some attempts to start such a dialogue and assesses lessons that can be drawn from these test cases.

Negotiators need to do a lot of information gathering, analysis and planning ahead of and during talks with their counterparts from other countries. This gives them a better understanding of their own interests, the interests of their counterparts, alternate strategies that might achieve a compromise, and the costs and benefits of different paths. Such analyses can facilitate creativity in the design of negotiation formulas that are at the heart of what the negotiators came to the table to achieve in the first place – effective outcomes that resolve or manage conflict, solve shared problems, or push forward cooperative programs that benefit all of the engaged parties.

Analytical support can take many forms, but the development of a set of systematic tools that can assist negotiators – decision support systems (DSS) – is a fundamental way for negotiators to prepare themselves to achieve successful results. This is not an analyst's dream. Since the mid-1970s, there have been several concrete examples of how analysts and negotiating practitioners have joined forces to develop and apply DSS effectively in international negotiations.

DOI: 10.4324/9781003314400-8

At the 1978 International Conference on Tanker Safety and Pollution Prevention, Ulvila and Snider describe quantitative decision analysis tools that were developed by analysts and used by US negotiators to evaluate alternate proposals, understand the negotiating positions of others, and communicate with domestic US advocacy groups.[1] The engaged practitioners assert that these tools indeed helped in finding compromise solutions. At bilateral negotiations over territorial issues concerning the Panama Canal in the mid-1970s, Raiffa describes how a group of analysts interviewed the negotiators and, based on this data, assigned weights to the range of issues addressed in the talks and offered practitioners a full set of alternative formulas.[2] Concerning negotiations on US military bases between the United States and the Philippines in 1978, external facilitators elicited preferences from both negotiation teams and developed a multi-attribute utility model that compared and weighed multiple issues and rated their perceived attractiveness to both sides.[3] This tool helped practitioners explore alternate packages of issues and construct arguments and formulas in favor and against each. The analysis also helped the practitioners become more creative – generating integrative approaches, not only distributive approaches for proposed tradeoffs.

Given these seemingly effective pilot tests, how can negotiation analysts become more engaged to support the needs of negotiation practitioners preparing for and in the midst of active negotiations? And how can negotiation practitioners be encouraged to take advantage of the analytical insights and projections of systematic decision support tools to guide their strategy and tactics rather than relying solely on their intuition? This essay seeks to extend what we now know about DSS and how they can be developed and best presented to negotiation practitioners. It describes a practical case study using DSS that I helped develop in the late 1970s for the US Government in preparation for what turned out to be the negotiations between Israel and Egypt, mediated by President Jimmy Carter, leading to the Camp David Accords. Lessons learned from this case are still relevant today.

Research on Decision Support Systems in Negotiations

There has been much research conducted on the range of information and decision support that could prove useful under different circumstances for negotiators. Spector identifies several important challenges that must be addressed in collaborative efforts between negotiators and analysts: the transformation of descriptive and explanatory analytical approaches into normative and prescriptive approaches; the synthesis of process and substantive models; the application of end user-focused strategies rather than technique-focused approaches to developing analytical support; and the design of effective presentation and delivery of practical analytical tools.[4] But the lack of significant dialogue between these communities is a major reason for the disconnect between the poor demand by practitioners and ample supply of analytical tools.[5]

There are guidelines for the type of information and analysis that negotiators need to prepare for international talks. In 1979, Winham developed a "Checklist for Negotiators" for the U.S. State Department's Senior Seminar on Foreign Policy.[6] It inventories the type of substantive information and planning that is generally required to prepare for international negotiations and defines three overarching tasks: (1) define problems and goals, establish a negotiating framework and procedures, and prepare an opening position; (2) conduct day-to-day negotiation (that is, attend meetings, analyze alternative proposals, liaise with the home government, accommodate positions on issues, and reach general agreement, if possible); and (3) assess the negotiation: reach agreement on major issues, if possible, and conclude the negotiation (that is, decide whether to accept available terms or discontinue negotiation). While they are not explicitly identified, the analytical support requirements implied by these substantive tasks can be readily derived.

Analytical tools include substantive models that seek to identify and prioritize alternate solutions to a conflict. An economic model that simulates alternate deep sea mining conditions was used in the Law of the Sea negotiations.[7] A meteorological model on acid rain emissions and depositions was used to assist the United Nations Economic Commission for Europe (UN/ECE) renegotiation of a sulfur protocol.[8] An economic model that places a monetary value on shared water resources in the Middle East was considered for application in the multilateral Middle East peace process.[9]

Kersten and Lai distinguish between several different kinds of support tools that can facilitate and aid in consensual negotiation processes.[10] Some are DSS that provide targeted analysis and projections for negotiators. These tools can help negotiators understand their own and their counterparts' priorities and constraints, predict the others' use of tactics, and advise on the impacts of compromise, among other critical pieces of information. Software tools are sometimes used to implement DSS, but not necessarily. DSS typically use models from the decision sciences and operations research fields.

Other tools combine DSS analysis with communications platforms among the negotiators – negotiation support systems. Yet others – e-negotiation systems – automate negotiation activities and may conduct negotiations on behalf of humans in an autonomous fashion. Experiments contrasting e-mediator software advice with negotiators' own intuition demonstrate that those receiving advice from the software resulted in more agreements and more positive perceptions of the outcomes from the negotiators.[11] The use of artificial intelligence is also being explored to support mediators in hybrid peacemaking efforts.[12]

Interviews conducted with senior, mid-level, and support staff of various Austrian negotiation delegations found that information analysis conducted to help them prepare for actual negotiation sessions were typically rather ad-hoc, very negotiation-specific, and mostly qualitative – focusing on assessments of the parties' interests and a range of alternatives for the negotiated solution.[13] If the negotiation was focused on economic issues, however, the analysis provided to delegations was more well organized, more quantitative and mostly centralized at the Foreign Ministry, not within the delegation itself. 74% of respondents felt that the analytical support they received had a positive effect on the negotiated outcome. Especially, where there was high issue complexity, more analytical support was provided that, in turn, motivated more strategizing within the delegation. The overall conclusion from these interviews was that systematic analytical support to negotiation teams helped them develop more acceptable tradeoffs, especially when multiple complex issues were at stake. The biggest problem was finding better ways to integrate these support tools into practical international negotiation planning, strategizing and execution.

An unintended consequence of the COVID-19 pandemic, starting in early 2020, has been the extensive use of the internet as a communications device for international negotiations. Chasek examines how the internet has facilitated many international environmental negotiation sessions during the pandemic when no face-to-face meetings were possible.[14] This support appears to have provided three different approaches to virtual forums where the internet was used as the communications platform. Some virtual meetings used a "silence procedure," where draft decisions or resolutions are presented to the negotiators and are adopted if there are no objections raised within a defined period of time. Other meetings were conducted as online information sharing sessions, and yet others were online negotiations, where negotiators could debate and present proposals, but without the typical face-to-face backroom discussions.

How DSS Are Used

The critical importance of DSS is how they are actually applied by negotiation practitioners. There are basically four types of systems that could be of value to negotiators.[15] *Planning and preparation systems* are used in the pre-negotiation phase to organize information, identify options, and prepare negotiation strategies and tactics. *Assessment systems* can be used to evaluate the implications of different strategies and tactics, and evaluate offers received from counterparts. *Intervention systems* can support mediation between parties, offering approaches to agenda setting and analyzing proposals. *Process systems* help the negotiating parties to communicate and respond to the information and analysis that is generated by the other analytical systems.

Unfortunately, most practitioners are not skilled in analytical techniques; they are not statisticians, researchers, or forecasters. To provide practitioners with the assistance they need in formulating the most successful negotiation processes, it is crucial to pay careful attention to how DSS functions and results are communicated to the negotiators. They must understand what the DSS are trying to assess, what their limitations are, and what their findings suggest to improve the negotiation process. Ultimately, it is how the DSS and their findings are actually used by the practitioners that is most important.

The initial point of entry for DSS is in the pre-negotiation phase, when the parties need information, diagnose different alternatives, and conduct tradeoff assessments. By offering support to negotiators, analysts can demonstrate how the information and analysis they can provide will help the practitioners assess risks, provide a platform for early dialogues and problem-solving, identify likely responses from the other, build trust and confidence among the negotiators, and generate domestic support for the negotiations and its likely outcomes.[16]

One obvious way to make negotiators aware of DSS – and to use them – is to conduct training for them and their staff analysts. Surprisingly, Druckman, Ramberg, and Harris found a reluctance at the US State Department's Foreign Service Institute to collaborate with negotiation analysts in preparing for and informing negotiation strategies and tactics.[17] But that was 20 years ago and hopefully attitudes have changed since then. As newer generations are recruited into the ranks of diplomats and negotiators – individuals who grew up in the digital age – it is more likely that they will be amenable to DSS and their assessments.

Another, and probably a better, more inclusive way of motivating the use of DSS is to engage negotiators, as well as analysts, in group workshops that are moderated by independent facilitators very early in the pre-negotiation process. Here, the practitioners can tell the analysts what information they need and the types of analysis that will be most useful, for example, projections of what would happen if a certain strategy is followed. The analysts can then tailor their toolkit to address the immediate needs of the negotiators, avoiding jargonistic or highly technical terminology. By assessing alternate scenarios of the negotiation process, simulating policy exercises, and estimating the implications of following different negotiation paths, negotiators can be helped to diagnose the situation more systematically, assess their own plans and strategies, and evaluate the likely reactions and outcomes for themselves and their counterparts.[18] By getting the practitioners engaged with analytical staff, each will better understand what the other needs and wants, and a learning process can ensue that can make negotiation practice more effective.

Cases where DSS have been used to support international negotiators reveal several lessons about how they should be introduced to practitioners.[19]

- Timing of support is critical: DSS will be listened to if the advice is provided at the time when agreements or disagreements need to be addressed.
- Credibility of the analytical results is important: The data, methodologies, and objectivity of the analysis need to be recognized and respected.
- Presentation must be staged effectively: DSS results should be presented to technical experts and then to the senior negotiators. The users should be able to ask questions and verify assumptions made by the DSS tools.
- Ease of use is essential: The tools and their findings need to be understandable to non-technical users.

Decision Support Systems that Assisted Middle East Negotiators

In the late Fall of 1976, as the Lebanese civil war and inter-Arab feuding began to subside, a diplomatic peace offensive commenced in the Middle East. Then Prime Minister Yitzhak Rabin of Israel quickly joined with moderate Arab leaders, with President Anwar Sadat of Egypt as their key spokesman, in discussing the possibilities of peace publicly. Jimmy Carter became the US President in January 1977 after strongly advocating for a resumption of the 1973 Geneva Middle East Conference during his election campaign. The reopening of that conference never materialized despite much diplomatic activity during 1977 to revive it. But in November 1977, President Sadat's visit to Jerusalem served as a trigger for more active exploratory consultations. Eventually, in September 1978, meetings were held at Camp David between Carter, Sadat, and Menachem Begin, who had become Israel's prime minister in June 1977, leading to the Camp David Accords, "A Framework for Peace in the Middle East."

Since before his presidency, Carter had the sincere hope of serving as a historic mediator who would try to bring peace to the Middle East. This desire, plus the wide-ranging national security interests of the United States in the Middle East region – maintaining uninterrupted flows of oil to the West, encouraging petrodollar recycling in the West, ensuring the survival and security of Israel while avoiding a regional arms race, containing Soviet influence and avoiding a direct superpower confrontation in the region, and limiting nuclear proliferation in the Middle East – resulted in a research contract issued by the International Security Affairs (ISA) office in the US Department of Defense in early 1977 to study potential outcomes of future negotiations. Whatever the future configuration and conclusion of Middle East negotiations, US security interests were viewed likely to be affected. By analyzing probable alternative futures prior to commitments that make them inevitable, the study was intended to help ISA plan effectively for critical turning points in upcoming Middle East negotiations and to influence events so as to avert potentially future destabilizing occurrences affecting the region and US interests. The surprising and innovative takeaway from this case is ISA's awareness that it could benefit from DSS analyses prior to and during negotiations. ISA took the initiative to find independent DSS analysts, have them conduct targeted analyses and projections, and then engage with government analysts and negotiators to better understand how such assessments could help guide practitioners to better negotiation outcomes.

Presented below is a case analysis of the forecasting study that was conducted for ISA and which supported other government agencies as well, including the State Department and the National Security Council (NSC), as they prepared for the anticipated negotiations.[20] I was the principal investigator of the study. Specifically, the case presented here focuses on the utility of the DSS conducted for these policymakers. The discussion provides a brief description of the substantive results of the study, but focuses on examining how the research was applied — the goals, technical approach, and communication and distribution of findings among policymakers. The responsiveness of each of these facets to the needs of policymaking practitioners preparing for negotiations and lessons learned, based on this case, will be examined. These conclusions do not presume to offer scientifically supported evidence on the best elements that should comprise negotiation DSS. However, they do provide some hard-learned propositions that may prove useful to others in similar substantive contexts, who are attempting to bridge the gap between scholar and policymaker.

DSS Objectives

Middle East regional desk officers in ISA are kept more than busy dealing with day-to-day occurrences, attempting to predict next moves and position changes, and recommending action alternatives for the United States should our national security interests become endangered. O'Leary, et al. found that analysts in the Department of State's Bureau of Intelligence and Research (INR) are also primarily involved in analyzing and forecasting the near-term horizon.[21] Given their focus on the near-term, ISA looked to the external research community for help in analyzing the probable long-term futures of potential Middle East peace negotiations and outcomes.

The principal objective of this ISA-sponsored study was to forecast the long-term stability of a range of hypothetical negotiated peace plans for the Middle East, focusing on how they might affect US national security interests. The results were intended to assist negotiators and policymakers by broadening their perspective from a peace settlement that might appear reasonable and attainable in the short term to a settlement that can provide a long-term durable and stable solution to the long conflict. Although certain solutions, such as the granting of self-determination to the Palestinian people to establish their own state, may appear to be politically expedient to many, only a few analyses have focused on the long-term economic viability of such a state, including its probable repercussions over the long run on Israel, Arab financial donors, and superpowers. ISA wanted sensitive issues such as these projected systematically so they could better advise the US negotiating/mediation team.

ISA was interested in having a detailed forecast of comprehensive, albeit hypothetical, peace plans. They wanted plausible projections, based on systematic analyses of data, to identify peace provisions and phased implementation strategies with high probabilities of minimizing the risk of breakdown in the peacebuilding process and maximizing the potential for long-term normalization and stabilization of relations. Peace terms that contained hidden seeds for future destabilization of the peace were to be pinpointed. If policymakers can anticipate those peace provisions or phasing arrangements that may cause difficulties in the long run, so the logic went, they can plan either to avoid using them or develop contingency strategies that will moderate their potentially negative consequences.

No systematic forecasts of this sort were available to ISA or INR from other government sources, as far as we know. Due to the highly volatile nature of politics in the Middle East, no prior study had attempted to tackle the joint problem of projecting what a comprehensive peace plan might look like as the outcome of negotiations, and what its long-term implications might be. While many analyses extant in the available literature at the time dealt with the potential viability of various elements of a peace treaty, none interpolated and projected the interactive complexity of a comprehensive settlement and took a systematic and replicable approach.[22]

Finally, there were no stipulations to advocate for any particular position in our charter from ISA. We were free to draw conclusions from what we found in the data. Our analyses were not meant to justify any entrenched bureaucratic position, but to provide new information to assist these policymakers in their tasks. However, forecasts were not desired that relied solely on the intuition and biases of particular area experts. It was believed that the results would be more justifiable and credible to a wider range of policymakers if they were based on a systematic and empirical approach, in which social science forecasting methods were used and conclusions could be logically and objectively reproduced.

Technical Approach and Findings

The DSS activity consisted of solving two sequential problems: What are the most likely potential provisions of an agreement resulting from Middle East negotiations in the near term? And what are the likely long-term consequences of these negotiated details and formulas for regional stability and US national security?

Several DSS techniques which are described below were employed to obtain plausible answers to these questions. Each research step yielded results that have critical policy implications.

1. The use of systematic methods to develop several possible comprehensive and phased peace solutions assisted policymakers in clarifying the interdependence of the various issues and the current possibilities for their resolution.
2. The study results distinguished between alternate peace provisions on the same issue to identify those that are potentially stabilizing or destabilizing over the long term. These findings can help policymakers anticipate problems if particular provisions are implemented, and either avoid these provisions or develop plans to ameliorate their impact.
3. The analysis also yielded conclusions on the overall shape of a comprehensive and phased peace plan. The results suggest a peace implementation strategy that may provide a stable approach to phasing the provisions.
4. The case analysis of a future Palestinian state's economic viability dealt with several scenarios of population growth and foreign assistance to determine the combinations likely to result in economic stability or instability. Nonviable outcomes are likely to yield renewed military confrontation.

The results of these analytical steps were presented to the policymakers who were also instructed on how they could use these tools on their own to test different projection parameters and assumptions, and update forecasts.

Position Range Analysis

First, our study team conducted a position range analysis to develop hypothetical peace plans. Considering that formal negotiations had yet to begin, the projection of probable negotiation outcomes had to rely on several assumptions that reduced particular uncertainties analytically, and on minimum and maximum positions held publicly by both sides at the time. The assumptions postulated that:

- A comprehensive and phased solution would emerge from negotiations,
- Public disclosure of positions would provide an accurate reflection of true starting positions,
- There would be no total position reversals from these initial sets of positions,
- No separate agreements would be signed between Israel and individual Arab states, and
- Specific stabilizing agreements would be implemented early in the negotiation process to enhance trust, bolster the feasibility of the diplomatic approach, and enable the talks to continue.

The sensitivity of alternate negotiated outcomes to changes in these assumptions was seriously considered in analyzing the modeling results.

Second, a list of fundamental agenda issues was decomposed into several more detailed sub-issues that were likely to circumscribe the resulting negotiated outcome. These included the signing of a nonbelligerency pact and resettlement plans for returning Palestinian refugees. Third, data were gathered from public sources on the then current minimum and maximum acceptable positions expressed by the Arab states and Israel on each sub-issue. These were used to define the pre-negotiation ranges of acceptability, from the softest to the toughest positions held by the two sides. The two adversarial continua on each sub-issue were superimposed to reveal any overlapping areas of agreement or gaps of disagreement requiring a negotiated compromise.

Iklé and Leites suggest a similar position range analysis to identify variable negotiator utilities and areas in which they may be modified to yield agreement.[23] Plausible gap-bridging measures between the minimum positions of both sides were developed, indicating potential convergences on each issue that might result from negotiation. Since these compromise measures usually were beyond the minimum acceptable boundary set by each side at the pre-negotiation phase, the probability of achieving such results depended on the likelihood of modifying utilities through the tactics and strategies of bargaining.[24] The product of these issue-by-issue position range analyses were hypothetical peace plans that demand compromises by both sides, are comprehensive in content, and are phased over time in terms of their implementation.

Two hypothetical peace plans were generated which would then be analyzed. Plan 1 was an "Israeli-tilted" scenario in which territorial withdrawals were delayed; Rafah, Sharm el Sheikh, and some West Bank settlements would be retained by Israel; strong economic ties would be established with a new Palestinian entity; and the Arabs would offer early recognition and movement toward normalization. Plan 2 was an "Arab-tilted" scenario in which there were early Israeli pullbacks from territory, essentially to the pre-1967 borders; Israel would maintain weak ties with a Palestinian entity; and the Arabs would withhold recognition and normalization measures until the end of the implementation process.

Projection Models and Peace Provision Simulations

Using these hypothetical peace plans as referents, attention was addressed to identifying their long-term implications for regional stability and US national security. Empirically based regression models were developed to forecast elements of Israeli viability and regional stability. They were used to facilitate simulations of the long-term consequences of the peace provision details in the plans.

First, the concepts of "Israeli viability" and "regional stability" were defined operationally in terms of their military, political, economic, demographic, and psychological components. Rather than using a nominal level dependent variable, such as "war-no war," explicit interval level variables on most of these dimensions were formulated for each of the combatant nations, plus Lebanon and the West Bank and Gaza Strip. Aggregate regional stability was represented by a series of variables tapping Arab-Israeli hostilities, military manpower ratios, and military force ratios. The goal in differentiating the dependent variable in this fashion was to make the ultimate projections as meaningful and as specific as possible for policymakers. For example, this procedure facilitated forecasts dealing with likely fluctuations in regional defense expenditures, terrorist activity, armed retaliation and regional conflict, domestic unrest, government stability, domestic economics, and public perceptions of security.

Data were collected on these and other relevant variables on a yearly basis from 1948 to 1976, when available. Hypotheses that postulate several predictors for each stability component were tested using these data and correlational techniques. Those hypotheses that were not disconfirmed were refined and the best predictors of each stability variable were entered into bivariate regression equations. The purpose in using bivariate regressions rather than multivariate models was twofold. First, it reduces the multicollinearity problem since many of the predictor variables were highly intercorrelated. Second, our interest lay in assisting policy analysis, not in complex or formal model building. Multiple bivariate equations provide the policy analyst with a set of early warning indicators (the predictor variables) of potentially stabilizing or destabilizing consequences to the peace. The goal was to identify these critical indicators for the policymaker;

the more complex interrelationships among the predictors and dependent variable were of heuristic, but little practical, value to the policy analyst.

The potential near-term impact of each peace provision was then hypothesized, assigned specific values, and simulated through relevant regression equations to determine their long-term consequences on stability. Historical and statistical criteria were established to specify numerical values for the near-term impacts and threshold ranges for long-term stability.

This simulation exercise was based on assumptions that historical trends, as captured by the regression equations, would continue. What the simulations tested then were the sudden, and sometimes drastic, impact of changes caused by implementation of peace provisions, as translated into changes in predictor values. For instance, if the signing of a nonbelligerency pact signaled a near-term impact of decreased military budgets, the simulation test would project the long-term consequences of reduced defense spending on future regional conflict, domestic unrest, and terrorist activity.

Alternately, the simulations could have been approached by postulating that any peace treaty would likely alter all of the historical trends established during the previous 30 years of hostilities. Under these assumptions, the regression slopes should be modified to reflect the step-level change in relationships that will occur among predictor and stability factors. While this argument has some merit, the specification of acceptable slope values would probably add more subjectivity and uncertainty into the analysis than would be gained from improved results. Thus, this approach was not pursued.

Substantively, the projection models found several potentially destabilizing issues:

- Two alternatives for a nonbelligerency agreement each yielded long-term projections that could waver between high stability and instability. One option exchanges an end-to-war pact for an Israeli statement of its intent to withdraw from territories, and the other is contingent on Israeli acceptance of Arab sovereignty over presently occupied territories.
- A first-step partial withdrawal from the Golan Heights, leaving Israel still on the ridge, possesses long-term properties that may lead either to high stability or instability.
- Two options for a first-step partial withdrawal from the West Bank and Gaza Strip were both found to have highly unstable consequences. In one case, this involves the return of some territory and demilitarization. The other case includes these elements plus the maintenance of Israeli settlements along the Jordan River in exchange for limited Palestinian immigration to Israel.
- Two alternate plans to deal with Palestinian refugee status each have uncertain long-term projections that lead to either high stability or instability. These two provisions allow citizenship to refugees in their current country of residence or encourage emigration and Palestinian state citizenship but allow residence in other Arab countries.

- Two plans for a settlement on Jerusalem proved to be highly unstable. One postulated a unified Israeli city with control over Muslim holy places in the walled city placed in the hands of the new Palestinian State. The other plan also viewed a unified Israeli city with an internationalized walled city and Israeli-Arab semi-autonomy in the north and east of the city.
- Superpower attempts to disarm the region have uncertain futures that could lead to either high stability or instability. In one tested alternative the United States and the Soviet Union agree to discuss arms transfer restrictions, and in another they put a freeze on arms levels and transfers.

The projection models also found some potentially stabilizing issues:

- If the PLO recognizes Israel's right to exist, either in exchange for Israeli acceptance of the PLO or Israeli withdrawal from the West Bank, moderately stable consequences are predicted.
- Agreement on a package of normalization measures to be implemented gradually is likely to yield highly stable results in the long term.
- A first-step partial withdrawal in the Sinai and demilitarization of the territory are likely to have stabilizing long-term consequences.
- A final West Bank and Gaza Strip withdrawal and demilitarization are indicated to be stabilizing for the region.
- Security guarantees in the shape of US early warning stations along the Arab-Israeli borders are highly stabilizing.

There were also some issues where a choice between alternatives made a difference in the models' projections:

- Arab recognition of Israel on a de facto basis is more stabilizing in the long term than on a de jure basis.
- A final-step Sinai withdrawal in which Israel retains the Rafah approach and leases Sharm el Sheikh is more stabilizing in the long run than demilitarization and withdrawal to the pre-1967 borders.
- A final-step withdrawal from the Golan Heights in which there are UN-Israeli and UN-Syrian joint forces patrolling the territory is more stabilizing in the long term than sole UN patrol forces.
- A Palestinian political agreement that creates a West Bank-Jordanian federation and an autonomous Gaza free port, both tied economically to Israel, is more stabilizing in the long term than a more economically autonomous West Bank-Gaza-Jordanian federation.

The analytical results indicate that on several issues neither of the two postulated peace alternatives are likely to offer long-term stability to Israel or the region. Moreover, on other issues, the results indicate an uncertain future, in which both peace alternatives possess the potential for creating highly stable or unstable situations. This is the case despite the fact that all of the alternatives were initially chosen on the basis of their promise for creating a stable environment. However, the empirical results indicate that, over the long term, these alternatives may be destabilizing. Among the issues in this category are a non-belligerency pact, partial withdrawal from the Golan Heights, partial withdrawal from the West Bank and Gaza Strip, Palestinian refugee status, the status of Jerusalem, and superpower attempts for regional disarmament.

These results emphasize the difficult and risky nature of Middle East peace-building efforts. If a comprehensive settlement is agreed upon, using these alternatives, it would increase the risk of long-term destabilization and divert achievement of peaceful US national security interests in the region. Further research is required to test other potential peace provisions on these issues using the same long-term projection models.

It is interesting that two issues prone to having long-term unstable consequences are the first-step partial withdrawals from the Golan Heights and from the West Bank and Gaza Strip. Two conclusions can be drawn from these findings. A total one-step withdrawal from these territories is probably unwise since it would multiply the shocks Israel would have to undergo over a short period of time and increase the causes of Israeli instability. Instead, the destabilizing impacts of these partial withdrawals can possibly be moderated by expeditiously scheduling the follow-up final withdrawals. Firm expectations of the time and shape of the final peace may help to ameliorate the causes of initial instability.

There were several issues that tended to have long-term stabilizing impacts on Israel and the region. These issues include PLO recognition of Israel, normalization measures, partial withdrawal in the Sinai, final withdrawal in the West Bank and Gaza Strip, and US security guarantees. On the following issues, one of the tested alternatives appeared to be more preferable than the other in terms of establishing the seeds for long-term stability: Arab recognition of Israel, final-step withdrawal in the Sinai, final-step withdrawal in the Golan Heights, and Palestinian political agreement.

Overall, the analysis was able to distinguish between those provisions that are potentially stabilizing and destabilizing over the long run. Policymakers can try to avoid the destabilizing provisions or plan ahead to ameliorate their negative consequences. This modeling and simulation exercise produced several practical results for policymakers:

- The relative long-term stability of specific peace provision details was projected on the basis of explicitly stated assumptions.
- An early warning checklist was prepared to facilitate the use of these results by policymakers. If an analyst observes a sudden change in any of the early warning signals subsequent to implementation of a peace provision, the checklist specifies the likelihood of long-term instability.
- The checklist also identifies those critical turning points that may require US action to avert future destabilizing trends and threats to US national security.

Event-Sequence Networking

A second forecasting methodology was used to identify the long-term implications of different phasing strategies. Each hypothetical peace plan was composed of peace provisions grouped into phases that would be implemented sequentially over time. The forecasting question here centered on determining which of the phasing alternatives appeared most stabilizing over the long term and which most threatening to a durable peace. A network of action-reaction sequences among the regional actors was developed to produce several plausible long-term scenarios emanating from the implementation of each peace phase. The endpoints of each network specified the potential for stalemate or successful continuation to the next peace phase.

The networks resembled large decision trees, although the alternatives at each node represented events that might be observed, rather than potential actions that might be selected by decision-makers. The grouping of peace provisions that comprise each phase was the starting point for each network. The plausible short-term reactions by each relevant actor to implementing a phase were defined and ranked from most to least favorable as they are likely to affect US national security interests. The plausible responses to these actions were then enumerated, enveloped, and appended to the network. This process of adding action and reaction nodes continued until it was judged that the addition of further plausible reactions to a prior event was not likely to change the situation significantly from one which is stabilizing to one that is destabilizing, and vice versa. In other words, branches of the network were terminated when it was judged that they had reached an equilibrium point. Each endpoint was then analyzed to determine whether circumstances at that point appeared to be stable and favorable for continuing the peace implementation process, or unstable and likely to produce a breakdown in the peace process.

While an infinite number of scenarios could probably be played out, only those deemed highly plausible and making a significant difference in Middle East stability were developed. A policy analyst can trace the path of many different scenarios by starting at any point in a network and reading sequentially from left to right, choosing the perceived probable event at each node. The analyst can view each event as a "what if" assumption. That is, the reader has the option to consider those events perceived to be most likely and follow them through to their downstream conclusions. These networks offer the following benefits to policymakers:

- Identification of the likely long-term implications of various peace phases, if there were no third-party attempts to intervene.
- Comparison of the stabilizing and destabilizing characteristics of alternate phasing strategies.
- Specification of critical turning points in the implementation process where US actions might avert negative consequences that could set back the peace-building process.

Substantively, the event-sequence networks presented an implementation plan that would minimize the probability of unstable or deadlocked conclusions, while maximizing the development of a stable and progressive peacebuilding process. This could consist of placing extensive pressure on Israel to make some important concessions in the early phases, but then switching gear and placing pressure on the Arabs to make substantial concessions to Israel in the mid- to late-phases.

The analytical results yielded two potential outcomes. Outcome 1 is based on a plan in which many Israeli demands for delay and maintenance of territory in the West Bank and northern Sinai supersede Arab demands. The implementation of this outcome is likely to become more stabilizing as each phase is introduced. While the first phase is projected to be highly destabilizing, the second and third phases may lead equally to stable or unstable endpoints, and the fourth phase is projected to have a higher probability of achieving a stable peace. Of course, if problems that arise during the first three phases are not resolved satisfactorily, the entire implementation process could deadlock early on. If this type of outcome was negotiated, the major task for its participants would be to overcome or avert the critical turning points that could destabilize the implementation process.

The long-term outlook for Outcome 2 is almost the inverse of Outcome 1. Outcome 2 assumes greater pressures exerted by the United States on Israel to make substantial concessions to Arab demands. As a result, initial Israeli pullbacks in the Sinai, the Golan Heights, the West Bank, and Gaza Strip occur in earlier phases than in Outcome 1. In this plan, Israel returns practically all territories to pre-1967 borders.

Given these results, the study found that the optimal peace plan would be one that mixed the initially stabilizing provisions of Outcome 2 with the subsequently stabilizing features of Outcome 1. Such a strategy would minimize the probability of pursuing peace provisions that could cause unstable conclusions, while maximizing the development of provisions that lead to a stable peacebuilding process. Operationally, a minimax peace plan for the Middle East would consist of placing extensive pressure on Israel to make some important concessions in the early phases, but then switching gear and placing pressure on the Arabs to make substantial concessions to Israel.

This plan would provide early and substantial rewards to the Arabs. These concrete benefits of peace could be offered as justification to hostile domestic Arab factions for pursuing a peaceful rather than militaristic strategy. Some of the humiliation of past military defeats could also be alleviated by these initial Israeli concessions. Moreover, this is likely to have stabilizing effects on domestic political and economic situations in the Arab states, and is likely to result in favorable attitudes by the Arab oil-producing nations, namely Saudi Arabia, toward the United States. In addition, if most of the affected Arab parties receive some concrete evidence of success in achieving their objectives, the impact of implementing concessions to the Israelis later on in the process could lose some of its sting.

Israel, on the other hand, may have to forego some of its initial demands and place its trust in the hands of the United States to achieve the "real" peace and normalization of relations it is seeking. Only by first reestablishing a normalized environment – free of occupied territory – can real peace truly be pursued. But to pressure Israel to make these early concessions with little initial compensation from the Arabs, the United States will probably have to establish an adequate plan to safeguard Israel's territorial security and bolster Israel's psychological sense of security and well-being. This could mean anything up to and including the temporary stationing of US troops near or on Israeli–Arab borders.

Following this difficult initial phase for Israel, subsequent phases could deal with issues from an Israeli perspective, including normalization measures, the status of Jerusalem, and resettlement of Palestinian refugees. Pressure could be applied on the Arab actors to make necessary concessions on these issues in exchange for initial Israeli good faith in returning the territories. According to the analysis, there is a high probability that such a minimax peace plan could be implemented peacefully, avoiding deadlock and satisfying both sides in the long run.

Communication and Dissemination of DSS Results

Since one of the major goals of the study was to motivate policy analysts, who are heavily immersed in short-term events, to think in terms of probable long-term events and actions, ISA wanted broad distribution of the findings to relevant policymakers. But it is often the case that busy foreign policy analysts do not have the time to set aside to read a 230-page report. As a result, the most direct method of communicating the study's results was through hour-long briefings, that facilitated face-to-face questioning and discussions, not only between the policy analysts and the study team, but among the analysts as well. Four major presentations were conducted for Middle East analysts in ISA, DoD's Middle East Task Group, the Defense Intelligence Agency, INR/State, and the NSC. The project was not new to many of the key attendees, because the study team had conducted many helpful conversations with them as the project was in progress.

It was interesting to note the obvious and appropriate differences in concern across bureaucratic lines.[25] INR expressed the most interest in the hypothetical comprehensive peace plans and the methodology used in formulating them. These analysts were also interested in examining the event sequence networks and following the specific actions and responses downstream. NSC analysts appeared concerned primarily with solutions to Palestinian status. DoD analysts focused attention on the long-term simulations, the sensitivity of the results to assumptions made, and the logic involved in projecting long-term consequences from likely near-term impacts.

The overall reaction of the audiences was favorable to the study's intent, methods, and results. It provided systematic insight and background on potential long-term problems that they might face in negotiating and implementing elements of a Middle East peace treaty. The comprehensive nature of the hypothesized agreements added an element of realism to the results. It also triggered many discussions among analysts on the probable nature of a comprehensive agreement – its content and how it might be phased, and on the complexity of forecasting its long-term implications. Moreover, the study was conducted at an opportune time to support the outset of negotiations – on schedule with pre-negotiation maneuverings and analyst concern over the situation.

The study also sparked the curiosity of many analysts to consider the consequences of changing or refining aspects of the DSS tools. Suggestions included a more accurate fix on the temporal framework, changes in some of the assumptions made by the model, modifications to the phasing process, analysis of alternative peace provisions, updates and reforecasts as Middle East positions change, the consequences of negotiation breakdown, forecasts of economic normalization in the region, the long-term nature of US guarantees, and analysis of various assumptions concerning the constitution of a potential Palestinian entity. There were also some analysts who dismissed the study's results, due to disagreement with the assumptions or mistrust and misunderstanding of the statistical methods employed.

Conclusions: Pursuing Relevant Paths for DSS Research

What did the DSS study team accomplish in this project that was responsive to the needs of foreign policymakers preparing for upcoming negotiations? Many issues can be recommended from this study to guide similar efforts in the future so that they address the requirements of practitioners. References are made below to relevant criteria in the literature that are supported by experiences in this project.

Research Goal Criteria

Focus on policymaker functions:[26] In our project, implications were drawn on how US national security interests might be affected by different peace plan formulations. These results were particularly relevant to ISA analysts who are concerned primarily with such questions.

Focus on reducing organizational limitations: Overworked and understaffed bureaucracies may find it difficult to keep abreast of the day-to-day tasks of interpreting events, making short-term predictions, and enumerating decision alternatives, as well as maintaining an active and unbiased perspective on the potential long-term implications of these occurrences. External researchers can assist policymakers by analyzing these gaps in information that often result from manpower constraints.

Focus on long-term implications: Foreign policymakers often become entrenched in formulating short-term details to the point that they lose sight of the larger picture. Analysis of long-term consequences can assist analysts design more effective and durable policy alternatives.

Focus on developing useful perspectives, not necessarily developing theories or providing answers:[27] Few conclusions that can be derived from international relations research will be undisputed. Rival hypotheses can often be found that enable the same facts to be interpreted differently and incompatible conclusions drawn. Thus, researchers should be cautious not to promise "answers" to policymakers. Moreover, data available within the government, but not to external researchers, put policymakers at a much greater advantage in coping with details on policy problems. However, external researchers can provide policymakers with broad perspectives on the issues, to spark thought processes, and facilitate balanced and unbiased attention to problems.

Methodological Criteria

Present research comprehensibly:[28] A practitioner audience may not be as conversant in the latest jargon, methods or theories as may international relations scholars. Statistical presentations may not be comprehensible to analysts with little technical expertise or background. While analyses may have to be conducted with precision and explicit methodological sophistication, the technical approach and results must be translated in an understandable and usable fashion to be of direct value to practitioners.

Provide systematic analysis: Studies conducted by international relations researchers have the potential advantage of combining substantive expertise in an area with the methodological skills of social science approaches. Such scholarly external research can be responsive to the needs of practitioners by relying on systematic, reliable, and reproducible methods that make its conclusions appear more credible than the potentially prejudiced judgments and raw speculations of government analysts.

Develop relevant dependent variables:[29] Highly specific dependent variables are likely to be more meaningful and useful to policy analysts who constantly deal with specifics, than gross, systemic level variables.

State assumptions explicitly: Assumptions are often made in research studies to reduce analytical uncertainty and enable conclusions to be derived. If these assumptions are stated explicitly, policymakers can judge the relevance of the results based on their knowledge of the facts, and alternate results can be approximated given modified assumptions.

Timing Criteria

Immediacy of impact: External research is most valued if its results can assist policymakers perform their current tasks more effectively. Results that impact directly on specific analyst concerns, such as those dealing with current negotiations, arms deals, crises, or domestic unrest, are likely to be most relevant and utilized.

Adaptability and Utilization Criteria

Focus on areas that can be manipulated, changed, or influenced:[30] The research conducted for this study focused on identifying specific elements of potential peace treaties that might destabilize the long-term peace. By pinpointing these peace terms prior to the onset of formal negotiations, it is possible for policymakers to use the study's findings to persuade negotiating parties to avoid such dangerous provisions. Moreover, the identification of early warning signals and critical turning points can help practitioners anticipate and avert potentially negative consequences. Awareness of potential hazards can lead policymakers to develop practical contingency plans in the event that critical points are encountered.

Develop adaptable research: Policymakers may be privy to information that scholars do not have. Thus, model parameters and assumptions should be fully explained to practitioners, and they should be given the option to test the impact of alternate assumptions and modified parameters on the sensitivity of the outcomes.

Know your audience:[31] Analysts in different bureaucratic units often have varying perspectives on the same situation that are derived from their particular functions, organizational backgrounds or precedents. To have a practical impact, DSS analysts must address the specific interests of the organization they are supporting. This does not require advocacy of a predetermined conclusion, but merely attentiveness and directed focus on certain substantive areas.

Notes

1 Ulvila, Jacob and Warren Snider (1980). "Negotiation of International Oil Tanker Standards: An Application of Multiattribute Value Theory," *Operations Research* 28: 81–96.
2 Raiffa, Howard (1982). *The Art and Science of Negotiations*. Cambridge, MA: Harvard University Press.
3 Ulvila, Jacob (1990). "Turning Points: An Analysis," in J. McDonald Jr. and D. Bendahmane, editors, *U.S. Bases Overseas*. Boulder, CO: Westview Press.
4 Spector, Bertram I. (1993b). "Introduction," *Theory and Decision* 34, 3: 177–181.
5 Zartman, I. William (1993). "Decision Support and Negotiation Research: A Researcher's Perspective." *Theory and Decision* 34, 3: 345–351.
6 Winham, Gilbert (1979). "Practitioners' Views of International Negotiation." *World Politics* 32: 111–135.
7 Raiffa (1982), op.cit.
8 Alcamo, J., R. Shaw, and L. Hordijkk (1990). *The RAINS Model of Acidification: Science and Strategies in Europe*. Dordrecht, the Netherlands: Kluwer Academic Publishers.
9 Fisher, Franklin (1994). "The Harvard Middle East Water Project: Overview, Results and Conclusions." Cambridge, MA: Harvard Institute for Social and Economic Policy in the Middle East, December.
10 Kersten, Gregory E. and Hsiangchu Lai (2007). "Negotiation Support and E-negotiation Systems: An Overview," *Group Decision and Negotiation* 16: 553–586.
11 Druckman, Daniel, James N. Druckman and Tatsushi Arai (2004). "e-Mediation: Evaluating the Impacts of an Electronic Mediator on Negotiating Behavior," *Group Decision and Negotiation* 13: 481–511.

12 Hirblinger, Andreas T. (2023). "When mediators need machines (and vice versa): Towards a research agenda on hybrid peacemaking intelligence," *International Negotiation* 28, 1.
13 Spector, Bertram I. (1997). "Analytical Support to Negotiations: An Empirical Assessment," *Group Decision and Negotiation* 6, 5: 421–436.
14 Chasek, Pamela (2023). "Is it the End of the COP as We Know It? An Analysis of the First Year of Virtual Meetings in the United Nations Environment and Development Arena," *International Negotiation* 28, 1.
15 Kersten and Lai (2007), op.cit.
16 Spector, Bertram I. (1992). "Developing the Negotiator's Tool Box: Practical Systems to Support Effective International Negotiations," *Control and Cybernetics* 21, 1: 21–35.
17 Druckman, Daniel, Bennett Ramberg and Richard Harris (2002). "Computer-Assisted International Negotiation: A Tool for Research and Practice," *Group Decision and Negotiation* 11: 231–256.
18 Ibid.; Spector, Bertram I. (1993a). "Decision Analysis for Practical Negotiation Application," *Theory and Decision* 34, 3: 183–199.
19 Kersten and Lai (2007), op.cit.
20 CACI (1977). *U. S. National Security Interests in Potential Middle East Peace Solutions: A Long-Term Perspective, Vols. 1–3.* Arlington, VA: CACI, Inc.-Federal.
21 O'Leary, M., W. Coplin, H. Shapiro, and D. Dean (1974). "The Quest for Relevance: Quantitative International Relations Research and Government Foreign Affairs Analysis," *International Studies Quarterly* 18, 2.
22 Bull, V. (1975). *The West Bank-Is it Viable?* Lexington, MA: D. C. Heath; Friedlander, D. and C. Goldscheider (1974). "Peace and the Demographic Future of Israel," *Journal of Conflict Resolution* 18,3 (September); Pelcovits, N. (1976). "Security Guarantees in a Middle East Settlement." *Foreign Policy Papers* 2, 5. Beverly Hills, CA: Sage Publications; Sakr, N. (1977). "Economic Viability: 3 Major Constraints," *The Middle East* (28 February); Van Arkadie, B. (1977). *Benefits and Burdens: A Report on the West Bank and Gaza Strip Economies Since 1967.* New York: Carnegie Endowment for International Peace; Zahlan, A. (1976). "The Economic Viability of a West Bank State," *Middle East International* (November).
23 Iklé, F. and N. Leites (1962). "Political Negotiation as a Process of Modifying Utilities," *Journal of Conflict Resolution* 6.
24 Spector, Bertram I. (1977). "Negotiation as a Psychological Process," *Journal of Conflict Resolution* 21,4 (December).
25 Whiting, A. (1972). "The Scholar and the Policy-Maker," in R. Tanter and R. Ullman, eds., *Theory and Policy in International Relations*. Princeton, NJ: Princeton University Press.
26 Ibid.
27 Young, O. (1972). "The Perils of Odysseus: On Constructing Theories of International Relations," in R. Tanter and R. Ullman, eds., *Theory and Policy in International Relations*. Princeton, NJ: Princeton University Press.
28 Brewer, G. and O. Hall (1972). "Policy Analysis by Computer Simulation: The Need for Appraisal." RAND Corporation (August) mimeo.
29 O'Leary, et al. (1974), op.cit.
30 Ibid.; CACI (1975). *Utilization of Computer Technology and Formal Social Science in Foreign Policy Decision-Making.* Arlington, VA: CACI, Inc.-Federal.
31 Whiting (1972), op.cit.; Allison, G. and M. Halperin (1972). "Bureaucratic Politics: A Paradigm and Some Policy Implications," in R. Tanter and R. Ullman, eds., *Theory and Policy in International Relations*. Princeton, NJ: Princeton University Press.

9
CITIZEN NEGOTIATION
Adding New Voices

There is a growing trend toward illiberal democracies. These states may hold elections on a regular basis, but they may be manipulated. They often place heavy constraints on civil liberties, they lack openness and transparency, and those who exercise power are not held accountable for their actions.[1] Citizens are deprived of their rights to advocate for their own interests with elected officials. They often believe that they must accept this situation as it is – there is no way out. Under these circumstances, what initiatives might initiate a turnaround toward greater democratic rights and civil liberties? What is the best way for citizen groups to stand up for their rights vis-à-vis government and promote change?

This essay provides an overview of how the negotiation process can be used by advocacy groups operated by nongovernmental organizations (NGOs) to promote and facilitate getting things accomplished in conjunction with government. The conditions needed for commencing negotiations are described, as well as the stages and activities that define negotiation behavior. Ultimately, moving from confrontation to achieving results and desired reforms requires an accepting "culture of negotiation" on the part of both advocacy groups and government agencies.

Achieving Advocacy Goals through Negotiation

The development of open democratic procedures in government naturally encourages the emergence and participation of many interest groups, both within and outside of government, in public policy decision-making. While on the one hand, these democratic approaches can produce balanced solutions to policy questions that represent the perspectives of many stakeholders, they can also incite battles among interest groups that feel threatened and can engender conflicts between government agencies and ministries, the executive and legislative branches, government and the public, and government and external

DOI: 10.4324/9781003314400-9

organizations, such as NGO advocacy groups. These conflicts can escalate if stakeholders perceive that their interests are at grave risk. In the worst of cases, stalemate on important policy issues can result.

Because of these tendencies, conflict resolution approaches have become an integral element of democratic decision-making procedures. The most frequently used of these conflict resolution mechanisms are negotiation practices. Formal or informal negotiation among stakeholders provides an outlet for conflicts of interest and opinion to be voiced, for these differences to be contrasted and debated, for common ground among the stakeholders to be sought, and for practical solutions to be found that accommodate the interests of all parties.

Negotiation is a mechanism that promotes the coordination of differing stakeholder interests in a constructive way; it is not a vehicle to force or coerce the capitulation of one side or the other. If practiced effectively, negotiation can help disputing parties find mutually acceptable agreements where the priority interests of each party are creatively cobbled together so that all perceive themselves as winners in the process. Well-crafted negotiated agreements offer face-saving provisions for stakeholders who may have compromised on lesser issues to achieve goals that are higher on their agendas.

Ultimately, negotiation is a process of democratic decision-making that facilitates the practical imperative of "getting things done." If the stakeholders have the political willingness to seek a solution to their differences, the negotiation process provides a mechanism for coordinating interests, resolving conflicts, and averting deadlock, thereby promoting more inclusive policy formulation and more effective policy implementation.

US President John F. Kennedy, while still a United States Senator, wrote about negotiation as the essence of democratic decision-making in government.[2] Making public policy, he writes, requires compromise between the desires of all stakeholders. Government decision-making is not a process that can tolerate rigid or inflexible positions; responsible legislators and government managers in a democratic system must practice flexibility, the willingness to adjust and modify positions to find mutual accommodation among stakeholders in a pluralistic society. This is not to say that government decision-makers or NGO advocates must abandon their principles, values, or beliefs. It is just that the "art" of getting things accomplished within democratic procedures requires that a way be found for multiple perspectives and interests to be represented and balanced, rather than having one interest overpower all alternative positions. Mutual concessions through the give-and-take of the negotiation process are the way this can be achieved.

Prerequisites for Negotiation

What does it take to get disputing parties to the negotiating table? Two factors are influential – the *willingness* of stakeholders to negotiate based on their perceptions that the issue is ripe for resolution and the *capacity* of the stakeholders to negotiate. Together, these factors combine to create a level of "negotiation readiness."[3] Negotiation readiness is defined as the motivation to resolve conflicts, as well as the ability to do so through negotiation processes. If any of the principal parties are not ready to negotiate, policy formulation or implementation may come to a halt and conflict may emerge.

In illiberal democracies and authoritarian states, citizens often do not have an option to sit down with government officeholders to dialogue about public policy. There are no active role models for citizens to hark back to, while government officials are likely to quash any attempts by citizens to advocate for change. Government can forcefully make their resistance to such citizen action well known by suppressing NGO activities and harassing citizen activists. Later in this essay, a case is described in which negotiation training of NGOs opened their eyes to the possibilities of dialogue.

Willingness *and* capacity are equally important in generating the decision to negotiate. Parties must believe that it is in their best interest to negotiate an agreement rather than to continue the conflict. If the disputing parties lack a sufficient level of capacity, they are *not* likely to decide to negotiate their differences, fearing a concessionary, or worse, an exploitative, interaction, even if they are motivated and the conflict seems ripe.

To be negotiation-ready, the parties must view the policy issue as being ripe; this depends largely on the magnitude of the costs which will be imposed or the rewards that will be foregone if a negotiated agreement is not achieved. Proposals offered by NGO advocacy groups, for example, must be persuasive and demonstrate that government interests, as well as the public's interests, will be well-served if they are accepted and implemented. Thus, the willingness to negotiate is influenced by this cost-benefit calculation. The willingness to negotiate is also determined by the relative power of the parties. Government authorities are usually viewed as possessing the power of the state, but they can be convinced to join in negotiations with NGO advocacy groups if these groups can demonstrate that they have broad and committed public support, public opinion is on their side, the law is on their side, or their position is upheld by the facts.

In addition, the parties must have sufficient capacity to negotiate, which depends on their skills, experience, and resources to perform adequately in the negotiation process – to be able to identify, defend, and promote their own interests effectively. They must be able to plan, strategize, persuade, advocate, and lobby on their own behalf.

Perceptions that benefits do not currently outweigh the costs or sensing asymmetry in capacity among the disputing parties can dissuade them from coming to the table to negotiate. On the other hand, better information and more realistic cost-benefit assessments, along with capacity building activities to enhance the negotiating skills of stakeholder groups, will increase the readiness of parties for negotiation and encourage them to come to the table.

Negotiation Activities

Once parties decide to negotiate, the process moves forward through various activities. The prominent activities change over time across several stages – from the pre-negotiation period, to the negotiations themselves, and finally to post-agreement negotiations. These activities do not vary whether the negotiations are government-to-government or government-to-NGO. But in most cases, both citizen groups and government authorities need to further develop their capacity to plan and conduct these negotiation activities, since they may not have much experience resolving policy conflicts with each other using this mechanism. In the *pre-negotiation stage,* the parties prepare, plan, and strategize for the upcoming talks. Activities include the following:

- Conduct fact-finding
- Identify your own interests
- Establish goals
- Identify acceptable fallback positions
- Assess the interests and goals of the other parties
- Assess the implications of differential power positions
- Develop strategies and tactics
- Test alternative demands and proposals
- Prepare or influence the structure and context of the upcoming talks
- Initiate confidence-building measures with the other side
- Build coalitions.

In the *negotiation stage* itself, the parties seek accommodation on the issues that have kept them apart through direct interaction. Many of the pre-negotiation activities to develop and evaluate the effectiveness of strategies, tactics, demands, and proposals still continue into the negotiation phase. New activities in the negotiation stage include:

- Present positions and interests to the other side
- Employ and modify strategies and tactics to encourage the other parties to see benefit in your proposals
- Defend and promote your interests
- Find general principles of justice and fairness upon which all parties can agree (these are called "formulas")
- Search for acceptable provisions that add detail to the agreed principles
- Overcome objections and impasses
- Conduct problem solving and find creative approaches to obtain mutually acceptable solutions
- Work within coalitions to further your interests.

The *post-agreement negotiation stage* is important in solidifying the ongoing relationship between parties. No matter how detailed the negotiated agreement, its implementation will always require additional interpretation and give-and-take to resolve differences or make adjustments. Post-agreement negotiations can be viewed as a process of sustaining relationships between advocacy groups and government authorities that need to work together but which may have conflicting interests. These negotiations provide a mechanism for them to resolve their differences through compromise and creative solutions. Activities at this stage include:

- Establish and participate in an ongoing forum in which the parties to an agreement can continue to dialogue and negotiate details, adjustments, and extensions
- Monitor and evaluate compliance with negotiated provisions
- Find ways to improve existing agreements
- Work with existing coalitions and develop new coalitions to implement agreements.

Across each of these stages, negotiation strategies and tactics are devised and employed by all parties. This bargaining behavior can be classified into a few basic categories, including issuing threats and warnings, offering promises and predictions, making commitments, feigning incapacity, making concessions, and bluffing, among others. Closely related to these strategies and tactics is negotiation style – whether the negotiator is tough (tendency to hold out for more) or soft (tendency to give in).

Developing a Negotiation Culture

What needs to be done to regularize negotiations between NGO advocates and government agencies? The readiness of the parties to negotiate must be developed and the institutional framework within which negotiation takes place must be established.

Building Negotiation Readiness

NGO advocacy groups and government agencies that need to work with one another must develop a perspective that the only way things can get accomplished and deadlock avoided is through continuing negotiation and compromise. There must be a mindset that greater benefits can accrue for the public good if advocates and government agencies work together to develop procedures to resolve their differences and get on with their work. They must not see each other as the enemy, but rather as stakeholders with which they can and should dialogue with to develop mutually acceptable results. The other part of the equation is to strengthen negotiation abilities and skills of the citizen advocates and government officers. This can be done through training, practice exercises, and observation.

Building Negotiation Platforms

Ongoing fora in which representatives of NGOs and government agencies can meet to negotiate their differences and find mutually acceptable solutions are essential. These can take the form of policy dialogue workshops or task forces. If these platforms have regularly scheduled meetings, negotiation norms and activities will likely become the favored approach over time to push progress on public policy issues.

Anticipated Outcomes

The anticipated benefits of promoting citizen negotiation with government are threefold:

- Deadlocks in policy formulation or implementation can be averted,
- Better policy solutions can be designed by including the perspectives of all stakeholders, and
- Policy formulation and implementation can be made more efficient through regularized processes of interaction between government agencies, the legislature, and the public.

Developing a culture of negotiation between advocacy groups and government is an acquired skill, one that can be institutionalized where there is a desire to make government decision-making the art of the possible. As policy issues increasingly require various government agencies, the legislature, and the public to interact and work in coordination with one another to get things done, each stakeholder must find a way to see beyond its own parochial organizational interests to avoid stalemate and find common ground to move policy issues forward. Negotiation is the principal mechanism to resolve such conflicts of interest in an inclusive participatory fashion.

Case Study: Russian Far East

When working within an illiberal democracy or authoritarian state, it is not easy to actively engage or mobilize citizen groups. Government typically resists citizen advocacy and negotiation efforts. And there are likely to be few examples of successful cases of citizen participation. In 2006, USAID awarded a contract to strengthen the foundations for effective citizen advocacy efforts and grassroots initiatives in Russia – of all places! It was well into the second term of Vladimir Putin's presidency. The *Community Participation and Regional Advocacy Project*, a three year project, focused its efforts in the Russian Far East – in particular, in the Khabarovskiy and Primorskiy krais.[4] The project sought to strengthen the capacity of municipal and regional organizations to develop and implement advocacy initiatives that would effectively address community priorities and reform policies to improve the quality of life. The proposed approach focused on promoting dialogue and collaboration between citizens and their local governments, not on conflict or confrontation. Activities included:

- Strengthening advocacy skills and capacities of local advocacy groups, primarily through training and coaching,
- Supporting public interest advocacy activities, initiated and implemented by local civil society groups primarily through grants and technical assistance,
- Facilitating networking and coalitions among advocacy groups, convening regional and interregional meetings, and encouraging network and coalition building around issues of common interest,
- Developing and disseminating advocacy tools and mechanisms, and scaling-up advocacy activities to reach out to other communities by engaging the local mass media and establishing civil society-local government dialogue, and
- Institutionalizing and building sustainability of citizen advocacy practices in the regions, primarily by establishing Public Advocacy Centers to serve as institutional hubs for future activity.

Over the life of the program, we worked with 435 civil society and business groups to engage in advocacy campaigns for legal and regulatory reforms; 34 groups took such action for the first time under the auspices of the program. 115 advocacy initiatives were conducted of which 55 were adopted or implemented by government entities (47.8% success rate). Nine of these initiatives were targeted specifically at improving the quality of life for women and/or youth. All of these initiatives were conducted by coalitions of advocacy NGOs. The reform campaigns were targeted at practical improvements in the budget process, small and medium business development, the environment, housing and communal services, public participation in decision-making, healthcare, support for vulnerable groups, land use and urban development, education, and increasing the transparency of authority.

As a result of advocacy campaigns supported by the program, new regulations were adopted to open government hearings and encourage public participation in future policies and planning. Administrative barriers to the development of local business were removed. Citizens influenced government decisions that would have harmed the environmental status of their communities. Housing and communal service providers were made to be accountable for providing quality and affordable work. The rights of pensioners and veterans were protected. And legal literacy was strengthened, thus mainstreaming civil, social, and human rights, and providing citizens with the knowledge to exercise and protect their rights.

Almost 38,000 citizens were mobilized by these advocacy campaigns. Over 650 representatives of NGOs and citizen initiative groups received advocacy and negotiation skills training. Seventeen regional and interregional events were conducted to encourage networking and coalition building among the advocacy NGOs. Many grants were made to NGOs and business associations that provided them with the resources and wherewithal to pursue their interests.

One set of training workshops for advocacy NGOs was in negotiation skills – to help them build their capacity to dialogue with local government authorities, present their interests, and generate agreements to change policies and improve service delivery. Advocacy is a two-way street – citizens make demands for change and, ideally, government officials listen and make reforms. But the interests of these two stakeholders often are not well-aligned. That is why citizen advocates must work hard to convince authorities to change their minds and their ways. To be effective, this requires a "results-oriented advocacy" approach that not only presents persuasive arguments in favor of its causes, but also employs negotiating techniques skillfully to achieve a consensus of interests between citizen advocates and government counterparts.

These training workshops focused on providing negotiation skills to citizen advocacy leaders to strengthen their capacity to transact collaboratively with government officials. To do this, the workshop strengthened their abilities to balance conflicting interests and reach agreement with the authorities to implement desired reforms. Training included techniques to understand the interests and motives of government counterparts and the constraints they operate under; understand the issues and priorities; understand, apply, and respond to negotiating strategies and tactics; achieve mutually acceptable agreements; and sustain negotiated solutions and follow-through on negotiated agreements.

Ultimately, the goals of the training provided practical skills to advocacy groups on how to achieve positive advocacy results through effective negotiations with authorities. The training workshop provided citizen advocates with the skills and tools to negotiate for their interests, but with a focus on achieving a "win–win" consensus solution that can facilitate implementation of their desired reforms. Role-playing exercises were used to reinforce the skills training.

Forty-five participants, including program grantees, NGOs, and local government and business representatives participated in the negotiation training. Participants were trained in various aspects of effective negotiation techniques and learned how to understand the interests and motivations of authorities when planning negotiations, plan negotiations and develop negotiation formulas, use different strategies and negotiation tactics, reach mutually satisfying agreements, sustain relationships established during negotiations, and follow-up on agreements. Several interactive role-play activities guided participants through all stages of the negotiation process, starting from carefully calibrated planning and development of negotiation strategies and tactics to conducting negotiations and sustaining post-negotiation agreements.

We experienced some positive and negative results during this program. Our project team met with the governor of one of the oblasts when we began the project to assess his willingness to participate and work with citizen groups. He said he was more than willing to talk with these groups, if there were any groups to talk with! He was not aware of many active or reasonable advocacy NGOs in his region. In another city, we trained members of several NGOs on how to negotiate with local authorities in a positive way – not to protest or complain about current decisions or services, but rather to dialogue and negotiate with the authorities to arrive at a mutually acceptable agreement on how to adjust and change the delivery of services. The NGOs had never heard of such approaches, but we provided examples of how this had worked in other places. This training opened their eyes to a new world in which NGOs could be more proactive and successful in achieving the changes they were seeking in policy and service delivery. We gave them a new set of tools and many of the training participants moved ahead and succeeded in negotiating policy change with local government authorities.

Unfortunately, there were also experiences where we saw active retaliation by government against NGOs that sought to advocate on behalf of citizens. A rule of law NGO in Vladivostok faced continual harassment for seeking to advocate and negotiate for improved services, to the point where the leader of the group was imprisoned. And based on comments from an executive branch official who participated in one of my negotiation workshops and reported back to Moscow, I became *persona non grata* in Russia and my travel visa was revoked. So much for illiberal democracies and their supposed opening for citizen participation!

Notes

1 Zakaria, Fareed (1997). "The Rise of Illiberal Democracy," *Foreign Affairs* 76, 6: 22–43.
2 Kennedy, John F. (1956). *Profiles in Courage*. New York: Harper Perennial: 5–7.
3 Spector, Bertram I. (2002). "Negotiation Readiness in the Development Context: Adding Capacity to Ripeness," in Ho-Won Jeong, editor, *Approaches to Peacebuilding*. New York: Palgrave Macmillan.
4 Management Systems International (2010). *Community Participation and Regional Advocacy Project in the Russian Far East, Final Report*. Arlington, VA: MSI. At: https://pdf.usaid.gov/pdf_docs/PDACQ845.pdf.

10
NEGOTIATED RULEMAKING

Regulations are a common mechanism used by governments to guide and facilitate the implementation, management, and enforcement of policy change. Through regulations, governments establish the rules that specify, control, and direct compliance with new decisions. However, if these rules are not complied with as intended, policy implementation may not proceed smoothly. Research has shown that the effectiveness of many regulations is strongly influenced by the process by which they were initially formulated. This essay describes an inclusive, participative, and problem-solving process – negotiation, with mediation built in to ensure progress – that is used to formulate regulations successfully. This application of negotiation is primarily used at local and national levels, although variants can also be relevant to rules developed at an international level to slow climate change, protect transboundary waters, and address hazardous and toxic substances, for example.

The traditional process of regulatory development is typically top-down. Government initiates, formulates, and proposes the rules. In centralized or closed systems, regulations are imposed; in more open systems, groups or individuals may comment on the proposals in public hearings, but with little possibility of making major structural and functional modifications to the regulations. This process, while well-intentioned, often leaves civil society stakeholders feeling far removed from the process and disempowered. They may feel that they have minimal voice in designing the regulations, standards, and provisions that must be obeyed, and, as a result, compliance may be low and enforcement costs high – a double-edged sword.

Stakeholder reactions to top-down regulatory development can have negative implications, as observed in a variety of countries.[1] If penalties are increased to discourage noncompliance, businesses may migrate into a "shadow economy," thereby fueling corruption, reducing tax revenues, and evading the regulatory

DOI: 10.4324/9781003314400-10

regime altogether. In some societies, lengthy and costly litigation in the courts is sometimes pursued by civil society groups to modify or eliminate imposed regulations. Antagonistic and adversarial relations between regulatory agencies and the regulated parties may ensue, resulting in delay or outright disregard for the regulation's intent. The lack of effective and frank dialogue between the regulators and the regulated is usually blamed for these negative consequences.

Regulation through Negotiation

There is an alternate approach to this traditional process of regulatory formulation and implementation – *negotiated rulemaking* or *regulatory negotiation (reg-neg)*. Negotiated rulemaking brings together affected stakeholder groups with the relevant government agency and a neutral mediator or facilitator to build a consensus on the features of a new regulation *before* it is proposed officially by the agency. Regulatory provisions are developed as a bottom-up participatory process of negotiation. Negotiated rulemaking is a fully collaborative process, in which all interested groups – government, business, and citizen groups – are convened in an Advisory Committee – a platform for dialogue and negotiation. Key issues and concerns are identified, the interests of all sides are compared and contrasted, negotiations take place, and hopefully, agreements based on consensus are developed. In the United States, negotiated rulemaking became the officially recommended approach to develop new regulations by federal government agencies in 1990 when the Negotiated Rulemaking Act (5 U.S.C. 561–570) was passed by Congress. A September 1993 Executive Order from the White House requires all federal agencies to consider applying negotiated rulemaking strategies in all future regulatory actions.

However, the approach has been used informally by government agencies since the 1970s. The Department of Labor, the Environmental Protection Agency (EPA), and the Department of the Interior, are its principal proponents. By far, the EPA has been the most frequent user of negotiated rulemaking. Over 50 federal negotiated rulemaking cases have been documented between 1982 and 1995; many more applications have been conducted in the United States at the state level.[2] Examples of environmental regulations developed using negotiated rulemaking in the United States include:

- Penalties for businesses for noncompliance with the Clean Air Act
- Exceptions for licensing pesticides
- Performance standards for wood burning stoves
- Controls on volatile organic chemical equipment leaks
- Standards for transporting hazardous wastes
- Standards for chemicals used in manufacturing wood furniture.

The negotiated rulemaking approach has been applied in other countries as well. The Council of State and the Economic and Social Council in France, the

Socio-Economic Council and Labor Foundation in the Netherlands, and the Council of State in Greece, have all applied consensus-building approaches to rulemaking.[3] Japanese and German business and government leaders also develop health and safety regulations collaboratively through negotiation.

Negotiated regulatory development has been practiced in New Zealand as well since 1985. Their approach dictates that a "regulatory impact statement" be prepared by the government regulatory agency to assess the likely costs and benefits of the regulation ahead of time.[4] The procedure includes exploration of "alternative compliance mechanisms" by which the regulated parties can propose and negotiate options on how they will comply with future regulations without degrading regulatory standards. Regulatory reform developed using consensus-building and negotiations was also introduced into East European countries by Western and international donor agencies.[5]

The experience with negotiated rulemaking in the United States has produced several benefits:[6]

- While negotiated rulemaking takes more time and effort upfront than traditional modes of developing regulations, all the stakeholders, including government agencies, are more satisfied with the results.
- Participants find that with a negotiated process, the resulting regulations tend not to be challenged in court. In contrast, about 80% of all non-negotiated EPA regulations have been challenged in court and about 30% have been changed as a result.
- Less time, money and effort are expended on enforcing the regulations.
- Final regulations are technically more accurate and clear to everyone.
- Final regulations can be implemented earlier and with a higher compliance rate.
- More cooperative relationships are established between the agency and the regulated parties.

Favorable Conditions for Negotiated Rulemaking

Certain societal conditions facilitate the application of negotiated rulemaking procedures. These include the existence of democratic procedures, an independent judiciary, basic governance capacity, and enforceable results of the process implemented in good faith. Practitioners considering this approach must also ask some basic questions:

- *Is there a willingness to negotiate?* The major stakeholders must be willing to negotiate and show some flexibility in their interests and position. One major motivation to negotiate a regulation's provisions is the belief that a better and more enforceable solution will be reached through negotiation than through the traditional top-down approach.
- *Is this the ripe moment?* The issues must be ripe for decision. The issues need to be known and commonly understood. Both governmental and

non-governmental parties need to be motivated to reach a mutually acceptable solution because of either impending and overwhelming costs that are predicted if they do not reach agreement *or* imminent and compelling rewards that will be made available if they do.
- *Is the process perceived to be fair?* The stakeholders must believe that the venue and atmosphere of the proposed negotiations will be fair and will enable each party to have an equal voice. There needs to be confidence that the playing field is level and that no party will dominate the talks. Moreover, the history of the issue and the history of past interactions among the stakeholders must suggest that any prejudices or biases among the parties can be overcome.

If these conditions are not met – if any of the parties believe that they can achieve their goals without the cooperation of the other stakeholders and at lower cost – they are not likely to be motivated to engage in negotiated rulemaking procedures. However, if they are interested in sustainable results that are not perceived as being imposed by more powerful stakeholders, instituting a negotiated rulemaking process is likely to be viewed as appropriate and can motivate the parties to come to the negotiating table.

Practical Procedures

How is negotiated rulemaking carried out in industrialized countries? There are several steps.

Step 1 Diagnose the Issue
The regulatory agency begins by conducting a preliminary assessment that examines the issue, the stakeholders, their interests and priorities, and the likelihood of success of applying negotiated rulemaking. If the issues are very contentious, there is a history of strong stakeholder animosity, or interests are highly divergent, the agency may decide not to use this regulatory negotiation process.

Step 2 Select the Facilitator
Selection of the "right" facilitator is critical to the success of the process. Making this selection is usually the responsibility of the regulatory agency that makes public, at this juncture, its intention to proceed with the negotiated rulemaking process. The facilitator must be perceived as a neutral and objective party, trusted by all stakeholders, and is usually selected from outside the organization. He/she must have both issue knowledge as well as process skills.

Step 3 Identify the Stakeholders and Obtain Their Commitment to the Process
The major stakeholders need to participate in the negotiations and be a part of the consensus if the process is to be a success. The identification of stakeholders is the responsibility of the facilitator, who must determine their willingness to participate in the process and their capacity

(training, infrastructure, and knowledge) to negotiate as equal partners. Commitment, capacity, and interest are the key criteria for selection. Certainly, who gets to sit at the negotiation table is a critical decision on which there needs to be early agreement. Each party needs to be contacted individually by the facilitator to pledge commitment to the process. The facilitator can then help prepare the parties for the upcoming negotiation by holding preliminary fact-finding meetings with each stakeholder.

Step 4 Establish the Advisory Committee

An Advisory Committee needs to be established and convened by the facilitator as the platform used to negotiate the regulatory provisions. Its membership consists of the stakeholders who have agreed to participate, including representatives from the regulatory agency (25 or fewer participants have been found to be the ideal number). Adequate resources should be pledged to enable the Committee to conduct its work. The relevant regulatory agency usually provides the financial support, but must be careful not to influence the process so as to ensure the independence of the Committee's deliberations. Fact-finding, preparation, and planning are essential elements of a reasoned process. Coming to a common understanding of the facts underlying the issues is a first step toward finding fair and appropriate agreements. The ultimate goals and anticipated products of the negotiation should be agreed among the Committee's members as the process commences. Deadlines, too, should be established by the Committee to stimulate reasonable progress in the talks.

Step 5 Conduct Negotiations

The negotiations are characterized by several activities:

- The issues, interests, and priorities of each of the stakeholders must be discussed openly by the Advisory Committee. Placing a diversity of issues on the table will yield a negotiation with more room to compromise and conduct tradeoffs.
- Points of agreement and points of difference must be identified.
- The negotiation must search for ways to resolve differences through creative problem-solving, tradeoffs among issues, and analogies to similar regulatory solutions, among others.

Throughout the negotiations, the facilitator should serve the role of stimulating the debate in the Committee – getting the parties to discuss their interests rather than their formal positions, highlighting points of commonality among the parties, and identifying solutions that will not cause stakeholders to compromise their fundamental values.

Step 6 Develop Consensus around a Single Text

Throughout, the facilitator needs to encourage the Committee to develop a single consensus text acceptable to all stakeholders. This document must address the key issues and interests of all stakeholders and present solutions that all can comply with and "sell" to their individual constituencies.

One way to generate such a document is for a small subcommittee to volunteer to write it, incorporating multiple perspectives and proposals, and expecting that it will serve only as a jumping off point for further negotiation and creative compromise.

Step 7 Present the Resulting Negotiated Agreement

When the Committee reaches consensus, it transmits its conclusions to the regulatory agency. This can be in the form of a draft regulation, a report, or recommendations. If a consensus could not be reached, minority reports may be filed along with the majority's findings. What the agency does with this input depends on what was originally promised when the negotiations began. Usually, the negotiated results are published and disseminated by the regulatory agency, which must be ready to act in good faith upon the results of the Committee.

Case Study

A real example helps to illustrate how negotiated rulemaking procedures work in a practical sense. This application involved the development of regulations in the United States concerning the emission of hazardous air pollutants from wood furniture manufacturing operations.[7] A two-year negotiating process involving representatives from industry, nongovernmental environmental groups, and state and federal government officials, resulted in a proposed regulation published by the EPA. This proposal was then open for public comments and hearings prior to promulgating the final rule. The Advisory Committee consisted of 23 members – representing 11 businesses (both large and small), three business associations, four environmental policy action groups, four state government environmental agencies, and the EPA. Two facilitators supported the Advisory Committee's work.

Even three years before the Advisory Committee was established, the industry association recognized that new emissions regulations soon would be required by EPA. In anticipation, the association commissioned a fact-finding study and began discussions with EPA that generated the negotiated rulemaking approach. Over an initial period of six months, plenary meetings of the Committee examined several issues including a protocol for the negotiations, reconciliation of industry and EPA databases, enforcement, industry segmentation, and the relative toxicity of the pollutants. Once the facilitators determined that there was significant consensus on most of the issues, small work groups, consisting of the Committee's members, were formed to negotiate the remaining outstanding issues simultaneously, speeding the process.

The draft regulation resulting from the negotiation yielded some novel provisions. A new measurement protocol for the pollutants was developed that was seen as a tool to encourage technological advances in the industry at the same time as it helped to limit emissions. The regulatory results also offered support to small furniture manufacturers that excused them from some of the more burdensome regulatory requirements. It could be said that the negotiation format stimulated new ideas for the proposed regulation that synthesized the interests of all the stakeholders, while still protecting the public interest represented by the regulatory regime.

Cultural Issues

To date, the application of negotiated rulemaking in developing countries is not a common occurrence. But that is not to say that similar consensus-building, negotiation, and mediation procedures do not already have deep cultural roots in all countries of the world. In fact, many traditional conflict resolution approaches in developing countries bear some resemblance to developed country approaches.[8] In Africa, for example, two frames of reference for traditional conflict resolution patterns are the practice of family or neighborhood negotiation facilitated by elders, and the attitude of togetherness in "the spirit of humanhood."[9]

Practitioners need to consider several issues that may lead them to consider adjusting and tailoring negotiated rulemaking as it is practiced in developed countries before applying it elsewhere[10]:

- *Legitimacy:* In most developed countries, legitimacy and acceptability of neutral facilitators is based on their professional expertise, reputation, experience, and objectivity. However, in other countries, neutrality may not provide the facilitator with credibility. Instead, factors such as social standing, resources, leverage, and age may be more important legitimizers.
- *Transparency:* Open and accountable decision-making fora are expected in most developed countries, but in other countries with different traditions and histories, such fora may be rare.
- *Commitment:* Negotiated rulemaking in most developed countries produces a contractual arrangement to ensure that commitments are honored. In other countries, where traditional, informal bonds of trust are at the basis of relationships, such legalistic outcomes might be inappropriate.
- *Role and responsibility of government:* In most developed countries, there are generally accepted public notions of the role for government in generating and enforcing regulations. In other countries, the balance between economic development and regulation may not be so clear; the need for stimulating rapid economic growth may take precedence over regulations that constrain business, even for admirable social objectives.

In the end, practitioners may decide that negotiated rulemaking is not an appropriate regulatory development mechanism for a particular issue or in a particular cultural setting. However, the procedure should be considered as an adjustable framework that promotes participatory engagement in regulatory development and, as such, its processes can be modified to accommodate local needs or traditions.

Costs and Benefits

Why use negotiated rulemaking? What are the implications for policy reform, the implementation of policy changes, and conflict between stakeholders and government? First, the process generates *an environment for dialogue* that facilitates the reality testing of regulations before they are implemented. It enables policy reforms to be discussed in an open forum by stakeholders and for tradeoffs to be made that expedite compliance among those who are directly impacted by the reforms. Second, negotiated rulemaking is *a process of empowerment*. It encourages the participation and enfranchisement of parties that have a stake in reform. It provides voice to interests, concerns, and priorities that otherwise might not be heard or considered in devising new policy. Third, it is a process that promotes *creative but pragmatic solutions*. By encouraging a holistic examination of the policy area, negotiated rulemaking asks the participants to assess the multiple issues and sub-issues involved, set priorities among them, and make compromises. Such rethinking often yields novel and unorthodox solutions. Fourth, negotiated rulemaking offers an *efficient mechanism for policy implementation*. Experience shows that it results in earlier implementation; higher compliance rates; reduced time, money, and effort spent on enforcement; increased cooperation between the regulator and regulated parties; and reduced litigation over the regulations. Regulatory negotiations can yield both better solutions and more efficient compliance.

There are some negative aspects to the use of negotiated rulemaking as well. First, it is *a resource intensive process* over the short term. More time and money must be spent to organize, find facilitators, involve stakeholders, and conduct meetings and negotiations than in the traditional top-down approach. Second, the process might produce greater contentiousness than the top-down approach, again in the short run, because more perspectives are brought to bear on the problem. Stakeholders are encouraged to promote their interests in the negotiations and this can lead to increased conflicts of interest and possible delay. Third, negotiated rulemaking commits the regulatory agency to incorporate the findings of the Advisory Committee in a serious way. If the regulatory body contradicts the Committee's conclusions, it could be seen as acting in bad faith and might generate future adversarial relations.

Conclusions

Negotiated rulemaking encourages participative and inclusive problem solving and decision-making. It provides a detailed structure and set of procedures for promoting inclusive participation in framing policy and formulating how policy can best be implemented by encouraging the stakeholders themselves to create the implementation approach. It provides a way of building public support for policy outcomes by involving those who will be regulated in the process of making the regulations. In its search for consensus among the stakeholders, negotiated rulemaking highlights and, hopefully, preempts conflicts among them which, in and of itself, will help to streamline the implementation of policy reforms. Unlike most negotiation and mediation approaches that are initiated by conflicts over a controversial policy reform or implementation, negotiated rulemaking targets elimination of disputes among stakeholders *before* they become manifest. It is a preventive technique.

Negotiated rulemaking has matured beyond the experimentation phase – it has been used, tested, and proven to be effective in many diverse, complex, and contentious situations. Applied rigorously, negotiated rulemaking can empower stakeholder groups, yield better policy reforms and implementation approaches, improve compliance with reforms, and generate more cooperative relationships between government and civil society. It also represents an important link between democratic governance and economic growth interests. While stimulating direct public involvement in policymaking, it also can enhance the business and investment climate, and reduce government's enforcement costs as well.

More research is needed to assess how best to expand the application of negotiated rulemaking to more countries. As well, the use of reg-neg approaches when designing international conventions that regulate environmental, trade, and other issues needs further examination, with the potential of making participation in the negotiations more inclusive by engaging citizen groups, the business community, and the media.

Notes

1 Pritzker, David M. and Deborah S. Dalton (1995). *Negotiated Rulemaking Sourcebook*. Washington, DC: Administrative Conference of the United States.
2 Ibid.
3 Perton, Victor (1997). "Regulatory Review - The Next Wave?" Wellington, New Zealand: Parliament of Victoria. At: https://www.parliament.vic.gov.au/images/stories/committees/lawrefrom/regulatory_efficiency/next_wave.pdf.
4 Ibid.
5 Moore, Christopher (1993). "'Have Process, Will Travel:' Reflections on Democratic Decision Making and Conflict Management Practice Abroad," *NIDR Forum* (Winter): 1–12.
6 Pritzker and Dalton (1995), op.cit.
7 National Paint and Coatings Association (NPCA) (1995). "Wood Furniture Regulatory Negotiation: A Summary," Washington, DC: NPCA.
8 Zartman, I. William, editor (1999). *Traditional Cures for Modern Conflicts: African Conflict "Medicine"*. Boulder, CO: Lynne Reinner; Faure, Guy Olivier, editor (2003). *How People Negotiate: Resolving Disputes in Different Cultures*. Dordrecht, the Netherlands: Kluwer Academic Publishers.
9 Malan, Jannie (1997). *Conflict Resolution Wisdom from Africa*. Durban, South Africa: African Centre for the Constructive Resolution of Disputes (ACCORD).
10 Susskind, Lawrence E. (1997). "Environmental Mediation: Theory and Practice Reconsidered," in Martin Gillian and Winfried Hamacher, editors, *Lessons Learned in Environmental Mediation: Practical Experiences in North and South*. International Workshop. Geneva/Bonn: International Academy of the Environment and Deutsche Gesellschaft für Technische Zusammenarbeit (GTZ).

11
PARADIPLOMACY AND THE DEMOCRATIZATION OF INTERNATIONAL NEGOTIATION

Traditionally, international negotiation is conducted among sovereign states. However, when it comes to cross-border issues, these sometimes can be considered local or regional, not national, problems, best addressed by the local authorities that reside on opposite sides of national boundaries. While in some sense, all cross-border issues can be said to deal with national sovereignty concerns, local communities that reside in different countries but share a common regional geography and common interests may be in the best position to resolve nearby problems and coordinate action to achieve joint goals.

Cross-border issues dealing with environmental protection, transport, trade, tourism, migration, economic development, emergency operations, and ethnic conflict, for example, regardless of their national implications, present challenges to local governments on both sides of the border. A natural way to address these challenges is through negotiation. Paradiplomacy is regional sub-state diplomacy – international negotiation conducted among local authorities in the region – rather than traditional negotiation among national governments.[1] Localization of cross-border negotiations devolves the responsibility for resolving problems to the grassroots level.

Local actors are not only assigned the role of the implementer of provisions that were negotiated and agreed to by central-level negotiators but they can also become empowered negotiators of their own future in a multilateral forum.[2] This devolution of negotiation authority, in a sense, democratizes international negotiation. It enables localities that share a common river basin, valley or mountain range to negotiate their own futures, rather than rely on national representatives at the center to do it for them. The local actors that understand the problem context, share certain common bonds, and must live with the consequences are empowered through localized international negotiations to interact with their local counterparts and address their own issues directly, rather than through surrogates.

DOI: 10.4324/9781003314400-11

This essay explores a critical aspect of paradiplomacy that has not received much research attention: how such negotiations by subnational governments are conducted and how they compare with more traditional international negotiation processes.[3] Most of the existing literature investigates case studies of paradiplomacy.[4] This essay describes this phenomenon, but then analyzes how its features can be distinguished from traditional state-to-state negotiation, derives propositions that can help explain these international negotiation processes, and identifies areas for further research.

Localization of International Negotiation

Typically, subnational governments do not interfere in international affairs. However, several trends have elevated and promoted the localization of international negotiation. Globalization trends have increased the sense of interdependence not only among countries but also among subnational regions.[5] National borders are no longer barriers to communication and cooperation as they once were. Rather, neighboring localities that share a common heritage, problems, and opportunities have found that they can work together in a coordinated fashion, perhaps better than they can with their respective central governments. At the same time, over the past decade, international donor organizations have encouraged local self-government movements in developing and transitional countries with the goal of devolving state power, strengthening democratic tendencies, and enhancing the delivery of quality public services. In doing so, they empowered local governments to deal with their own issues directly and to seek help and support from nearby localities in the same region, distinctly deemphasizing a dependence on the central government.

Research describes a growing number of cases of paradiplomacy in many policy areas – especially, in finance, defense, and the environment – since the 1960s. These include border commissions involving state governments in the United States with their counterparts in Mexico and Canada; US states and Canadian provinces dealing with climate initiatives and trade agreements; and regional governments in Mexico, India, and Spain that focus especially on attracting foreign direct investment, promoting exports and tourism, fostering border security, and developing international cooperation on education, culture, science, and technology.[6] In 2017, for example, when the US federal government announced its upcoming withdrawal from the Paris Climate Accords, 12 state governors created the US Climate Alliance (ultimately endorsed by 30 governors) that refused to abandon the Paris principles.[7]

Localized cross-border diplomacy has emerged as a new and viable international structure that provides an alternative to (or an addition to) traditional international negotiation structures.[8] This localization of international negotiation gives new meaning to the adage, "think globally, but act locally."[9] Transboundary negotiation that is more grassroots, more participatory, and more democratic can give rise to fairer and more implementable solutions that local stakeholders are more likely to comply with because they were a part of creating them. It also creates a new and increasingly relevant structure of international negotiation that has yet to receive extensive research attention.[10] Some of the major questions that need to be addressed about localized negotiation concern how national sovereignty versus local empowerment challenges are resolved, how local interests get reconciled with national interests, how local negotiation processes may differ from traditional international processes, how multilayered diplomacy is coordinated administratively across levels, and if locally negotiated agreements achieve greater compliance.

There are three types of paradiplomacy negotiations.[11] First, transborder regional paradiplomacy can occur in formal or informal structures across localities that share proximity and common problems. Euroregion Associations are an example of this first type. Second, transregional paradiplomacy occurs across localities that are not in contiguous regions, but whose nations are neighbors. For example, provincial trade missions from Canada can negotiate agreements with cities or states in the United States. Third, global paradiplomacy occurs among noncentral governments (NCGs) from distant nations. The Congress of Local and Regional Authorities of Europe, a consultative organization of the Council of Europe, brings local and regional government representatives together in a broad assembly to deal with issues of self-governance that are common to all European cities, towns, and regions.

By decentralizing international negotiation, the practice of diplomacy is becoming democratized. Localities are empowered to deal with issues that affect them directly without having to lobby national bodies that must balance national interests with local concerns. Communities that have a problem with their neighbors across the border can deal with such issues directly, thus averting conflicts locally that otherwise could escalate into major international flashpoints.

The democratization of international negotiation has also increased public participation because it deals with grassroots issues that are understandable and close to constituents' aspirations. Subnational issues attract the interest and participation of local governments and local nongovernmental organizations because they impact directly on daily life, economically or socially. These are concrete and practical issues that affect people where they live, work, and play. Localized international negotiations do not deal with large, distant, or abstract concepts like "national security," "trade balance," or "disarmament" where solutions might appear impersonal or theoretical. Rather, they deal with highly personalized issues that impact on the lives of people through their pocketbooks, their workplace, or their community. Thus, local constituencies are easily attracted to participate.

Example: Euroregion Negotiations

An example of decentralized international negotiations occurs in the context of the Euroregions. Localities participating in Euroregion Associations have been empowered by their national governments to deal with transboundary regional issues – devolving international negotiation to subnational actors to address shared economic and environmental problems. Originally promoted by the Council of Europe,[12] the first Euroregions date back to 1958, though a large number were established in the aftermath of the Cold War, incorporating Eastern and Central European regions. As of 1992, there were 36 Euroregions; after the end of the Cold War, that number exploded to close to 100. Each Euroregion Association has members (cities) from two or more countries that have devolved authority to negotiate transborder agreements and coordinate transborder activities at the local/regional level. The European Union's PHARE program has supported many Euroregions which are part of the EU's regional strategy. Examples of Euroregion negotiations have included:

- Developing agreements on cross-border transport links (border crossing points, linked infrastructure, regional planning, etc.) — Nisa Euroregion
- Developing trade and tourism initiatives — Euroregio
- Developing cooperation in fighting fires and natural disasters — Euroregion Pomerania
- Developing cross-border tariff associations to deal with transboundary transport — Regio Basiliensis
- Developing cross-border regulations on damage to the environment, decontamination, and safety in the aftermath of the Sandoz catastrophe — Regio Basiliensis
- Developing cross-border economic development and environmental protection regimes — Carpathian Euroregion
- Developing partnerships among regional universities — Carpathian Euroregion
- Establishing joint research institutions to promote scientific and cultural cooperation — Euroregion "Pro Europa Viadrina"

Other examples of localized international negotiation have involved the reduction of environmental conflicts[13] and cultural/linguistic promotion.[14]

Once these Euroregions are established through negotiation, they operate as a *regional regime* structure – based on agreed norms and procedures – to deal with prescribed issues. Their mode of operation to make joint decisions and act upon them is through post-agreement negotiations.[15] Their negotiation process tends to be characterized by consensus.

Building Blocks of Localized International Negotiation

International negotiations are typically described in terms of several features – actors, issues, situation, structure, process/strategy, and outcome.[16] The distinguishing elements of localized international negotiations are described below.

Actors

Perhaps the most distinctive feature of localized international negotiations are the participants. Much has been written about the growing active role of nongovernmental organizations in international negotiations, but little has been written about the role of NCG as actors in negotiation. Countries with federal systems or decentralized government structures have been increasing within the European Union – 19 of 27 states in the European Union are formulated in this way. Forty percent of the world's population live in a country with a federal type of governmental system.[17]

Local governments can be accorded *legitimacy* as agents in international negotiation by a decision from their central governments to be official representatives. In the best of circumstances, in addition to this bestowed legitimacy, NCGs also assume a certain degree of *autonomy* to make decisions that affect their region, while not harming the national interest or other regions.

Typically, NCGs have minimal *experience* as negotiators, though they will understand the issues and the context very well. Their *knowledge* will help them in the preparatory stages before negotiations begin, but their inexperience as negotiators may hinder their abilities to reach mutually acceptable outcomes efficiently. By their very nature, localized international negotiations may involve participants who know each other on a personal level or have worked together in other cooperative projects in the past. This *prior personal interaction* may be helpful in mobilizing consensus.

Issues

The issues that localized international negotiations are concerned with are another distinctive feature. They are not abstract; they are *local, understood, and concrete*. The NCG participants all have a common interest in finding a resolution to the problem or issue because it can directly affect their economy or way of life in their shared region. Paradiplomacy addresses common issues including, for example, economic and trade promotion, attracting foreign investment, education, science and technology, energy, environment, labor mobility, international development, human rights, and border security.[18]

Proximity of the actors has an impact on the types of issues to be negotiated. While proximity often yields issues or problems that demand *cooperation* or coordination of effort, it can also sow the seeds for *contention* and conflict where shared resources are scarce.[19] At a regional level, many mutual assistance requirements are related to the economy or the environment; they can produce negotiations to deal with natural emergencies, water and sewage management, air and water pollution, and energy transfers – where superordinate goals dictate that all parties must cooperate to achieve their joint objectives or else none of them will obtain the benefits. Other cooperative issues can relate to attracting trade, investment, and tourism to the region and joint economic development programs that will benefit all parties. Security-related problem areas on which cooperation is required can deal with border checkpoints, customs, drug trafficking, smuggling, population migration, civil defense, and transport issues. In regions where there are scarce resources, any of these issues can turn competitive and contentious; the role of negotiation, in these cases, is to find solutions that can ameliorate the conflict and yield positive sum results.

Situation

The situation in localized international negotiations is distinctly grassroots. That means that local constituencies are likely to get involved directly, seeking to influence the process and outcome. Interested NGOs and private sector actors, as well as the local media, are likely to want to influence the negotiation process because it deals with issues that they, and the entire regional community, are concerned with. National governments may also seek to intervene to impact localized negotiations.

Because the negotiations take place in and are concerned with a particular region, ethnic and/or cultural issues may become important situational elements. Homogeneous ethnicities or cultures can promote cooperation, while diverse ethnicities and cultures can produce conflict in the negotiation.

External events can also affect the negotiations. Economic slumps, natural disasters, related international agreements, and regional political change, for example, can change the context within which negotiators make decisions for tradeoffs and settle for certain outcomes.

Structure

Because of the continuous nature of most local and regional issues, the formation of a stable platform for negotiation, typically a *regional regime,* is common. Within the Euroregions, for example, working committees are established on transport, trade, border crossing, economic development, and other issues to set agendas, seek opportunities for cooperation, find ways of dealing with problems as they arise, develop declarations, and work on joint projects. Regional regimes provide a regular forum for representatives from the constituent localities to meet, discuss, and negotiate. They also provide a set of rules, procedures, and norms within which negotiated agreements can be implemented, adjusted, and any conflicts resolved.

The establishment of the regime itself is a product of negotiation. Then, the operation of the regime is conducted through post-agreement negotiation processes.[20] Continuity within the regime structure promotes the development of relationships among negotiators, coordination, and joint activities across localities, and a deepening sense of commitment to the region.

Process/Strategy

The negotiation process can be distinctive in localized international negotiation. *Consensus* is most likely to be the procedure by which outcomes are achieved.

Situations that demand cooperation and coordination among the stakeholders – typical in the localized negotiation context – will tend to operate through nonconfrontational processes that seek mutual benefit for all parties. Concession-making or formula-detail bargaining processes are not likely to be appropriate, especially if the actors are relatively equal in their power and resources. Regional governments typically do not have military power at their disposal to use as a negotiating tactic, but they have others. They can often access international negotiation and diplomatic networks to push their agendas, if agreed to by their central governments.[21]

These negotiations tend to be *concerned more with technical than political issues*. This derives from the fact that the politics of national sovereignty are *not* a central feature of these negotiations. To the contrary, a common regionalism motive rather than national differences catalyzes the negotiation, with the goal of fixing something that has gone or will go wrong in the region, or upgrading the opportunities to work together to better the region.

Outcome

Localized international negotiations demand positive sum results where all can benefit. The underlying reason to establish local regimes to start with is to accrue benefit to the local actors through joint action.

Implications for Negotiation

The different context of localized international negotiation can yield some new and interesting insights for the practice of traditional state-to-state international negotiation.

Process and Structure

The increasing trend toward devolution of power and authority in many developing countries from central governments to their regions and municipalities has resulted in local governments becoming more adept at solving local problems. This trend has extended beyond the boundaries of sovereign states where now, localities on different sides of the border find ways of working together directly to build, strengthen, or fix their common cross-border region, rather than wait for their centers to deal with these issues from afar. To accomplish this, they have established platforms and structures (regional regimes), and processes (negotiation) with localities as the stakeholders, to deal with shared issues on a continuous, rather than episodic basis.

These regimes tend to be small and focused on clear sets of concrete, non-abstract issues. They are built around not only a shared geographic space that they inhabit, not only shared goals and objectives for their neighborhood, but also a common vision that the only way to reach these goals is to work together cooperatively. Working independently or worse, at cross-purposes, would defeat their vision. Superordinate goals – those that can be achieved only if all parties pull their weight together – are the glue that holds these regional regimes as one.[22]

What lessons can be gleaned for traditional international negotiations? These are stated as propositions.

- *Proposition 1.* Regime structures based on geographic proximity rather than common issue interest provides a tighter bond among participants and a stronger cooperative motive.
- *Proposition 2.* Negotiation objectives that are formulated to require the participation of all on an equal basis, for all to benefit, should reduce defections or vetoes by any of the actors, and it should build a sense of oneness among the stakeholders. They are not in it alone and they can learn to rely on each other to achieve mutually acceptable goals.

Constituency Development

There are many examples of successful international negotiation that produce unsuccessful outcomes. The process may yield what appears to be a useful agreement, but that agreement is very difficult to implement effectively by the signatories. The problem is often that the negotiation process becomes effectively divorced from the constituencies that must implement the outcomes. It is often the case that centralized political elite negotiate a solution in isolation from and with limited or no consultation from the citizens, businesses, and parliamentarians who will be entrusted with implementing the negotiated provisions.

One of the arguments made to explain the collapse of the Israeli-Palestinian Oslo agreements was the lack of constituency development that occurred on either side. First, the negotiations themselves were conducted in secrecy by a political elite. Second, after the terms of the solution were publicized and implementation was taking place, the leadership did not make the major efforts that were necessary to educate their most vehemently opposing publics of their vision and the vision of the negotiated agreement. For the elite, the conflict, and the way out of the conflict, may have been reframed, but for their constituencies who were entrusted with carrying out the agreement, this reframing had not occurred. Thus, they were not willing parties to the solution and its implementation disintegrated back into violence.

What can be learned from localized international negotiations is the very critical issue of constituency development. At the local/regional level, constituencies are the very engines that move the negotiation process. The local authorities are members of regional regimes and negotiate with their neighboring towns and cities, but grassroots movements in civil society and the private sector are also clearly involved in the negotiations and the formulation of solutions. The issues under negotiation, after all, will affect them directly – economically, environmentally, in the delivery of basic services, in civil defense, etc. So, the development of constituencies is an organic element of localized international negotiation and, as a result, implementation is likely to be more forthcoming and effective.

Early in their development, people did not think of themselves as part of a Euroregion.[23] They viewed themselves as citizens of a city or a country, but not in a supranational way; early on, the Euroregion concept was novel and untested. Over time, however, an attitude and sense of allegiance has developed regarding these regions to the point where real Euroregion constituencies exist, have common interests, and seek results.

- *Proposition 3.* To ensure reliable implementation of negotiated agreements, there needs to be a constituency that has bought into the vision of the resulting solution. Sometimes, this constituency needs to be created or found. If there is no stable constituency, the results of even a successful negotiation process may be ultimate failure in implementation.
- *Proposition 4.* Constituency development cannot be left out of the picture; it should be an integral element of the negotiation process. Consultations with NGO and private sector representatives should be a mandatory feature of the negotiation process – helping to formulate each parties' base of interests and solution options. Tight linkages between negotiators and their constituents could be institutionalized in terms of citizen advisory boards to the negotiation process, for example. Engaged constituencies are the engine by which negotiated agreements are implemented.

Conflict Prevention

Paradiplomacy can offer the possibility, not only for conflict resolution – especially on border-related disputes – but also for conflict prevention as well. By dealing with and localizing what are now minor irritants, future escalations of conflict at the national level can be moderated. In the best of circumstances, if escalatory seeds can be transformed into joint cooperation programs, not only will larger conflicts be averted but also cooperation will be promoted.

NCG negotiations over sticking points between localities within a region can often avoid cross-cultural communication problems and ethnicity clashes that nation-to-nation negotiation over the same issues would ram right in to. There are certain commonalities and sensitivities to the other parties that are second nature to localized international negotiation situations.

Moreover, the intimate involvement of grassroots constituents in the negotiation process ensures that they have a strong sense of ownership over the process that can follow through into the post-agreement phases.

Can localized international negotiation become a close adjunct to official Track 1 diplomacy? Would official negotiations in conflict situations be well assisted by parallel negotiations that can occur at a local/regional level? Perhaps, paradiplomatic negotiations can be allocated certain issues that are locally/regionally targeted, leaving larger and more abstract issues to the national-level negotiations.

- *Proposition 5.* By establishing a regularized structure and process for localized international negotiation, local flashpoints that could escalate into serious international conflict can be moderated early, diverted from national attention, and transformed into cooperation.
- *Proposition 6.* Large multi-issue international negotiations can best be served by segmenting issues so that appropriate ones are devolved to localized negotiations for resolution.

There are many open questions about localized international negotiation that still need to be addressed by the research community. They deal primarily with how paradiplomacy processes fit into or expand our understanding of international negotiation theory and processes.

- What are the skills and experiences of these new local actors entering the international negotiation sphere? Are they up to the challenge?
- How can local interests be reconciled with the national interest?
- Does the concrete and practical nature of local international negotiation yield a different type of process, different outcomes, different perceptions of fairness and justice, and different rates of compliance? Is there a commonly practiced negotiation mode at the local level – consensual, problem-solving, formula-detail, or concession-making?
- Is the common geography possessed by negotiators likely to yield shared interests over common problems and more successful negotiations *or* heightened competition over scarce resources and contentious negotiations?
- Are these negotiations likely to be more sustainable because they are conducted by the very people who are needed to comply with them? Do such local and participatory negotiations solve Putnam's problem of two-level negotiations because both international and domestic levels are merged into one?[24]
- Are negotiated agreements more stable and implementable because constituencies are naturally part of the negotiation process?
- Is localized international negotiation an effective preventive conflict technique to avert threatened conflict escalation from reaching the national level?
- What can traditional international negotiations learn from the practice of subnational negotiations, especially in terms of constituency development, interest development, and conflict prevention?
- What are the larger implications of devolved sovereignty and the local democratization of international negotiation for the current structure of international relations based on nation states?

These are questions for future research. This essay provides a very preliminary step toward explicating a framework that might support such research.

Conclusions

This line of inquiry leads in two related directions. First, what are the implications and future of this relatively new formula that democratizes international negotiation? Will new platforms and structures be developed to promote more localized negotiation venues? Are the processes by which outcomes are reached significantly different than in traditional nation-to-nation negotiations due to the different level and venue? Are outcomes fairer, more sustainable, more implementable and complied with by key stakeholders? Does localization and democratization yield greater cooperation or conflict in the negotiation process? Does localization of negotiation provide a platform for early and preventive conflict management?

The second direction seeks to find lessons from paradiplomatic negotiation that can apply to traditional nation-to-nation negotiation. Are actors involved differently and do they relate to each other differently? Does the localized process operate differently and better? Is the existing structure of international negotiation likely to be better served by a change in level or structure? How can the practice and experience of localized negotiation inform improved practices to develop tighter implementing constituencies and produce more stable and sustainable outcomes?

Notes

1 Paquin, Stéphane (2020). "Paradiplomacy," in Thierry Balzacq, Frédéric Charillon, and Frédéric Ramel, editors, *Global Diplomacy: An Introduction to Theory and Practice*. London: Palgrave Macmillan.
2 Lequesne, Christian and Stéphane Paquin (2017b). "Federalism, Paradiplomacy and Foreign Policy: A Case of Mutual Neglect." *International Negotiation* 22, 2: 183–204.
3 Lecours, Andre (2002). "Paradiplomacy: Reflections on the Foreign Policy and International Relations of Regions," *International Negotiation* 7, 1: 91–114; Alvarez, Mariano (2020). "The Rise of Paradiplomacy in International Relations," At: https://www.e-ir.info/2020/03/17/the-rise-of-paradiplomacy-in-international-relations/.
4 Lequesne, Christian and Stéphane Paquin (2017a). *Federalism and International Negotiation*, special issue. *International Negotiation* 22, 2.
5 Michelmann, Hans J. and Panayotis Soldatos, editors (1990). *Federalism and International Relations: The Role of Subnational Units*. Oxford: Clarendon Press.
6 Lequesne and Pacquin (2017a), op.cit.
7 Alvarez (2020), op.cit.
8 Aldecoa, Francisco and Michael Keating, editors (1999). *Paradiplomacy in Action: The Foreign Relations of Subnational Governments*. London: Frank Cass.
9 Hocking, Brian (1993). *Localizing Foreign Policy: Non-Central Governments and Multilayered Diplomacy*. New York: St. Martin's Press.
10 Lecour (2002), op.cit.; Duchacek, Ivo, Daniel Latouche and Garth Stevenson, editors (1988). *Perforated Sovereignties and International Relations: Trans-Sovereign Contacts of Subnational Governments*. New York: Greenwood Press.
11 Michelmann and Soldatos (1990), op.cit.
12 The Council of Europe sponsored the establishment of a consultative body, the Congress of Local and Regional Authorities of Europe (CLRAE) in 1994, to support local grassroots self-governance and regional democratic development. Members of the Congress represent many of the localities and regions throughout Europe. They meet

to develop overall programs, codes, and charters and conventions related to local and regional democratic development. The Congress represents an intergovernmental body focused at national level membership, not the local level.

13 Petzold-Bradley, Eileen, Alexander Carius, and Arpad Vincze (2001). *Responding to Environmental Conflicts: Implications for Theory and Practice.* Dordrecht: Kluwer Academic Publishers.
14 Lecour (2020), op.cit.
15 Spector, Bertram and I. William Zartman, editors (2003). *Getting It Done: International Regimes and Post-Agreement Negotiation.* Washington, DC: United States Institute of Peace Press.
16 Kremenyuk, Victor, editor (1991). *International Negotiation.* San Francisco: Jossey-Bass.
17 Lequesne and Pacquin (2017b), op.cit.
18 Ibid.
19 Spector, Bertram (2001). "Transboundary Disputes: Keeping Backyards Clean," in I. William Zartman, editor, *Preventive Negotiation: Avoiding Conflict Escalation.* Lanham, MD: Rowman and Littlefield.
20 Spector and Zartman (2003), op.cit.
21 Pacquin (2020), op.cit; Lecours (2002), op.cit.
22 Sherif, Muzafer (1967). *Social Interaction: Process and Products.* Chicago: Aldine Publishing.
23 Grodzinski, Michael (2000). "Carpathian Euroregion: 'Locomotive' or 'Platform' of Transboundary Cooperation," unpublished paper. University of Kyiv, Ukraine.
24 Evans, Peter, Harold Jacobson, and Robert Putnam, editors (2000). *Double-Edged Diplomacy: International Bargaining and Domestic Politics.* Berkeley: University of California Press.

12

VALUES IN NEGOTIATION

The Case of International Development Assistance

Are negotiations concerning international development assistance and humanitarian support conducted empathetically? After all, if the objectives are to help countries that are in need economically, politically, or socially, or in the midst of a violent crisis or environmental disaster, one would think that the principal motivators driving negotiation strategies, tactics, and behaviors would be altruism, caring, and compassion. While empathy must play some role in most of these negotiations, self-interested goals are almost always present as well – on both sides – and this impacts the negotiation process.

For the past 25 years, I have been engaged in designing and implementing international development assistance projects, specifically those supporting improvements in governance and accountability mechanisms in developing countries. While the objectives of these projects – all offered by countries and organizations in the Global North and conducted in agreement with the recipient country – have been to enhance how the host carries out its governmental functions and to reduce corruption in their ranks – there are typically benefits to the donor country as well: the likelihood of increased trade, other economic advantages, and sometimes, favorable political and military implications. This essay examines the nature and dynamics of negotiations concerning international development assistance, and the special case of humanitarian negotiations – from the perspective of the core values that should motivate and shape these negotiation dynamics.

The Role of Values

Negotiations are conducted to resolve problems or conflicts where it is hoped that all parties can agree on a solution. While negotiators seek to maximize their own interests in the agreement, they always operate within the framework of some basic values.[1] Among these values, *reciprocity* is very basic to the negotiation

DOI: 10.4324/9781003314400-12

process: exchanging things with others for mutual benefit. *Equality* in the negotiation process and in the outcome, as well, is another core value; all parties should be treated impartially, justly, and fairly. *Ethics* is yet another key value that frames how negotiations proceed; each party decides on moral principles that will guide their actions and decisions at the negotiating table.

Based on these and other basic values, particular negotiation strategies are developed to persuade the other parties to arrive at the ultimate agreement. At one end of the spectrum, totally *self-interested* values focus on one's own needs and desires; the goal is to maximize the outcome for oneself. A *win-lose* solution is usually the consequence of this approach to negotiation. Power tactics can sometimes be used to push the other party to concede and accept an outcome that it might not otherwise agree to.

At the other end of the spectrum, a negotiator could operate out of a sense of *altruism*. The issues under negotiation may address sensitive problems that only one of the parties is coping with. They may be particularly painful or cause difficulties for its population, but with the help of other parties, it may be possible to alleviate the distress. Compassion – the capacity to perceive the other's problems and situation – is a first step toward acting in a way that can relieve the others' pain.[2] Through negotiation, it may be possible to coordinate efforts, and design and implement a caring and altruistic agreement that can also strengthen political, economic, or social institutions and processes that can boost development or reduce suffering due to a humanitarian or environmental crisis. Such concern for the welfare of the other can be spurred by a sense of selflessness, charity, or humanity.

Mediation workshops that promote problem-solving through empathy for the other have been conducted with Israeli and Palestinian participants.[3] By evoking personal narratives from both sides, greater healing, trust, and empathy across the groups was evident. Might there be some label that depicts altruistic values, perhaps, a *caring-win* outcome, where the providers of the assistance hone in to maximize their empathetic goals (caring) and the recipient of the assistance gets what it needs to survive (win)? The altruistic party may offer help, money, and resources to the needy country without receiving anything in return that make it a winner or loser; it is just a caring party.

Midway on this continuum, negotiators seek out just and fair outcomes for all parties. Based on values of *justice and fairness*, negotiators are willing to compromise and find an acceptable outcome for everyone. Interests in justice and fairness can motivate negotiators to develop strategies that will lead all engaged parties to find acceptable compromise solutions to their problem. This is a *win-win* solution.

In the context of negotiating international development assistance, parties can be motivated by all of these values. Altruism would seem to be at the top of the list; providing support to another country that truly needs help is something that a developed country should be willing to promote, with the overall goal of reducing fragility and maintaining stability. At the same time, developed countries are likely to be motivated to help another country in need if they can get something in return – some political treaty or some economic reward. And the interest in just and fair outcomes is also entwined in this type of negotiation; all countries – the strong and the weak – are susceptible to environmental or humanitarian crises and may need help from the outside at some time in the future. Finding a solution that supports all parties to come to an agreement that is perceived as fair and impartial for all may require some compromises, but can promote a stable outcome.

Dynamics of International Development Assistance Negotiations

Negotiations about international development assistance are, at their core, asymmetrical.[4] The recipients of this assistance are typically in a subservient position; they may desperately need support due to crises that they do not have the resources to manage on their own, or they require help to boost or reorganize their economies, for example. The donor may offer very little latitude concerning the amount, form or delivery of the support. Especially, when negotiation occurs in a nonemergency situation, development assistance can be offered and implemented in a way that treats the beneficiary essentially as a passive actor. The donor always has some reason and motive driving their interests in offering aid: sometimes it is altruistic, but often, it is tied to promoting a particular foreign policy, or social or economic agenda.

Zartman and Rubin studied the negotiation dynamics between weak and strong parties.[5] Such situations create the potential for exploitation and submissiveness, where the more powerful can seek to dominate. But their case studies led them to conclusions that demonstrate that the weaker parties usually adopt counterstrategies that voice their demands, protest the stronger parties' terms, or seek to gain acceptance of detailed outcomes that are beneficial to them. Typically, the weak do not just give in. In the case of international development negotiations, the ultimate agreement usually highlights the beneficial provision of donor support and assistance to the developing country, while the donor gets something it wants in return; so, it can be a win-win outcome.

According to data collected by the Organization for Economic Cooperation and Development (OECD), the United States led all countries in its total net official development assistance (ODA) in 2020 with $US35.5 billion, followed by Germany (US$28.4 billion), the United Kingdom (US$18.6 billion), Japan (US$16.3 billion), and France (US$14.1 billion), at the top of the list.[6] These amounts were boosted in 2020 in large part because of COVID-19 relief assistance. The ratio between ODA and donors' combined gross national income increased to 0.32%, only one-half of the amount recommended for donor countries in multiple international agreements. There are more than 1,000 donor agencies disbursing funding, including over 50 bilateral and over 200 multilateral institutions.[7] This profusion of actors introduces many challenges for recipients; they must dedicate resources to negotiations with a wide variety of potential funders which may duplicate each other's efforts or be leveraged against one another to the recipient's advantage.

Donor countries usually want something from their assistance. On one hand, there is sincere interest in helping developing countries, because if they thrive in stability and peace, it will accrue to everyone's benefit. The altruistic goals of aid include alleviating poverty, overcoming problems to growth and stability economically, politically, and socially, and sustaining those achievements. Certainly, there can also be self-interested reasons for providing assistance: gaining access to a country's resources, attracting the recipient into the donor's sphere of influence, and influencing and supporting the political opposition if the donor seeks regime change, among many others. The developed countries seek to achieve these goals through carrots (the development aid of various sorts) and sticks (conditions imposed on the aid or threats of withdrawal of the assistance).

For example, policy-wise, China's stated strategies for providing international development support have evolved over the years.[8] Starting in the 1950s, China's support was motivated by helping developing countries seek their own political and economic independence, in a way, seeking fairness for others while building China's national prestige. Then, in the late 1970s, China began to focus on what it called "mutual benefit": how international development could help both the developing nations as well as boost the economic interests of China – more of a self-interested approach. In the latest stage, starting in 2013, China has formulated its interests in providing development aid as altruistic, doing so because of "righteousness rather than mere benefit." But, sometimes, stated goals paper over true interests. China's development assistance goals have always been closely intertwined with its own economic policy, suggesting that its interests are primarily focused on strengthening its own access to raw materials and exporting its own labor and goods through this assistance.

Of course, developing countries also have interests regarding the aid: improving their health or educational framework, enhancing their economic situation, strengthening governance, and generating clean energy infrastructure, for example. Recipients also want to be able to sustain these improvements and that often requires strengthening institutional and human capacities. Overall, their goals usually entail enhancing the economic, social, and political well-being of their citizens. They can go about doing this – asserting their interests with donor nations – by presenting their own plans and proposals on how to implement the aid and by seeking direct control over the funds and resources.

Negotiation is typically the path taken to promote developed and developing country interests related to development assistance. Recognizing the potential asymmetrical relationship that can characterize these negotiations, Sunshine wrote a negotiation handbook for developing country practitioners to strengthen their capacity to assert their interests and mitigate the assumed consent of the recipient.[9] On one side of such negotiations are the donors, which can be countries, international and multilateral organizations, private voluntary organizations, and foundations. In many situations, there are multiple donors seeking to assist recipient countries, especially in times of crisis. But negotiations typically proceed for each one separately over time; post-agreement negotiations among the donors and the recipient often need to occur later on to properly coordinate and achieve synergy across different development aid programs. Recipient countries are usually represented by central governments, but regional or local governments, civil society, and business organizations can be invited in as well. Aid negotiations can be initiated by either side: in some cases, developing countries request assistance, but in other situations, developed countries offer programs to promote their larger economic, trade, or foreign policies.

In international development negotiations, the issues that are most contentious are usually not the extension of the aid itself, but the terms and conditions by which that aid is delivered. There can be heated discussion about which sectors should benefit from the aid – health, education, infrastructure, environment, or business, for example; priorities between the donor and the recipient might be at odds. But major disagreements typically surround important ancillary issues, including the following:

- *Direct budget funding.* Will the development aid involve a transfer of funds to the recipient country's budget that they will control directly or will it involve the provision of supplies, resources, or technical assistance delivered by the donor with limited funds transfer? In the first case, the recipient wields much more power over how the funds ultimately are used, while in the latter case, the donor maintains that control.
- *Conditionalities.* Many aid agreements place certain restrictions on the beneficiary country to ensure that the assistance is used appropriately for the intended purposes and is exercised within strict financial standards. Conditions can also be implemented to achieve other donor objectives, such as reducing corruption or conflict cessation. For example, many World Bank loans and grants come with special terms that require the recipient to adopt good governance principles, establish anti-corruption commissions, and practice accountability and due diligence with regard to the donor funds.
- *Working with government versus nongovernmental entities.* If developing country governments are seen as hostile, uncooperative or disinterested, donors can sometimes bypass central governments entirely by providing assistance directly to nongovernmental groups or local governments. This obviously reduces the degree of central government control and could be a significant point of contention in development talks.
- *Sensitive interventions.* Many development aid programs are targeted at sensitive, often political, issues, such as enhancing the rule of law and democracy strengthening efforts, reducing public sector corruption, addressing the rights and needs of ethnic or minority populations, and focusing on women's rights. These could be viewed as impinging on the recipient's sovereignty and, thereby, be a point of contention in negotiations.

Strategies used by the parties in the negotiation process tend to reflect and adjust for these asymmetrical conditions. The donor countries are in a position to impose their interests through forceful strategies and tactics. The recipient developing countries, on the other hand, seek to equalize the power balance by exercising creative negotiation approaches. For example,

- *Protest conditionalities.* Developing countries can protest against terms and conditions in aid agreements that they view as dysfunctional. In October 2009, in Pakistan, street protests were unleashed in reaction to conditionalities placed on a four-year US$7.5 billion nonmilitary development assistance package from the United States. The terms required Pakistan to monitor and report back to the United States on its use of the funds, to strengthen anti-corruption programs, to provide the United States with access to Pakistani agents of nuclear proliferation, and to plan military assistance annually instead of on a multi-year basis. While the government finally acceded to the US demands, the protesters complained that the condescending terms, and the proposed micro-management were humiliating and undermining of Pakistani sovereignty.
- *Play off one donor against another.* Most developing countries receive assistance from many donors. As a result, one can be played off against another to "up the ante" – to get more assistance and on better terms. This is a feasible strategy especially in those circumstances where the donors do not coordinate their aid programs adequately.
- *Pay only lip service to conditionalities.* Many recipients accept the terms and conditions placed on them in silence. They implement what is required, but do not enforce the provisions vigorously. For example, many developing countries have established anti-corruption agencies as a result of requirements in their World Bank loans and grants. However, these agencies are often not provided adequate budgets, resources, or mandates to conduct the job intended.
- *Accept onerous conditions now but plan for negotiated changes in the post-agreement period.* Conditions can be accepted in order to get the development aid now, but once the agreements are signed, the developing country can initiate post-agreement talks focused on the details of how funds get allocated, for what programs, and under revised terms and conditions.
- *Form coalitions.* Because negotiating aid is often a transaction between one donor and one recipient, it does not lend itself to an obvious strategy for the weak. However, in multilateral negotiations – related to trade or environmental regimes – where development assistance is but one element of a larger outcome, coalitions of weaker parties can materialize and press their interests effectively against ostensibly stronger parties.

Humanitarian Negotiations

One would think that negotiations over such a sensitive, conflict-driven, and risky issue as humanitarian assistance, a particular type of development aid, would proceed in a more selfless, altruistic, and collaborative manner. But that is often not the case. These talks are usually conducted among vastly asymmetric actors – humanitarian organizations which are nonstate groups seeking to access and protect civilians affected by armed conflict, armed nonstate groups who are using violence to gain control but have no legal standing, or the existing state government which is under siege. The armed groups are the ones endangering civilians that the humanitarian groups are trying to help.[10] The humanitarian groups approach the situation with few resources to trade, no weapons, and no territory. They are motivated to do their job, but without an agreement, they are not likely to be able to do it. Talks with the armed groups are typically ad hoc and decentralized, resulting in only short-term and verbal agreements at best.

Despite their position of weakness, humanitarian actors have found tactics they can leverage to reduce this power asymmetry with armed groups.[11] They have been able to persuade armed groups to yield and allow them to do their work using moral, religious, and legal arguments. In addition, they have sometimes been able to demonstrate to the armed groups that through reciprocity, they can gain some legitimacy in the eyes of others. Coalition building and mobilizing third party support can also be used to increase the influence and resources available to humanitarian groups. Representing fairness and acting in an impartial fashion, humanitarian actors can often influence armed groups to treat them with some respect and allow them to proceed with their work. Despite these strategies, humanitarian groups obviously face many risks and challenges in negotiating with armed groups in a violent context.

Even when humanitarian actors need to negotiate with the existing state government to gain access and protect civilians, they often face similar obstacles and the outcomes are not always positive. When more powerful parties are confronted with these empathetic situations, but still feel threatened themselves, self-interested values are elevated and altruistic values get trumped.

Rapid provision and distribution of COVID-19 vaccines to developing countries is a good case in point. Soon after vaccines were tested and approved for use, several developed countries, including the United States, announced major programs to supply lower-income countries with vaccine doses. In addition, in late 2020, India and South Africa put forward a proposal to waive some provisions of the World Trade Organization Agreement on Trade-Related Aspects of Intellectual Property Rights (TRIPS), which would suspend intellectual property protections for pharmaceutical companies, allowing vaccines to be produced around the world.[12] The waiver was seen as a solution to vaccine inequity in that it would add to the number of vaccine manufacturers. The proposed waiver was praised by many lower income countries and others as an altruistic initiative, prioritizing people's lives over corporate profits. Higher income countries, obviously influenced by the drug industry, were mainly skeptical, citing possible adverse effects on future innovation and drug quality. In response, India, South Africa, and others in the Global South proposed a modified waiver to seek more support; it limited the waiver to only a three-year period and only for COVID-related vaccines and technologies. Support broadened from some higher-income countries, but the United States, for example, voiced its support for yet a narrower concept of the waiver.

However, by the end of 2021, this proposed waiver was a nonstarter. International negotiations over the waiver proposal never occurred; there was strong opposition from the European Union and the pharmaceutical industry worldwide. Rather than a universal waiver, these negative parties pushed for half measures – limiting export restrictions on the vaccines and encouraging voluntary licensing. Their interests were clearly to protect the patent rights of the drug companies; self-interest won out over altruism. They did not offer any realistic alternatives and the WTO negotiations were hopelessly deadlocked. Despite more than 100 countries that backed the India-South Africa waiver proposal, the handful that opposed were most powerful, as WTO generally reaches agreements through consensus. So, while millions of people around the world continued to get infected by COVID, and many thousands continued to die in the Global South, the developed countries prioritized their profits over humanitarian concerns.

Conclusions

Values held by negotiating parties sometimes do not get translated directly into actionable strategies. The negotiating context and negotiator perceptions appear to play important roles here. Even if the desired negotiated outcome is morally driven to relieve pain and help civilians in great need, a negotiating party that knows it is at physical risk itself or perceives itself to be in a fragile situation may defer to self-interested values. Altruistic values will get pushed aside in favor of what the negotiator perceives as a decision for self-preservation. The irony is that the party in need of humanitarian support, in this case, is operating from a weak and dependent stance, but so is the party that can agree to allow the charitable assistance.

Is there a way for insecure negotiators to overcome their fears and negotiate based on their higher core values? One approach might be for the negotiating parties to dialogue with one another at the negotiating table in the manner discussed earlier between Israeli and Palestinian actors: by relating their personal narratives of past pain and injustice to build trust and empathy. If such perceptions for the other side can be built, both sides might feel safer to proceed with the needed negotiation of humanitarian assistance. Alternatively, impartial mediators can be brought in to moderate the dialogue of narratives, so both sides can feel in touch with the other and move forward with the negotiation.

Notes

1 Zartman, I. William (1999). "Negotiating Cultures," in Peter Berton, Hiroshi Kimura, and I. William Zartman, editors, *International Negotiation: Actors, Structure/Process, Values*. New York: St. Martin's Press.
2 Marshall, Colin (2018). *Compassionate Moral Realism*. Oxford: Oxford University Press.

3 Babbitt, Eileen F., et al. (2009). "Combining Empathy with Problem-Solving: The Tamra Model of Facilitation in Israel," in Craig Zelizer and Robert Rubenstein, editors, *Building Peace: Practical Lessons from the Field*. Sterling, VA: Kumarian Press.
4 This section updates and expands upon Spector, Bertram I. and Lynn M. Wagner (2010). "Negotiating International Development." *International Negotiation* 15, 3: 327–340.
5 Zartman, I. William and Jeffrey Z. Rubin, editors (2000). *Power and Negotiation*. Ann Arbor: University of Michigan Press.
6 Organization for Economic Cooperation and Development (2021). "COVID-19 spending helped to lift foreign aid to an all-time high in 2020, Detailed Note," April 13. At: https://www.oecd.org/dac/financing-sustainable-development/development-finance-data/ODA-2020-detailed-summary.pdf.
7 United Nations Department of Economic and Social Affairs (UNDESA) (2007). *UN Millennium Development Goals Report 2007*, New York, NY: Inter-Agency and Expert Group on MDG Indicators, United Nations.
8 Gu, Jing, Xiaoyun Li and Chuanhong Zhang (2021). "Whose Knowledge? Whose Influence? Changing Dynamics of China's Development Cooperation Policy and Practice," *IDS Bulletin* 52, 2: 1–18. At: https://bulletin.ids.ac.uk/index.php/idsbo/article/download/3129/3143?inline=1.
9 Sunshine, Russell B. (1990). *Negotiating for International Development: A Practitioner's Handbook*. Dordrecht: Martinus Nijhoff Publishers.
10 Clements, Ashley J. (2020). *Humanitarian Negotiations with Armed Groups*. London: Routledge.
11 Clements, Ashley J. (2018). "Overcoming Power Asymmetry in Humanitarian Negotiations with Armed Groups." *International Negotiation* 23, 3: 367–393.
12 Congressional Research Service (2021). "Potential WTO TRIPS Waiver and COVID-19," *In Focus*, September 13. At: https://crsreports.congress.gov/product/pdf/IF/IF11858; Krishnan, Vidya (2021). "How to End Vaccine Apartheid." *Foreign Policy*, November 9. At: https://foreignpolicy.com/2021/11/09/vaccine-apartheid-covid-pandemic-covax-us-trips-waiver/.

13
NEGOTIATING FOR GOOD, NEGOTIATING FOR BAD

The international negotiation process should be a value-free mechanism meant to resolve problems in a nonviolent way. But it can take on value-laden meaning based on the nature of the issues for which the process is applied. Typically, we think of international negotiation as addressing political, security, environmental, ethnic, economic, business, legal, scientific, and cultural issues, and conflicts among nations, international and regional organizations, multinational corporations, and other non-state parties. But the negotiation process can also be used to delay progress to buy time, rearm, and resume conflicts. The process can also be put to use to disadvantage weaker actors for the benefit of the more powerful. And the process can promote corrupt transactions across national boundaries.

How can a process that resolves difficult disputes and solves complex problems peacefully among state and non-state actors also be used effectively for such negative purposes? The primary underlying feature of negotiation – no matter what the goal – is to offer parties a chance to dialogue, present their ideas and options for a resolution, and hopefully, find a mutually acceptable outcome. One subprocess that is evident in every instance of negotiating involves the use of persuasion. To get the other party to agree to your proposed solution, you may offer something to the other side that they want in order for them to agree to what you want. In the best of situations, this results in a win-win outcome, where both sides get something that they need while resolving the conflict or solving the problem. This is considered the tit-for-tat, the give-and-take, or the offer-and-demand of negotiating. But sometimes, the result is not equal for both sides. There could be a win-lose outcome, where one side believes they are gaining more from the negotiated settlement than the other, but the other is willing to accept it because it is better to come to a resolution than to continue the state of conflict or dispute.

So much has been written about the "good" side of negotiating and the benefits that come from reaching successful agreements, but little about the "bad"

DOI: 10.4324/9781003314400-13

side. A few examples of the sometimes negative application of negotiations at the international level are examined in this essay.

Negotiation Put to Bad Use
Delay Tactics

Negotiations can be sabotaged if one side uses the process explicitly or implicitly to cause delay in the resolution of a transnational problem. Placing a pause on negotiations can be used to buy time, regroup or rearm. Often such delay tactics are used by the weaker party to frustrate the other side and produce a more desirable outcome despite the power asymmetry.[1] This tactic offers the weaker party a pathway to maintain some semblance of control. There are many ways by which delay in negotiations can be achieved: through silence, introducing new issues, making objections, providing excessive information, and asking questions, among others.

A recent example of the use of this tactic is Iran's delay in resuming negotiations to return to the 2015 Joint Comprehensive Plan of Action (JCPOA) agreement.[2] The United States exited the agreement in 2018 and reimposed sanctions on Iran, but since the Biden presidency began in January 2021, there have been seven rounds of talks just to restart the negotiation. But due to delays introduced by Iran, they only agreed to return to the negotiation in November 2021. The goal of these delays was to seek concessions from the United States – the lifting of sanctions and other technical issues. But during this delay period, Iran breached the JCPOA limits on uranium enrichment, refining to a higher purity, and installing advanced centrifuges. The delay tactic had a definite purpose: advancing Iran's nuclear program, even though it probably believed it would have to rejoin the agreement anyway. From 2018 through 2021, Iran felt confident that it could delay and pursue its nuclear goals without consequence since the United States did not indicate it would react militarily.

Agreeing to negotiate, but for the purpose of causing delays in problem-solving, sabotages the process; it also offers a new way out for the weaker party. It gives them the space to pursue their own goals that might be contrary to the goals of the negotiation itself. By changing the foundational context of the negotiation during the delay period, the party can unhinge the talks in a very negative way.

Taking Advantage of the Weak

Power asymmetry at the negotiating table has always been an opportunity for the strong to take advantage of the weak. For example, there have been many critics of international development assistance negotiated by China with developing countries since the 1950s. Chinese practices are often seen as predatory.[3] While agreeing to needed infrastructure projects that are promoted by the Chinese, the developing country takes on high levels of debt. These projects, while certainly of great help to the recipient country, also helps China – by increasing their access to production and natural resources. The debts are often difficult for the developing country to repay, creating a state of dependency into the future. China has been very aggressive in building these dependent foreign aid relationships, increasing its share of bilateral debt that developed nations have lent to developing countries from 45% in 2015 to 63% in 2019. In essence, the Chinese get the weaker developing nations to buy off on the needed aid, and then gain advantage over them for trade and resources for the long-term future. Despite Chinese denial of such a strategy, the facts over many years confirm their objectives.

Looking more broadly, Drahos examines the inequalities of bargaining power between developed and developing countries in both bilateral and multilateral negotiations.[4] The weak often face pressures and are forced into unwanted tradeoffs when confronted by strong nations banding together to push for their interests. Similarly, humanitarian agencies that negotiate with armed groups in conflict situations typically enter from a position of weakness. Without any raw power resources, they are often forced to concede on most of their demands so that they will be allowed to provide assistance to a few civilian groups.[5]

On the other hand, not all weaker parties are taken advantage of. Increasingly, weak parties in international negotiations have realized how to bargain to their own advantage over time. Examining six international negotiation cases with clear asymmetry or symmetry among the parties, Zartman and Rubin find that negotiations between weak and strong nations tend to be more efficient and effective than symmetrical negotiations.[6] When the strong confront the weak at the negotiating table, they each typically know their roles and adjust their strategies so that they can each achieve benefits in the outcome.

In a case study of Sino-British negotiations on the handover of Hong Kong, Wanglai found that the weaker party, in this case Great Britain, used the pressure of timing, the importance of frequent high-level communications, and empathy with the interests of the more powerful party to obtain many of its own objectives in the negotiation.[7] Singh also argues that weak countries are not necessarily overwhelmed by powerful nations in the negotiation setting.[8] The weak often use negotiation tactics effectively – setting agendas, linking issues, building coalitions, and lobbying in other countries, for example. The weak do not necessarily suffer at the negotiating table, though the odds are against them unless they pursue creative and flexible strategies. Dinar, analyzing negotiations between weak and strong nations over shared international river basins, agrees that the weak downstream state may be at a disadvantage in achieving its interests at the negotiating table.[9] But he also indicates that cooperation and coordination between the weak and strong parties has been shown to offer clear benefits to both in the negotiation setting.

Enabling Corrupt Behavior

Bargaining is an integral element of corrupt practices. To seek a bribe or kickback when providing a government service or signing off on a public procurement, for example, government officials can start the corruption process. It's the start of a give-and-take transaction. Their demand for a bribe is followed either by a concession from the citizen – providing the bribe or kickback – or a counteroffer from the citizen – a smaller bribe, a threat to report them to the police, etc. The corruption negotiation can also happen in reverse. A citizen or businessperson can seek certain favors from a civil servant – faster processing, extra services, awarding of a contract – by offering them a bribe, and the government authority can respond by accepting it, making a counteroffer, or rejecting it. Unfortunately, these negotiations are all too common in most countries. But they can happen across countries as well.

In the United States, the Foreign Corrupt Practices Act (FCPA) of 1977 regulates US businesses in terms of their financial dealings with foreign officials. Over the years, the FCPA has been responsible for many investigations and indictments of US companies for corrupt practices overseas.[10] Just a few recent cases are provided here as examples. In 2008, Siemens pled guilty to paying $1.5 billion in bribes to government officials in countries all over the world in exchange for public contracts. Also in 2008, KBR Inc. and Halliburton Company were found to have made more than $200 million in bribes to Nigerian government officials in order to get government construction contracts valued at $6 billion. Total S.A., an oil and gas company, paid over $60 million to Iranian officials to get government approval for a contract to develop Iranian oil and gas fields – a bribe that accrued to over $150 million in benefits to the company.

The leak of 11.5 million documents in 2015 from the Panamanian law firm, Mossack Fonseca, revealed data about many corrupt individuals, corrupt companies, and money launderers who sought to take advantage of moving their funds to offshore companies that the law firm established for them.[11] Analyzed by over 300 investigative journalists from 76 countries, and coordinated by the International Consortium of Investigative Journalists, the findings were published in 2016. While not all of the over 200,000 offshore entities were established for corrupt purposes, many were. Apparently, the goal of these offshore accounts was to avoid or minimize taxes and provide untraceable ways to do illegal business. These data exposed bribery, financial fraud, tax evasion, illegal arms deals, and drug trafficking conducted across borders.

What all of these cases have in common is the negotiation exchange that facilitated their illicit activity. They present a give-and-take swap. Bribes were offered to government officials as the "give" and the awarding of public contracts was the "take." It can be considered an integrative bargaining encounter where mutual gains were achieved by both parties by offering tradeoffs that benefited each. Unfortunately, the encounter utilizes the negotiation process for illegal purposes.

Conclusion

We typically think of negotiation – when it succeeds – as leading to good, constructive, and positive outcomes. But that is not always the case. The negotiation process can also be subverted to achieve bad goals. Are there ways to reduce the benefits of negotiation when used for negative purposes?

As discussed earlier, negative impacts of delay tactics at the negotiating table can be ameliorated by setting hard and fast deadlines in the negotiating agenda for getting things done. Powerful countries taking advantage of weaker parties in the negotiation process can be modulated by making sure the weak know how to adjust their negotiating strategy vis-à-vis the stronger party to steer the process toward more collaborative results.

Perhaps the hardest problem is reducing negotiation in corrupt enterprises. The negotiation paradigm is a common tool used by parents to get their kids to do what they want. Toys, candy, and gifts are offered to quiet down the children, get them to eat the vegetables on their plate, or get them to take a vaccination. It's a give-and-take exchange that is in our DNA from early life experiences. It is not unusual, then, to see the negotiation process employed in business dealings and in citizen-government interactions, not only to solve problems in a coordinated way but also to achieve illicit goals of one or both of the parties.

Is there a solution? Creating and then enforcing greater transparency and accountability in government-citizen and government-business interactions is one path to decommission the utility of the negotiation tool in these corruption encounters.[12] If all government decisions, operations, and actions are subject to sunshine laws and are conducted in the open, then situations that have led to corrupt negotiations will disappear, and the possibilities for offering bribes or extorting businesses or citizens will become very difficult. As well, if there is more extensive monitoring and auditing of government departments – both by internal investigators and citizen watchdogs – then this public scrutiny will also reduce opportunities for bribery negotiations. Other approaches, such as more extensive use of e-governance applications to get licenses and permits, and apply for public contracts, for example, will reduce direct personal contact between officials and citizens/businesses, at the same time as making the transactions more transparent and accountable.

There are no solutions that will guarantee that negotiations are not employed for bad purposes. But there are approaches that have been piloted and can be scaled-up that will start making a difference.

Notes

1 Spangler, Brad (2003). "Decision-Making Delay." *Beyond Intractability*, July. At: https://www.beyondintractability.org/essay/delay/.
2 Radio Free Europe (2021). "U.S. Iran Envoy Warns Tehran May Be Delaying Talks to Advance Nuclear Program," October 25. At: https://www.rferl.org/a/31528864.html; Amidror, Yaakov (2021). "Why is Iran Returning to the Negotiating Table?" November 16. *Israel National News*. At: https://www.israelnationalnews.com/News/News.aspx/316993.
3 Cordell, Kristen (2021). "Chinese Development Assistance: A New Approach or More of the Same?" March 23. Washington, DC: Carnegie Endowment for International Peace. At: https://carnegieendowment.org/2021/03/23/chinese-development-assistance-new-approach-or-more-of-same-pub-84141.
4 Drahos, Peter (2003). "When the Weak Bargain with the Strong: Negotiations in the World Trade Organization." *International Negotiation* 8, 1: 79–109.

5 Clements, Ashley Jonathan (2018). "Overcoming Power Asymmetry in Humanitarian Negotiations with Armed Groups." *International Negotiation* 23, 3: 367–393.
6 Zartman, I. William and Jeffrey Z. Rubin (2000). "Symmetry and Asymmetry in Negotiation," in I. William Zartman and Jeffrey Z. Rubin, editors, *Power and Negotiation*. Ann Arbor, MI: University of Michigan Press.
7 Wanglai, Gao (2009). "Negotiating with China in Power Asymmetry: The Case of Sino-British Negotiations on the Handover of Hong Kong." *International Negotiation* 14, 3: 475–492.
8 Singh, J. P. (2000). "Weak Powers and Globalism: The Impact of Plurality on Weak-Strong Negotiations in the International Economy." *International Negotiation* 5, 3: 449–484.
9 Dinar, Shlomi (2009). "Power Asymmetry and Negotiations in International River Basins." *International Negotiation* 14, 2: 329–360.
10 Price Benowitz LLP (2021). "FCPA Famous Cases." At: https://whitecollarattorney.net/fcpa/famous-cases/.
11 Fitzgibbon, Will and Michael Hudson (2021). "Five years later, Panama Papers still having a big impact." International Consortium of Investigative Journalists, April 3. At: https://www.icij.org/investigations/panama-papers/five-years-later-panama-papers-still-having-a-big-impact/.
12 Spector, Bertram (2008). "Perverse Negotiations: Bribery, Bargaining, and Ripeness," in Terrence Lyons and Gilbert Khadiagala, editors, *Conflict Management and African Politics: Ripeness, Bargaining, and Mediation*. London: Routledge.

14
REFRAMING NEGOTIATION TO AVERT DEVELOPMENT CONFLICTS

After the end of the Cold War, much research and policy attention that previously was addressed to managing strategic superpower conflicts became refocused on dealing with national and subnational conflicts over economic development, resource scarcity, environmental change, and ethnic cleavages, mostly in the developing world.[1] Although these newly targeted conflicts were not necessarily transnational in nature, their consequences are prone to spilling over state boundaries, and as such, they may be perceived as threatening international security. As the venue, level, and nature of these conflicts have shifted, so have the types of conflict resolution and diplomatic approaches that are appropriate and required to deal with them.

The question that arises is how to evaluate and reframe international diplomacy and negotiation approaches to deal with one of these newly perceived threats to security interests: conflict spurred on by inequitable growth that is inadvertently stimulated by international development programs. Ironically, international development assistance, which is meant to improve the well-being of a society and takes a pledge to "do no harm," has been shown to be a major contributing factor to escalating internal instability and violent conflict if it results in drastically unbalanced or inequitable growth patterns.[2]

Development-Induced Conflicts

There are many opportunities for disagreements and disputes to arise among stakeholders when a country's policies are being changed or reforms are being implemented. Attempts to reform laws, regulations, procedures, or institutions may impact a variety of interested parties on all sides of the issue. It is easy to imagine how disputes can emerge if resources are redistributed: certain groups are empowered at the expense of others; latent political, economic, social, and

DOI: 10.4324/9781003314400-14

cultural problems rise to the surface; new grievances are aired; and strict regulation and enforcement are imposed.

While there is the potential for conflict in the midst of change, there is often also the opportunity for greater coordination. Stakeholders often see the benefits of pulling together in the face of change. In effect, change can produce a problem situation that stakeholders can manage effectively only if they find a way to cooperate and act interdependently, despite their differences. Thus, the implementation of change provides a simultaneous, and sometimes contradictory, stimulus to seek a resolution to conflict *and* build a new consensus. Happily, most techniques that are labeled as "conflict resolution mechanisms" are equally useful in helping parties recognize their commonly shared problems and find mutually acceptable ways to cooperate. When groups or individuals are confronted with conflicts that divide them *or* mutual problems that demand their cooperation and interdependence, conflict resolution methods can help them find common ground, agree, cooperate, and move forward. Understanding and activating the *agreement motive* in development assistance situations can be a powerful tool for consultants and managers to remove barriers to implementation and stimulate effective policy execution.

The unintended impacts of international development assistance programs gone awry have been highlighted in several studies. Esman, Renner, Levine, and Lund all provide evidence of how inequitable access to economic growth opportunities can result in domestic conflicts.[3] The NATO Committee on the Challenges of Modern Society (CCMS) sponsored a multinational study on how environmental stresses generated at national and subnational levels – with many of these stresses stimulated by economic development projects – produce domestic conflicts that can escalate into international threats to security which NATO and other policymakers ought to be concerned about.[4] The study highlights a large number of environmental, developmental, and foreign policy responses to such threats, including preventive diplomacy, conflict settlement mechanisms, and negotiations within regimes. Other initiatives sponsored by the United States Agency for International Development (USAID) promote negotiation, mediation, and other forms of conflict resolution to prevent and/or manage disputes that arise due to local resource scarcity, economic issues, or ethnic/religious differences, and that may escalate into international security threats.

In these and similar programs and studies, the threatened local and transnational consequences of such development-induced conflicts strongly suggest that a newly reframed approach to negotiation and diplomacy is required to address these circumstances. In effect, traditional international negotiation and diplomatic approaches need to be adjusted so that they are accessible *at a local level*, and can be exercised by local actors to deal with domestic conflicts before they escalate into the international sphere.

Countries undergoing economic development or extensive democracy and governance reforms are highly prone to the outbreak of conflict. There are usually many groups in society that fear they will lose power, influence, and resources if policies, institutions, and procedures change. The provision of development assistance by multilateral and bilateral donor agencies, by itself, can be a catalyst for such disputes and disagreements because of the very fact that this assistance can threaten current power bases and reallocate resources among key stakeholders.[5]

An example from West Africa's central corridor can illustrate the nature and operations of a dispute management system in a relatively stable and nonviolent situation.[6] In the early 1990s, National Coordinating Committees (NCC) were established in Mali, Burkina Faso, and the Ivory Coast as part of the Nouakchott Plan to promote cooperation among these countries with regard to cross-border livestock trade. Membership in the committees included the major stakeholder groups – governmental ministries and agencies, livestock producers and traders, butcher syndicates, private transporters, professional organizations, and consumers – each with its own interests to maximize.

Through the dispute resolution mechanisms of the NCCs, these groups were able to negotiate with one another and build consensus within and across countries on such contentious issues as taxes, fees, services, and corruption. For example, the NCCs stood ready to manage potential disputes and rivalries between the transporters and brokers over new fees for customs services and the excesses of uniformed security services. They also lobbied and negotiated successfully with their respective governments over the threatened imposition of higher taxes and fees for customs clearances. By providing fora for continuing public policy dialogue on livestock trade issues and the mechanisms for resolving disputes before they escalate into hardened positions, deadlock, and even violence, the NCCs proved to be important dispute management structures that helped to prevent conflicts from expanding both within and across these three countries on this particular issue area.

What particular types of activities do economic development and democratic reform programs set in motion? They redistribute land or resources, empower new civil society organizations, reform laws, change institutions, and enforce new regulations, among many other activities. Directly or indirectly, these changes can stimulate latent political, economic, social, and cultural problems to come to the surface, because they alter the stakes in society. Conflicts may arise as a result. Development programs conducted to promote post-crisis reconstruction/reconciliation are particularly sensitive to the eruption of factional conflict. Depending on how serious these conflicts are, they can cause development programs to become hopelessly deadlocked, frustrating not only external donors, but also host country reformers, and they can escalate beyond national boundaries. These conflicts may not evoke violence, but they may be serious, nonetheless. Some examples of such conflicts that were initiated by development programs can be illustrative:

- During the implementation of the NCC regional livestock trade program in West Africa, described above, conflicts at border crossings dealing with taxation, tariffs, and deregulation came to the fore in Mali, Burkina Faso and the Ivory Coast. Mediation by a team of outside neutrals was required

to resolve these disputes through compromise so that the development program could proceed.[7]
- The distribution of food relief in Sudan in the early 1990s became a pivotal development activity that spurred domestic conflict and factional rivalries.[8]
- The 1990 IMF stabilization requirements in Rwanda, including currency devaluation, increased prices for basic commodities and removed consumer subsidies. These requirements were viewed as failed development strategies that could lead to bloodshed.[9]
- Several regional development projects related to the sharing and utilization of water resources have produced local conflicts and threats that have flared into broader regional conflicts, sometimes, though not always, involving violent clashes – for example, the Gabcikovo-Nagymaros dam project (Slovakia and Hungary), the Farakka barrage on the Ganges (Bangladesh and India), and the Senegal River Valley dam project (Senegal and Mauritania).[10]
- The World Bank's Inspection Panel receives and investigates complaints from NGOs that are negatively affected by World Bank-financed projects. Between 1994 and 1997, 10 complaints were received, largely dealing with the socio-economic impacts on local populations of internationally sponsored development projects. In some cases, these impacts involved population migration across national borders, potentially triggering security conflicts.[11]

Development professionals are usually not prepared to deal with such conflicts caused by their own development programs. Technical assistance programs generally require people who possess different skills than do conflict resolution programs. Moreover, conflict forecasting or conflict impact assessments are not generally commonplace when planning development programs. Thus, it is unusual to have early diagnoses and warnings of potential conflicts in development situations which might help development personnel manage such cases.

How widespread and significant is this problem? First, USAID budgetary resources in fiscal year 2021 amounted to US$37.5 billion, covering support to programs in democracy and governance, economic growth, education and training, environment and energy, humanitarian response, and population and health. While representing only a small fraction of the entire US budget (0.3%), such programs are substantial to the recipient countries and can produce major reactions by local stakeholders who feel threatened by the consequences of these programs. Many other major industrialized countries provide significant development assistance as well.

Second, international development assistance is meant to yield positive effects in the host countries. If they do not, and if they sometimes achieve conflict instead of cooperation, such assistance is viewed as detrimental and must be fixed. What is required is a reassessment of:

- How development assistance is provided,
- How safeguards can be embedded in such programs to prevent conflict from emerging, and

- How the international community can adjust approaches to international diplomacy and negotiation so as to manage and resolve conflicts that do emerge and for which they are in part responsible.

While the problem of development-induced conflict is acknowledged by USAID as a major challenge, very little research or literature has been published on the linkages between such conflicts and diplomatic responses. In fact, a special issue of *World Development* that focused on these very problems of implementing policy change via development programs admits the problem's existence, but offers no further analysis or solutions.[12] White's classic work on participative methodologies to implement development assistance programs alludes to the problem that major reforms often breed conflict.[13] Rigidity, unwillingness to cooperate, and direct opposition by stakeholders to development programs can present potent barriers to achieving the objectives of development assistance. If the degree of conflict is great, White asserts that stalemate can emerge or, worse, violence can break out, but little is said as to how to alleviate this conflict. Matland also conceptualizes how conflict can emerge in development assistance programs, but does not move beyond this to identify methods for resolving or preventing such conflict.[14] More data collection and analysis are required.

Reframing Negotiation and Diplomacy

How can negotiation be reframed to satisfy the new demands of this type of development-induced security threat? As has been described, development-induced conflicts involve both governmental and civil society actors. In developing countries, civil society often has not matured, commands only small constituencies, lacks capacity, and feels disempowered in comparison to governmental authorities. Thus, one of the major problems to resolving development-induced conflicts is to create an inclusive environment that is conducive to negotiation, that is, where civil society can be engaged as an equal player and where all parties perceive that fair and just outcomes can result.

To deal with this, it is necessary to reframe traditional preventive diplomacy and negotiation approaches to meet the special contingencies of subnational development-induced conflict. From a preventive perspective, it will be necessary to:

- *Anticipate potential conflict when designing development assistance programs.* This might involve conducting conflict impact assessments, similar to environmental impact assessments, before the development program is launched to assess areas of sensitivity and points of potential risk. This should include a stakeholder analysis. Based on such assessments, development programs could be modified and emergent conflicts could be dealt with in advance and possibly averted.
- *Embed dispute management systems in development assistance programs.* This might involve incorporating an ombudsman, grievance offices, periodic

problem-solving and negotiation workshops, and alternative dispute resolution (ADR) techniques into the functioning of development programs.
- *Ensure that all major stakeholders in development have the capacity to negotiate.* The development program might include training and other stakeholder capacity strengthening activities in negotiation techniques, so that each stakeholder group, especially those in civil society, can represent and support their own interests effectively.
- *Train local development providers in diagnostic techniques.* Donor representatives, voluntary organizations, nongovernmental organizations, and local development providers should be trained in diagnostic techniques so that they are sensitive to and can assess the likelihood of future conflict and design appropriate responses.
- *Train local development providers in negotiation and diplomatic approaches.* Ensure that development program implementers are trained in these conflict resolution techniques.

If conflict emerges, it may be necessary to:

- Involve local-level third parties to serve as mediators and facilitators.
- Deal with problems of perceived power asymmetry across groups, which is likely to be prominent in development-induced subnational conflicts.
- Create opportunities and venues for informal meetings of the effected parties so they can hear the others' narratives, hopefully to generate a sense of empathy.
- Create opportunities for equal information access and assessment of options.
- Create opportunities and the environment for parties to perceive the process as mutually beneficial and fair.
- Evaluate the effects of external actors and occurrences.
- Design and implement institutions, regimes, and procedures at the national and subnational levels to support and sustain conflict resolution responses.

Researchers also need to examine past cases of development-induced conflicts in greater detail to see what patterns emerge that can help policymakers better predict and avert future problems. In particular, they need to analyze the confluence of three factors: the development context, the conflict type, and the response to the conflict situation. Importantly, these factors can also be assessed for any currently emerging case, so that general trends deduced from past examples can be helpful in a practical sense.

The *development context* can be evaluated in terms of the following factors, among others:

- Cleavages – political, economic, social, ethnic, religious
- Institutional strengths and capacities
- Rule of law
- Civil society strengths
- The nature of development assistance.

Conflict types can be elaborated in terms of Crosby's typology:[15]

- Conflicts over the legitimacy of change
- Conflicts over changing constituencies and power bases
- Conflicts over the reallocation of accumulated resources
- Conflicts over the redirection of future resources
- Conflicts over the restructuring of rights, privileges, and procedures.

Conflict responses run the gamut from:

- Retreat (doing nothing)
- Conciliation (including preventive diplomacy, negotiation, mediation, and other approaches)
- Coercion (including military or police action).

The cases collected can be assessed and coded in terms of the variables in this framework. Its fundamental underpinnings suggest that development conflicts are a function of the nature of the development assistance and the development context. These situational factors determine whether conflict will emerge at all and the capacity of the country to manage conflict that does emerge. The interaction between the context, the conflict, and the response defines a "case profile." The desired results of analyzing these cases will produce useful and practical guidance for policymakers by identifying and specifying distinct case profiles, understanding the dynamics in each, and forecasting the likely effectiveness of each in terms of conflict reduction.

The analysis will yield implications, lessons learned, and recommendations for both researchers and policymakers about what to do to avert conflict or deal effectively with conflicts that emerge. As indicated earlier, these conclusions will address preventive diplomacy, for example, anticipating conflict in the design of development assistance programs, embedding dispute management systems in these programs, giving stakeholders the capacity to negotiate, and training local development providers in diagnostic techniques and in conflict resolution approaches. The analytical results will also help in reframing negotiation methods for local development situations, for example, involving local third parties, dealing with perceived power asymmetry, providing for informal meetings and equal information access, creating a level playing field, assessing the effects of external actors and occurrences, and designing institutions, regimes, and procedures at the subnational level to sustain conflict resolution responses. To disseminate these findings, a handbook can be produced based on these results for development assistance practitioners, private voluntary organizations, and nongovernmental organizations to help them plan future development assistance programs that avert or prevent conflicts, and use effective negotiation and diplomatic techniques that can reduce and manage any conflicts that might emerge.

Future Paths

Development programs are commonly used as a channel for foreign aid and typically seek cooperative and beneficial outcomes. However, these programs can also unleash the undesirable results of escalating conflict that can extend beyond national borders and produce international security threats. New approaches to negotiation and diplomacy — practiced at a more local level — are required to avert and/or manage such conflicts. Future research needs to evaluate the characteristics of evolving threats in the context of development assistance programs and identify new directions for negotiation and diplomacy that can be practiced effectively at the national and subnational level to avert or manage such conflicts.

It is anticipated that the study of past cases will suggest new ways to reframe negotiation and diplomacy to make them more amenable to development-induced conflicts. These results will have special meaning to USAID and other donors, private voluntary organizations, NGOs, and development consultants. Some likely implications of such analyses would include the following:

- Negotiation options need to be brought down to a local level to be effective, that is, diplomacy needs to deal with the sources of development-induced conflict between local stakeholders.
- To accomplish this, negotiation needs to be based on a detailed, "on the ground" understanding of development conflict and all its local stakeholders, so that the practical opportunities for negotiated solutions are properly understood in context.
- Local representatives of bilateral and international donor organizations need to be trained in negotiation approaches since they are more likely to understand the situation on the ground than officials back home.
- Preventive diplomatic mechanisms need to be developed to avert development conflicts in their very early stages. This includes the design and implementation of institutions, regimes, procedures, and dispute management systems. It also implies designing development programs with the capability to anticipate conflict and/or manage it.
- Local government and civil society leaders need to be empowered with these negotiation and diplomatic tools. This requires that donors include training and implementation of these mechanisms as an integral part of development assistance programs.

Notes

1 Carnegie Commission on Preventing Deadly Conflict (1997). *Preventing Deadly Conflict*. New York: Carnegie Corporation of New York.
2 Ibid.
3 Lund, Michael (1997). *Preventing and Mitigating Violent Conflict: A Guide for Practitioners*. Washington, DC: Creative Associates International Inc.; Esman, Milton J. (1991). "Economic Performance and Ethnic Conflict," in Joseph Montville, editor, *Conflict and Peacemaking in Multiethnic Societies*. New York: Lexington Books;

Renner, Michael (1996). *Fighting for Survival*. New York: W. W. Norton and Co.; Levine, Alicia (1996). "Political Accommodation and the Prevention of Secessionist Violence," in Michael E. Brown, editor, *The International Dimensions of International Conflict*. Cambridge, MA: The MIT Press.

4 NATO/CCMS (1998). *Environment and Security in an International Context*. Edited by EcoLogic, EBR Inc., and the Center for Negotiation Analysis. Brussels: NATO.

5 Spector, Bertram (1997b). "Managing Disputes and Building Consensus: A Guide to Applying Conflict Resolution Mechanisms when Implementing Policy Change." USAID's Implementing Policy Change Project, Working Paper No. 9 (April).

6 Brinkerhoff, Derick W. (1996b). "Enhancing Capacity for Strategic Management of Policy Implementation in Developing Countries," Washington, DC: Management Systems International. IPC Monograph No. 1 (September); Kulibaba, Nicolas (1995). "Good Governance in Sheep's Clothing: Implementing the Action Plan for Regional Integration of the Livestock Trade in West Africa's Central Corridor. Washington, DC: Management Systems International Inc., IPC Working Paper (May).

7 Spector, Bertram (1997a). "Policy Implementation, Conflict, and Dispute Resolution." Washington, DC: Management Systems International. USAID's Implementing Policy Change Project, Working Paper No. 11 (August).

8 Lund (1997), op.cit.

9 Ibid.

10 Baechler, Günther, V. Böge, S. Klötzli, S. Libiszewski, and K. Spillmann (1996). *Kriegsursache Umweltzerstörung: Ökologische Konflikte in der Dritten Welt und Wege ihrer friedlichen Bearbeitung*. Band 1. Chur, Zurich: Rüegger; Homer-Dixon, Thomas and Valerie Percival (1996). Environmental Scarcity and Violent Conflict: Briefing Book. Toronto: University of Toronto.

11 World Bank (1997). *The Inspection Panel, Annual Report, August 1, 1996 to July 31, 1997*. Washington, DC: The World Bank.

12 Brinkerhoff, Derick, editor (1996a). "Implementing Policy Change" *World Development* 24 (9), September.

13 White, Louise (1990). *Implementing Policy Reforms in LDCs: A Strategy for Designing and Effecting Change*. Boulder: Lynne Reinner Publishers.

14 Matland, R.E. (1995). "Synthesizing the Implementation Literature: The Ambiguity-Conflict Model of Policy Implementation." *Journal of Public Administration Research and Theory* 5:(2): 145–174.

15 Crosby, Benjamin (1996). "Policy Analysis Units: Useful Mechanisms for Implementing Policy Reform." Washington, DC: Management Systems International. USAID's Implementing Policy Change Project Working Paper No. 10 (October).

15
EVOLUTIONARY NEGOTIATION

Important negotiations take time. Most problems involving international actors are not peacefully resolved in just one go-around. The negotiation process, when applied to ending complex conflicts, resolving major mutual problems, or developing consequential collaborative programs, is usually an incremental process carried out over a long period of time. The process can involve many informal dialogues leading to formal talks at the negotiating table and then back to informal discussions to better understand the interests and positions of all parties and what an acceptable solution might look like. One-off negotiations resulting in an agreement and then ratification by all parties, on the other hand, are usually the product of more straightforward and simpler problems.

An initial negotiated agreement might be effective at generating a ceasefire between warring parties, for example, but it logically would require much additional work to move beyond the cessation of violence to a more peaceful resolution. That takes time. It requires all parties to adjust their perceptions and behaviors to the new reality. It also requires new assessments of the agreement's effects by all parties to determine what else is needed to maintain or improve upon the new situation. As well, successful negotiations in other problem-solving domains may yield useful close-in results, but can require periodic updates over time.

Sometimes, a drawn-out negotiation process can be attributed to one or more parties trying to delay the talks for various reasons. Delay can be used as a bargaining tactic to seek out better offers from other parties or it can be a way to keep a conflict situation at bay while strengthening your own position to resume the conflict. While delay tactics, by definition, can extend the time for negotiations to reach a conclusion, this essay focuses on the more positive approaches by which the negotiation process can evolve in search of positive outcomes.

DOI: 10.4324/9781003314400-15

Declaring success and walking away from the negotiating table upon signing an agreement is perhaps too abrupt. In most cases, signing the agreement is not the end but only the beginning of the negotiation process. The research literature has developed several different frameworks to describe and explain these longer term incremental negotiations.

Evolutionary Frameworks

We examine four related evolutionary approaches that the negotiation process can pursue. The first is *incremental trust-building*, where parties slowly try to understand the other sides, where they are coming from, what they need and want, and build trust and empathy. This can take the form of multiple informal dialogues and meetings, until the parties feel sufficiently comfortable to proceed with designing and negotiating potential agreements. The second evolutionary approach, *formula-detail-reframing*, is an incremental process that starts with the parties developing and agreeing on an overarching solution plan for the agreement and then filling in the details over time. As circumstances change over the longer term, the formula may need to be reframed and new details negotiated.

A third evolutionary approach to conducting negotiation is to move through the *functional process stages*. This involves the information gathering and analysis of the pre-negotiation stage, the give-and-take of the negotiation stage, executing the agreement in the implementation stage, revising the agreement provisions in the post-agreement stage, and possibly reopening the negotiations once again to make major changes in the re-negotiation stage. The fourth evolutionary approach takes the form of negotiating within institutionalized processes and structures established within *international regimes* – monitoring, adjusting, and revising the negotiation agreement in the post-agreement period.

Incremental Trust-Building

Osgood put forward an interesting incremental approach to negotiation.[1] His evolutionary Gradual Reduction In Tension (GRIT) process is a tactic to use in conflict situations where the negotiation process is deadlocked. He suggested that an incremental de-escalation could begin with one side making a small, unilateral concession to the other side, while also asking for a reciprocal gesture from the opponent. If there is a positive response, then another concession could be made and an incremental peace spiral will have been initiated. However, if the opening concession is ignored, the first party could continue trying through additional steps to build trust, but not to indicate weakness. The idea is that positive baby steps in the right direction over time can provide positive incentives to transform the conflict to a cooperative and less adversarial situation. Babbitt employed a similar process of dialogue among Israelis and Palestinians to instill a sense of trust and empathy for the other side before moving on to problem-solving discussions to reach negotiated agreements on local issues.[2]

The value of Osgood's GRIT process can be visualized in many international negotiation situations. Climate change is recognized as a global problem that requires all nations to pitch in their share of actions so that all can observe and share the benefits.[3] This is why negotiating a global, binding, and comprehensive climate change agreement is the ultimate goal. However, the costs of implementing these actions are large and local. There is also a large deficit of trust among countries that they will all live up to their word and comply with such an agreement. Without mutual trust, countries resist negotiations that will lead to a comprehensive agreement and are incentivized to take a free ride on the actions of others in the interim. But success in the climate change arena is only possible with universal cooperation and coordination of actions, and that is only possible if the parties build trust that the others will live up to their commitments. The potential path toward building this trust could be through a strategy where the parties agree to much smaller partial agreements to take smaller, but concrete, steps in the right direction, where all can take note of the mutual benefits when all actors participate. Over time, mutual trust will be built and eventually enable a comprehensive agreement to be established.

Formula-Detail-Reframing

Rarely do all engaged parties come to the table with the same concept for resolving the conflict or problem at hand. It is through dialogue and discussion that they come to understand the other parties' interests and commitments issue-by-issue, are able to compare these with their own interests, and then devise an overall formula that includes and organizes all interests into a framework that could lead to an acceptable agreement.

Once the formula is reached, then the negotiation turns to the nitty-gritty details of how the formula's objectives can be achieved. With the details in hand that are acceptable to all parties, a pact can be formulated and agreed to, and then implemented. But it is in the implementation phase that nuances not recognized earlier can come to light – where some aspects of the formula or particular agreed details do not materialize as anticipated. Or the situation may have changed significantly over time to make the existing agreement obsolete.

Over time, this can lead to the need for reframing the agreement – reformulating how interests are handled and accounted for in the agreement, and reassessing the details that implement the new formula. If the originating agreement has not entirely fallen apart, the reformulation, re-detailing, and re-implementation can proceed, using the originating agreement as the stepping stone to a new one.

The Abraham Accord agreements of 2020 are a case in point.[4] Brokered by the United States, Israel negotiated and then signed agreements with several Arab states – Morocco, the United Arab Emirates, Bahrain, and Sudan – to normalize bilateral relations. The texts call for the initiation of diplomatic relations and promote bilateral economic cooperation for the first time. Unlike most previous attempts to negotiate an Israel-Arab peace agreement that were framed as broad regional efforts to primarily address the Israeli-Palestinian conflict, the Abraham Accords do not attempt to tackle the Palestinian question at all. They engage Arab states that are not border states with Israel and have not been directly involved in past wars. As such, the goal of the negotiations leading to the Accords was to totally reframe the issues being addressed under the agreements: to promote bilateral relations with no mention of the Israeli-Palestinian conflict. Earlier regional formulas were put aside, and reframed in the Accords to be constructive for bilateral agreement.

Functional Stages

The negotiation process has often been considered a multi-stage effort: from pre-negotiation, to negotiation, to implementation, to post-agreement negotiation, and to re-negotiation. In pre-negotiation, the parties plan for the upcoming negotiation. They assess their own interests and commitments on the issues at hand, the other parties' interests and commitment, power dynamics, and the situation if agreement is reached or not, among many other issues. They also plan out their tactics and strategies to achieve their own interests and influence the other parties to achieve a compromise agreement.

The negotiation stage is where all parties come to the table to discuss and seek to influence the others. The bargaining can occur over multiple sessions and may not result in an immediate outcome. Negotiators may need to go home, confer with country leaders, readjust their negotiating tactics and strategies, and then reassemble to finalize a deal. This may go on for multiple return sessions.

Once an agreement is reached, the crucial implementation stage occurs. This might start with national ratification of the agreement, but then proceeds to executing the provisions that had been agreed to. Depending on capacities, funding, resources, political will, and coordination, among others, this implementation process can be a period in which the parties see the concrete results of their negotiating – both positive and negative. In either situation, the experience of implementing the agreement can lead the parties to a post-agreement negotiation stage.[5] Here, with some understanding of how the agreed provisions really operate, the parties might want to adjust them so they can be better implemented and produce the desired outcomes.

Even after modifications are made in the post-agreement stage, re-negotiation may be required.[6] The context or the parties may have undergone significant change over time to make the existing agreement obsolete. With the history of that agreement under their belts, a re-negotiation stage might pick up from where the parties left off or push the negotiation to totally new issues and solutions.

The re-negotiation of international agreements can be rather dramatic. What we know as the European Union today was subject to many negotiations and re-negotiations between 1952 – when the European Coal and Steel Community was agreed to – and 1993, when the European Union was negotiated to incorporate three different collaborative entities. The re-negotiations were always focused on modernizing, but also changing the formulas, rules, and provisions by which member states could coordinate their policies and transactions.[7]

International Regimes

International regimes – such as those related to climate change, biodiversity, and nuclear test bans, for example – generate administrative commissions, other structures and procedures, and subsequent conferences that continue to meet and operate after the originating agreement was negotiated and signed to ensure that the provisions are implemented as planned and the agreement is adjusted as issues and interests change over time. This institutional regime framework anticipates the evolutionary process of negotiation to keep the agreement up-to-date, meaningful and fully executed.[8] Post-agreement negotiation within the context of international regimes is built into the process, not only to update the agreement but also to correct it, extend it, and deal with any unresolved issues over time. The original authors of the initial agreement anticipated the need to adjust the agreement over time and established the mechanisms to do just that.

Recursive negotiations within regimes help them adjust through post-agreement negotiation.[9] These are corrective rounds – to fix mistakes that might have been made in the initiating agreement, modify the regime to deal with unexpected complexities, adjust the regime to changing conditions, or make it better through adding and expanding to the original agreement. Negotiations within regimes are not one-off events.

The 1972 United Nations Conference on the Human Environment (UNCHE) and the 1992 United Nations Conference on Environment and Development (UNCED), also known as the Rio Earth Summit, placed in motion an international regime focused on establishing sustainable development programs and goals. The ultimate agreements from these conferences planned for subsequent meetings to take stock of implementation and review adjustments that might be needed: the World Summit on Sustainable Development was held in Johannesburg 10 years out (in 2002) and a 20-year review was conducted at the UN Conference on Sustainable Development (Rio+20) in 2012. A myriad of post-agreement negotiations emanated from this regime that produced agreements creating the UN Environment Program, the Commission on Sustainable Development, several conventions to combat desertification and address biological diversity and climate change, and agendas that outline future environmental objectives and goals, among others.[10] The need for post-agreement negotiation in the case of UNCHE and UNCED does not imply, by any means, that they were failed negotiations. Rather, the negotiators understood clearly that scientific advances and political will would build over the years, requiring that updates, adjustments, and expansions of the initial agreements would become obvious and needed. The annual meetings established by UNCED were built-in post-agreement negotiation sessions, employed to maintain the initial agreements' currency and relevance.

Why Is Evolution Necessary?

Incremental negotiation in the international context makes sense. In many cases, it advisable to go slowly. Countries can fear dramatic changes in the situation if it comes too quickly. It may take signatories some time to build their resources and capacity to effectively follow-through on agreed provisions, so it could make sense to stretch out the implementation period by generating smaller sequential steps leading to the desired end state. It also might take some time to unify domestic factions around an agreement, so the incremental approach might be useful in selling the program at the national level and generating sufficient support.

In the international arena, there are so many complicated and interlaced issues, multi-party interests, power dynamics, and contexts that change over time that it is hard to see an agreement struck at one point in time that would not need to be adjusted or completely overhauled to remain viable. Some change factors emerge from the political-economic context. The progression of events, power interactions, and improved understanding of the issues can require that a negotiated agreement be updated. Sometimes, the initial agreement might have just gotten it wrong; its provisions may not address the issues appropriately or sufficiently and the problem still persists. Equally consequential are human factors related to the decision-making approaches of the negotiators and country leaders back home; there may be certain psychological and behavioral factors that can be pinpointed as critical in understanding why the negotiation takes an incremental trajectory. Several of these human factors are discussed here.

Experimentation

Reopening negotiation of agreements that have already been reached can suggest a desire for experimentation. There may be new hypotheses as to what changes will work best at achieving the desired outcomes. Negotiators may start with particular approaches that they think will work, but after a while may suspect that other actions will be more effective. If the opportunity is available, why not try them out? Experimentation can take the form of sequenced options. After conducting several of these experiments to find a good solution, the negotiators may feel they have done their best.

Experimentation is also an approach that can be used when the negotiators are uncertain about the relative impacts of several options they have available. Some may work and some may fail. Restarting the negotiations to pursue these experimental possibilities or establishing a structure within the initial agreement that allows for experimentation extends the period within which the ultimate negotiated outcome is achieved.

Psychology of Regret

What if you make a decision as the nation's negotiator to accept certain offers or demands from the other side? If the results are good or at least what you expected, you made the right choice. But if things go wrong as a result of your decision, the responsibility lies with you. You can be blamed. This is what is called the psychology of regret.[11] For those who anticipate this regret over making a bad decision, it may be better to just do nothing or let others make the decisions for you. By not making a proactive decision, you cannot blame yourself, and hopefully, others will not blame you either.

When at the point of making decisions, negotiators typically look at the cost-benefit of taking action, but they can also look at the worst-case scenario and that might cause them to refrain from making offers or agreeing to others' offers at the negotiating table. This fear of regret can cause negotiations to grind to a halt or to slow down. This situation is more likely to happen among negotiators who represent weaker parties in the talks. If they do move forward, the negotiators may steer toward progressing with baby steps, which can be the safer strategy.

Fear of Noncompliance

All negotiators should have some fear that the provisions they agree to at the negotiating table may not be implemented as intended. Starting with ratification at the national level and then the actions required of each party, if some provisions are difficult to implement or ultimately disagreeable, that could spell the failure of the agreement. Negotiators can respond to this fear by establishing a monitoring board within the agreement that will oversee implementation once the agreement is signed and ratified. If there is noncompliance with any provisions, the agreement can mandate fines or sanctions on parties that fail to live up to their commitments or negotiations can be restarted to address any technical or substantive problems parties had with particular provisions to adjust or upgrade the agreement.

Conclusion

International negotiation is a step-by-step, evolutionary process, not one that advances by decree or by revolution. Through dialogue and the exchange of offers, agreements can eventually be made. Then, through implementation, the agreements' provisions can proceed to resolve conflicts, solve problems, or support coordination. Alternatively, implementation efforts can demonstrate over time that changing situations, ideas, orientations, and behaviors require that the negotiated agreement must be modified to continue to yield its desired impacts.

That a particular negotiated agreement is the only and best solution that can last forever is not realistic. Establishing a mechanism for incrementally improved settlements, and continuous updates and repairs to keep negotiated outcomes current and relevant is logical and good practice. This implies that most well negotiated agreements should incorporate provisions for updates and adjustment over the long term. Given this evolutionary tendency, two areas stand out as in need of further research.

Planning Mechanisms

In the pre-negotiation stage, negotiators and their staff need to spend much of their time analyzing the situation, the other parties, and their own strategies. An essential element of this analysis period should be developing an understanding of the short- and long-term ideas that all negotiating partners have for solving the problems at hand. There may be some issues that have obvious quick solutions that will satisfy all sides. But there are likely to be more complex issues that are dynamic and can move the negotiations along many alternative paths. These are the ones that are likely to result in prolonged or multi-pronged talks over time. At least by identifying that these issues require more attention early in the process, and considering multiple or step-by-step options for them to reach resolution, the agenda can be set more realistically for when the parties sit down at the table. As well, such early analysis can help negotiators plan for establishing administrative mechanisms such as monitoring committees, and prepare themselves for the likely future need for continued negotiations on certain issues.

Adjustment Provisions

After negotiated agreements are under way, what are the best and least disruptive ways to adjust and update the agreements if that is deemed necessary? First, how is it determined that changes to the agreement are required? Agreement monitoring results can be analyzed on a regular basis to see if the expected objectives are being achieved. If the political-economic dynamics have changed significantly, analysis can be done to assess if new outcomes should be sought. If the agreement's provisions have been implemented well but have not achieved their results, it could be that an update or expansion of the agreement is called for. What might that look like? Analysis and projections of the future could be relevant to planning effectively for this situation.

Notes

1 Osgood, Charles (1962). *An Alternative to War or Surrender*. Urbana: University of Illinois Press.
2 Babbitt, Eileen F., et al. (2009). "Combining Empathy with Problem-Solving: The Tamra Model of Facilitation in Israel," in Craig Zelizer and Robert Rubenstein, editors, *Building Peace: Practical Lessons from the Field*. Sterling, VA: Kumarian Press.
3 Keohane, Robert and David Victor (2016). "Cooperation and discord in global climate policy." *Nature Climate Change* 6: 570–575.

4 Makovsky, David (2020). "How the Abraham Accords Look Forward, Not Back," September 16. Washington, DC: Washington Institute for Near East Policy. At: https://www.washingtoninstitute.org/policy-analysis/how-abraham-accords-look-forward-not-back.
5 Spector, Bertram I. and I. William Zartman, editors (2003). *Getting It Done: Post-Agreement Negotiation and International Regimes*. Washington, DC: United States Institute of Peace Press.
6 Spector, Bertram I. (2020). "Ripe for Renegotiation?" *International Negotiation* 25, 1: 69–77.
7 Ibid.
8 Zartman, I. William and Bertram I. Spector (2013). "Post-Agreement Negotiating within Multilateral Regimes." *International Negotiation* 18, 3: 325–332.
9 Spector & Zartman (2003), op.cit.
10 Wagner, Lynn M. (2013). "A Forty-Year Search for a Single-Negotiating Text: Rio+20 as a Post-Agreement Negotiation." *International Negotiation* 18, 3: 333–356.
11 Galinsky, Adam (2021). "The 'Psychology of Regret' Helps Explain Vaccine Hesitancy." *Washington Post*, November 14. At: https://www.washingtonpost.com/outlook/2021/11/11/vaccine-hesitancy-psychology-regret/.

16
FUTURE PATHS

The refrain in the 1969 Rolling Stones' song, "You Can't Always Get What You Want," has always brought me back to the essence of the negotiation process. Mick Jagger shouts that you can't always get *what you want*, but sometimes, if you try hard enough, you can get *what you need*.

I'm sure that the writers of these lyrics had something else in mind, but for me it depicts how the negotiation process works. Negotiators often start by voicing their *positions* on a particular issue; they tell the other parties *what* they want. But no matter how hard they try, as the lyrics say, they cannot always get what they want.

At the same time, negotiators come to the table with an understanding of their own interests and, hopefully, the interests of the other parties, along with some core negotiating values and a strategy in their pocket that they believe can help them achieve their interests in an ultimate agreement. In the end, a negotiator's *interests* – what they really *need*, as the song says – is the most important thing in the negotiation. It is what negotiators desire in the outcome, it says *why* they want it, and it represents their "interests," as Fisher, Ury, and Patton suggest.[1] Not always getting what you want, but getting what you need is a basic and accepted principle in the negotiation literature.

This collection of essays examines a wide range of issues and questions about international negotiation dynamics that have concerned me – where we already have some analysis but not enough, where more deep-dive study is needed. I hope that these essays extend our understanding of these issues and open new doors to advance our conceptual understanding and practical implementation of negotiations. As we dig deeper, new questions and new paths for research always arise. Pulling together the findings of these essays, here are some key issues that I think merit further examination.

DOI: 10.4324/9781003314400-16

Creativity and Experimentation

Experiments are tests of theories. That is just what negotiations are about. Will various tactics and strategies succeed in moving other parties to a compromise solution? Will the ultimate agreement really end the conflict or solve the problem at hand? Can the parties find reasonable ways to implement the agreement and then adjust the agreement as needed over time? Each of these questions lays out another experiment of hypothesized relationships between dependent and independent variables. In any one negotiation, there can be multiple hypotheses being tested simultaneously or consecutively, making it a complicated real-time field experiment.

The hypotheses to be tested are usually derived from either past experience, or better yet, creative thinking. More assessments of creative tactics and strategies are needed to see if they do yield more effectiveness and efficiency in reaching acceptable outcomes, and under what conditions. These assessments can be accomplished by comparing a wide range of case studies, but also through simulation experiments. What are the best creativity approaches to achieve outcomes under different circumstances: using analogies, roleplaying, flowcharting, brainstorming, extrapolating, or inserting new actors into the situation? And how can creativity be stimulated in the first place; is it a matter of personality, cognition, or situation? Can creativity in negotiation be trained – allowing negotiators to recognize opportunities, but also to formulate unusual and exceptional options?

Engineering Negotiation Situations

Negotiators can gain control of what happens at the negotiating table if they are able to smartly engineer the situation in such a way as to promote their interests. They need to go well beyond their intuition, experience, and instinct to yield a positive outcome. Negotiators will improve their ability to reach a successful agreement if they are aware of and can adjust key situational factors. Based on systematic research, important situational factors that can make a difference include, for example, introducing a third-party facilitator, better planning in the pre-negotiation stage, conducting informal talks first, considering the extent of media coverage for the negotiations, setting firm deadlines, and using creativity approaches. These are only a few factors that can be introduced and engineered to steer the negotiation process and outcome toward agreement. More research – both qualitative and quantitative – can be conducted to analyze which factors can be engineered effectively under different circumstances to achieve the desired outcomes. To promote these initiatives, more targeted training for negotiators is warranted, and better communications between practitioners and researchers are needed to assess the value of these situational factors and identify efficient ways of engineering the practical situation.

The Psychology of Negotiation

Getting down to the basic human level, negotiation is highly influenced by the psychology of the engaged individuals – their personality, perceptions, persuasion, understanding, past experience, and reactions, etc. More research should be conducted to assess how and if different personality profiles tend to produce different bargaining strategies. Do different personality types perceive strategies differently? As well, do different perceptions of the situation and strategies used by other parties make negotiators more cautious, defensive, or aggressive?

And it is not only a matter of each negotiator's psychology, but the complex mix of these psychologies as they interact around the bargaining table to find solutions. Research based on interviews with practitioners, as well as experimental simulations, should help us understand these factors better and assist in translating these findings into practical lessons for real-life negotiators.

Negotiability

A critical piece of information that negotiators need to properly strategize is the negotiability of the other parties at the table. Are they trained and capable, trustworthy, believable, and reliable? What are the best ways of measuring these factors – going beyond subjective cultural factors? More research can help by finding the best ways to formulate negotiability as a multi-dimensional index. Does this phenomenon change over time? Does it manifest itself differently across different issue areas that might be the subject of negotiation? Is such an index correlated with negotiation success?

Incomplete Negotiations

What do successfully negotiated agreements that fail to get implemented tell us? Were certain essential issues ignored, misread, or mistakenly assessed? Does this situation have something to do with the reliability and commitment of certain signatories to the agreement who did not follow through, or were some key factors missing from the agreement? To avert such problems, negotiating agendas from the outset should incorporate a special round of talks to negotiate the implementation formula – the plan of action – assuming that a basic agreement on the substantive issues has been reached. What should such an implementation formula include? What mechanisms can be developed to monitor the implementation process so that any disruptions to the original plan can be adjusted over time?

Implementing Agreements

Looking again at the post-negotiation period – particularly, at the implementation of agreed provisions – countries often find themselves in a quandary. After what appears to be a successful negotiation, obstacles can come in the way of properly implementing the agreement. Our analysis of international environmental agreements suggests that power asymmetry between the signatories is often viewed as the primary factor determining whether implementation happens or not. But our findings also demonstrate that problems in implementation can be traced to issues relating to technical incapacities on both sides, deriving from spoiler factions among domestic stakeholders, a lack of financial or technical resources, and enforcement complications. One practical approach to get out of this conundrum is to engage nongovernmental organizations and other role models in society to present new visions of how to address these incapacities and differences to implement negotiated provisions more effectively. Are there other approaches?

Decision Support Systems

Decision support systems (DSS) for negotiating teams already exist and specialized ones that focus on the issues at hand can always be developed. The practical problem is getting them used. Coordination between the analytical developers of DSS and the practical negotiators seems to be the key factor. How can these teams best communicate their information needs and pilot test the DSS approaches? Can the DSS be developed to assist in short-term, as well as long-term, strategies? Can the DSS be designed to test out a range of negotiation strategies? How can the results of the DSS best be presented to be actionable for the negotiation practitioners? Can the DSS approach be made adaptable to changing negotiation conditions?

Negotiated Rulemaking

Inclusive negotiations and decision-making are at the heart of negotiated rulemaking. It is a process that brings government together with stakeholder representatives from civil society and businesses to cooperatively design future regulations and how they will be implemented. It has worked well in the United States and other countries, but there are conditions under which negotiated rulemaking might meet up with some obstacles. How can the process be adjusted to deal with different cultural issues about how different stakeholders interact? The process takes some time and money to produce results; can the process be implemented faster? Bringing a large number of stakeholders together to discuss future regulations in a particular issue area can open the doors to contentious debates. Are there ways that trusted facilitators can reduce the potential for combative negotiations?

Citizen Negotiation

Bringing citizens into a negotiation space with government creates new opportunities for democracy, transparency, and accountability. But such openness requires preparation both for citizens, citizen groups, and government officials. How can these actors get themselves ready to interact in an efficient and civil manner to negotiate issues of common interest? Some training is needed not only to understand the negotiation process but also to develop the skills needed, and to collect the information for strategy development. Dialogues where each party presents their narrative is also essential to build a sense of empathy among the actors. And what are the best frameworks within which to establish forums to conduct such negotiations? This may vary by level of government and according to cultural norms. As citizen engagement in negotiation with government expands, it is critical for all parties to make negotiation an efficient mechanism to find common ground, avert deadlock and stalemate, and adjust policy and services as circumstances change over time.

Paradiplomacy

With an increasing number of international negotiations being conducted by authorized and legitimate subnational or regional governments, the international negotiation field is becoming democratized. It is no longer only the central governments that have a say in designing and negotiating solutions to transborder problems and conflicts; noncentral governments and their citizens are getting engaged and developing solutions that they can design, implement, and live with. Many questions are raised by these paradiplomatic encounters. How does this negotiation process differ from traditional international negotiations, given that the negotiators and the subnational territories they represent are likely to have a lot of shared interests, beliefs, and perceptions? Are their outcomes better implemented and more sustainable? What are the implications for justice and fairness in negotiated agreements when the negotiators are more inclusive of the affected stakeholders? Are there lessons from paradiplomacy that can benefit traditional nation-to-nation negotiations?

Negotiating Values

Especially when negotiating sensitive life-saving problems, such as assistance during humanitarian crises and emergency situations, it is essential that negotiators find a way to conduct their problem-solving by applying altruistic and empathetic values first, despite any self-serving interests that may need to be put aside. They need to go beyond a search for win-lose or even win-win outcomes by examining *caring-win* solutions, where compassion and good will for others take precedence. There also may be ways to generate greater empathy and understanding of other parties at the negotiating table through trust-building facilitation exercises.

Reframing Development Assistance Negotiations

Do negotiations surrounding international development assistance to low-income countries need to be reframed to make them more sensitive to potential economic inequalities and development-induced conflicts that may arise from such agreements? Despite their anticipated impact on strengthening social, economic, and political pathways, the resulting programs can have unintended and negative consequences as well. Can development workers from donor countries get trained in practical conflict resolution mechanisms? How can local stakeholders become engaged more closely in the design of such development programs from the outset to avert potential problems? How can local governments and civil society become empowered so they can exercise dispute management approaches early on if necessary? And can the initiating negotiations incorporate the establishment of local level institutions and mechanisms to moderate any future problems that arise?

Negotiating for Good and Bad

What are the best ways of subverting the use of the negotiation process for bad purposes? We have discussed several approaches – establishing and enforcing greater transparency and accountability in government-citizen and government-business transactions, generating better sunshine laws, conducting more extensive internal and external monitoring and auditing within government, and greater use of e-governance applications to reduce direct personal contact between officials and citizens/businesses. What other approaches might be worth trying that are context-sensitive? After pilot testing these approaches, what is the best way to bring them to scale and monitor their effectiveness?

Evolutionary Negotiation

Given the step-by-step evolution of the international negotiation process, it is reasonable to plan for future changes and adjustments over time. Once agreements are struck, administrative mechanisms need to be established to monitor the commitment of all parties to the provisions and implementation. What options appear to be the most effective in different contexts? And as political-economic-social circumstances change, what are the best approaches to restart negotiations or adjust the existing agreements so they continue be implemented and relevant?

International negotiation is an incredible process for transforming conflicts into peaceful relations, and complex problems into mutually beneficial coordination efforts. It has been an obvious tool supporting human existence since the beginning, but we are still learning how best to apply it and adjust it to particular circumstances. Imagine how much more economical and life-saving it would be to resolve international problems through negotiation dialogues rather than through military warfare. It is certainly worth the investment of time by researchers and practitioners to discover and rediscover the dynamics and intricacies of the negotiation process so that peaceful and collaborative resolution of conflicts and problems can be maximized.

Note

1 Fisher, Roger, William Ury, and Bruce Patton (1991). *Getting to Yes: Negotiating Agreement Without Giving In*, 2nd edition. New York: Penguin Books.

BIBLIOGRAPHY

Alcamo, J., R. Shaw, and L. Hordijkk (1990). *The RAINS Model of Acidification: Science and Strategies in Europe.* Dordrecht, the Netherlands: Kluwer Academic Publishers.

Aldecoa, Francisco and Michael Keating, editors (1999). *Paradiplomacy in Action: The Foreign Relations of Subnational Governments.* London: Frank Cass.

Allison, G. and M. Halperin (1972). "Bureaucratic Politics: A Paradigm and Some Policy Implications," in R. Tanter and R. Ullman, eds., *Theory and Policy in International Relations.* Princeton, NJ: Princeton University Press.

Alvarez, Mariano (2020). "The Rise of Paradiplomacy in International Relations," At: https://www.e-ir.info/2020/03/17/the-rise-of-paradiplomacy-in-international-relations/.

Amidror, Yaakov (2021). "Why is Iran Returning to the Negotiating Table?," November 16. *Israel National News.* At: https://www.israelnationalnews.com/News/News.aspx/316993.

Aquilar, F. and M. Galluccio (2008). *Psychological Processes in International Negotiations: Theoretical and Practical Perspectives.* New York, NY: Springer.

Babbitt, Eileen F., et al. (2009). "Combining Empathy with Problem-Solving: The Tamra Model of Facilitation in Israel," in Craig Zelizer and Robert Rubenstein, eds., *Building Peace: Practical Lessons from the Field.* Sterling, VA: Kumarian Press.

Baechler, Günther, V. Böge, S. Klötzli, S. Libiszewski, and K. Spillmann (1996). *Kriegsursache Umweltzerstörung: Ökologische Konflikte in der Dritten Welt und Wege ihrer friedlichen Bearbeitung.* Band 1. Chur, Zurich: Rüegger.

Baldwin, John D. (1969). "Influences Detrimental to Simulation Gaming," *American Behavioral Scientist* 12, July-August.

Bekoe, Dorina A. (2005). "Mutual Vulnerability and the Implementation of Peace Agreements: Examples from Mozambique, Angola and Liberia," *International Journal of Peace Studies* 10, 2: 43–68.

Benedick, R. (1991). "Lessons for Practitioners," Presentation at the conference on International Environmental Negotiation at the International Institute for Applied Systems Analysis, Processes of International Negotiation Project, Laxenburg, Austria.

Bouchard, T. (1972) "A Comparison of Two Group Brainstorming Procedures," *Journal of Applied Psychology* 56: 418–421.

Bibliography 181

Brewer, G. and O. Hall (1972). "Policy Analysis by Computer Simulation: The Need for Appraisal," RAND Corporation (August) mimeo.

Brinkerhoff, Derick W. (1996b). *"Enhancing Capacity for Strategic Management of Policy Implementation in Developing Countries,"* Washington, DC: Management Systems International. IPC Monograph No. 1 (September).

Brinkerhoff, Derick, editor (1996a). "Implementing Policy Change," *World Development* 24 (9), September.

Bull, V. (1975). *The West Bank-Is it Viable?* Lexington, MA: D. C. Heath.

CACI (1975). *Utilization of Computer Technology and Formal Social Science in Foreign Policy Decision-Making.* Arlington, VA: CACI, Inc.-Federal.

CACI (1977). *U. S. National Security Interests in Potential Middle East Peace Solutions: A Long-Term Perspective*, Vols. 1–3. Arlington, VA: CACI, Inc.-Federal.

Carlin, Robert (2019). "Negotiating with North Korea," February 19. Stimson Center. At: https://www.38north.org/2019/02/rcarlin021919/#:~:text=As%20a%20general%20rule%2C%20North%20Korean%20negotiators%20proceed,carve%20out%20room%20for%20flexibility%20down%20the%20line.

Carnegie Commission on Preventing Deadly Conflict (1997). *Preventing Deadly Conflict.* New York, NY: Carnegie Corporation of New York.

Chasek, Pamela (2023). "Is It the End of the COP as We Know It? An Analysis of the First Year of Virtual Meetings in the United Nations Environment and Development Arena," *International Negotiation* 28, 1.

Clements, Ashley J. (2018). "Overcoming Power Asymmetry in Humanitarian Negotiations with Armed Groups," *International Negotiation* 23, 3: 367–393.

Clements, Ashley J. (2020). *Humanitarian Negotiations with Armed Groups.* London: Routledge.

Cohen, Raymond (1997). *Negotiating Across Cultures.* Washington, DC: United States Institute of Peace Press.

Congressional Research Service (2021). "Potential WTO TRIPS Waiver and COVID-19," *In Focus*, September 13. At: https://crsreports.congress.gov/product/pdf/IF/IF11858.

Cooper, Chester L. (1975). "The Iron Law of Negotiations," *Foreign Policy* 19, Summer.

Cordell, Kristen (2021). *"Chinese Development Assistance: A New Approach or More of the Same?,"* March 23. Washington, DC: Carnegie Endowment for International Peace. At: https://carnegieendowment.org/2021/03/23/chinese-development-assistance-new-approach-or-more-of-same-pub-84141.

Crosby, Benjamin (1996). *"Policy Analysis Units: Useful Mechanisms for Implementing Policy Reform,"* Washington, DC: Management Systems International. USAID's Implementing Policy Change Project Working Paper No. 10 (October).

DeCallieres, Francois (1963). *On the Manner of Negotiating With Princes.* Notre Dame, IN: University of Notre Dame Press.

DeDreu, Carsten, Bianca Beersma, Wolfgang Steinel, and Gerben van Kleef (2007). "The Psychology of Negotiation: Principles and Basic Processes," in A. W. Kruglanski and E. T. Higgins, eds., *Social Psychology: Handbook of Basic Principles* (2nd edition). New York, NY: Guilford Press.

DeFelice, F. (1976). "Negotiations, or the Art of Negotiating," in I. William Zartman, ed., *The 50% Solution.* New York, NY: Doubleday Anchor.

DeRouen Jr., Karl, Mark J. Ferguson, Samuel Norton, Young Hwan Park, Jenna Lea and Ashley Streat-Bartlett (2010). "Civil war peace agreement implementation and state capacity," *Journal of Peace Research* 47, 3: 333–346.

Bibliography

Deutsch, Morton (1960). "Trust, Trustworthiness, and the F Sacle," *Journal of Abnormal and Social Psychology* 61.

Dinar, Shlomi (2009). "Power Asymmetry and Negotiations in International River Basins," *International Negotiation* 14, 2: 329–360.

Douglas, Ann (1957). "The Peaceful Settlement of Industrial and Intergroup Disputes," *Journal of Conflict Resolution* 1.

Drahos, Peter (2003). "When the Weak Bargain with the Strong: Negotiations in the World Trade Organization," *International Negotiation* 8, 1: 79–109.

Dreistadt, R. (1969) "The Use of Analogies and Incubation in Obtaining Insights in Creative Problem Solving," *Journal of Psychology* 71: 159–175.

Druckman, Daniel, editor (1977). *Negotiations: Social Psychological Perspectives*. Beverly Hills, CA: SAGE.

Druckman, Daniel (1993) "The Situational Levers of Negotiating Flexibility," *Journal of Conflict Resolution* 37: 236–276.

Druckman, Daniel, James N. Druckman and Tatsushi Arai (2004). "e-Mediation: Evaluating the Impacts of an Electronic Mediator on Negotiating Behavior," *Group Decision and Negotiation* 13: 481–511.

Druckman, Daniel, J. Husbands and K. Johnston (1991) "Turning Points in the INF Negotiations," *Negotiation Journal* (January).

Druckman, Daniel, Bennett Ramberg and Richard Harris (2002). "Computer-Assisted International Negotiation: A Tool for Research and Practice," *Group Decision and Negotiation* 11: 231–256.

Duchacek, Ivo, Daniel Latouche and Garth Stevenson, editors (1988). *Perforated Sovereignties and International Relations: Trans-Sovereign Contacts of Subnational Governments*. New York, NY: Greenwood Press.

Esman, Milton J. (1991). "Economic Performance and Ethnic Conflict," in Joseph Montville, ed., *Conflict and Peacemaking in Multiethnic Societies*. New York, NY: Lexington Books.

Evans, Peter, Harold Jacobson, and Robert Putnam, editors (2000). *Double-Edged Diplomacy: International Bargaining and Domestic Politics*. Berkeley, CA: University of California Press.

Faure, Guy Olivier, editor (2003). *How People Negotiate: Resolving Disputes in Different Cultures*. Dordrecht, the Netherlands: Kluwer Academic Publishers.

Faure, Guy-Olivier, editor (2012). *Unfinished Business: Why International Negotiations Fail*. Athens, GA: University of Georgia Press.

Faure, Guy Olivier and Jeffrey Rubin (1993). *Culture and Negotiation*. Newbury Park, CA: SAGE.

Fisher, Franklin (1994). *The Harvard Middle East Water Project: Overview, Results and Conclusions*. Cambridge, MA: Harvard Institute for Social and Economic Policy in the Middle East, December.

Fisher, Roger (1983) "Negotiating Power: Getting and Using Influence," *American Behavioral Scientist* 27, 2: 149–166 (November/December).

Fisher, Roger, William Ury and Bruce Patton (1991). *Getting to Yes: Negotiating Agreement Without Giving In*, 2nd edition. New York, NY: Penguin Books.

Fitzgibbon, Will and Michael Hudson (2021). "Five Years Later, Panama Papers still having a big impact," International Consortium of Investigative Journalists, April 3. At: https://www.icij.org/investigations/panama-papers/five-years-later-panama-papers-still-having-a-big-impact/.

Fortna, Virginia Page (2003). "Scraps of Paper? Agreements and the Durability of Peace," *International Organization* 57, Spring: 337–372.

Friedlander, D. and C. Goldscheider (1974). "Peace and the Demographic Future of Israel," *Journal of Conflict Resolution* 18, 3 (September).
Galinsky, Adam (2021). "The 'Psychology of Regret' Helps Explain Vaccine Hesitancy," *Washington Post*, November 14. At: https://www.washingtonpost.com/outlook/2021/11/11/vaccine-hesitancy-psychology-regret/.
Gick, M. and K. Holyoak (1983). "Schema Induction and Analogical Transfer," *Cognitive Psychology* 15: 1–38.
Grodzinski, Michael (2000). "Carpathian Euroregion: 'Locomotive' or 'Platform' of Transboundary Cooperation," unpublished paper. University of Kyiv, Ukraine.
Gu, Jing, Xiaoyun Li and Chuanhong Zhang (2021). "Whose Knowledge? Whose Influence? Changing Dynamics of China's Development Cooperation Policy and Practice," *IDS Bulletin* 52, 2: 1–18. At: https://bulletin.ids.ac.uk/index.php/idsbo/article/download/3129/3143?inline=1.
Güiza-Gómez, Diana Isabel and Rodrigo Uprimny-Yepes (2021). "Legitimizing and enshrining peace commitments: Inclusivity and constitution-building in the Colombian peace process," in Jorge Luis Fabra-Zamora, Andrés Molina-Ochoa, Nancy C. Doubleday, eds., *The Colombian Peace Agreement: A Multidisciplinary Assessment*. London: Routledge.
Habeeb, William M. (1988). *Power and Tactics in International Negotiation: How Weak Nations Bargain with Strong Nations*. Baltimore, MD: The Johns Hopkins University Press.
Habeeb, W. M. and I. W. Zartman (1986). "The Panama Canal Negotiations." Foreign Policy Institute, School of Advanced International Studies. Washington, DC: The Johns Hopkins University.
Hare, A. P. and D. Naveh (1985). "Creative Problem Solving: Camp David Summit, 1978," *Small Group Behavior* 16, 2, 123–138.
Hirblinger, Andreas T. (2023). "When Mediators Need Machines (and vice versa): Towards a research agenda on hybrid peacemaking intelligence," *International Negotiation* 28, 1.
Hocking, Brian (1993). *Localizing Foreign Policy: Non-Central Governments and Multilayered Diplomacy*. New York, NY: St. Martin's Press.
Holst, J. J. (1993) "Reflections on the Making of a Tenuous Peace, or the Transformation of Images of the Middle East Conflict," Presentation to the School of International and Public Affairs. New York, NY: Columbia University.
Homer-Dixon, Thomas and Valerie Percival (1996). *Environmental Scarcity and Violent Conflict: Briefing Book*. Toronto: University of Toronto.
Hopmann, P. Terrence and C. Walcott (1977). "The Impact of External Stresses and Tension on Negotiations," in D. Druckman, ed., *Negotiations: Social-Psychological Perspectives*. Beverly Hills, CA: SAGE.
Iklé, Fred C. and Nathan Leites (1962). "Political Negotiations as a Process of Modifying Utilities," *Journal of Conflict Resolution* 6.
Jarstad, Anna K. and Desiree Nilsson (2008). "From Words to Deeds: The Implementation of Power-Sharing Pacts in Peace Accords," *Conflict Management and Peace Science* 25, 3: 206–223.
Jonsson, Christer (1981) "Bargaining Power: Notes on an Elusive Concept," *Cooperation and Conflict* XVI: 249–257.
Joshi, Madhav, Jason Michael Quinn and Patrick M. Regan (2015). "Annualized implementation data on comprehensive peace accords, 1989–2012," *Journal of Peace Research* 52, 4: 551–562.
Kennedy, John F. (1956). *Profiles in Courage*. New York, NY: Harper Perennial.

Kerlinger, Fred N. and Elazar J. Pedhazur (1973). *Multiple Regression in Behavior Research.* New York, NY: Holt, Rinehart, and Winston, Inc.

Kersten, Gregory E. and Hsiangchu Lai (2007). "Negotiation Support and E-negotiation Systems: An Overview," *Group Decision and Negotiation* 16: 553–586.

Kidder, L. (1987). "Breaking a Stalemate with a Creative Alternative," *Negotiation Journal* (April).

Kremenyuk, Victor, editor (1991). *International Negotiation.* San Francisco, CA: Jossey-Bass.

Krishnan, Vidya (2021). "How to End Vaccine Apartheid," *Foreign Policy,* November 9. At: https://foreignpolicy.com/2021/11/09/vaccine-apartheid-covid-pandemic-covax-us-trips-waiver/.

Kulibaba, Nicolas (1995). "*Good Governance in Sheep's Clothing: Implementing the Action Plan for Regional Integration of the Livestock Trade in West Africa's Central Corridor.*" Washington, DC: Management Systems International Inc., IPC Working Paper (May).

Language of Peace (2021). *Language of Peace Database.* At: languageofpeace.org.

Lecours, Andre (2002). "Paradiplomacy: Reflections on the Foreign Policy and International Relations of Regions," *International Negotiation* 7, 1: 91–114.

Lequesne, Christian and Stéphane Paquin (2017a). *Federalism and International Negotiation,* special issue. *International Negotiation* 22, 2.

Lequesne, Christian and Stéphane Paquin (2017b). "Federalism, Paradiplomacy and Foreign Policy: A Case of Mutual Neglect," *International Negotiation* 22, 2: 183–204.

Levine, Alicia (1996). "Political Accommodation and the Prevention of Secessionist Violence," in Michael E. Brown, ed., *The International Dimensions of International Conflict.* Cambridge, MA: The MIT Press.

Licklider, Roy (1995). "The Consequences of Negotiated Settlements in Civil Wars, 1945-1993," *American Political Science Review* 89, September: 681–690.

Lund, Michael (1996). *Preventing Violent Conflicts: A Strategy for Preventive Diplomacy.* Washington, DC: US Institute of Peace Press.

Lund, Michael (1997). *Preventing and Mitigating Violent Conflict: A Guide for Practitioners.* Washington, DC: Creative Associates International Inc.

Lynch, Catherine (2005). "Implementing the Northern Ireland Peace Settlement: Factionalism and Implementation Design," *Irish Studies in International Affairs* 16: 209–234.

Madron, Thomas W. (1969). *Small Group Methods and the Study of Politics.* Evanston, IL: Northwestern University Press.

Makovsky, David (2020). "*How the Abraham Accords Look Forward, Not Back*," September 16. Washington, DC: Washington Institute for Near East Policy. At: https://www.washingtoninstitute.org/policy-analysis/how-abraham-accords-look-forward-not-back.

Malan, Jannie (1997). *Conflict Resolution Wisdom from Africa.* Durban, South Africa: African Centre for the Constructive Resolution of Disputes (ACCORD).

Management Systems International (2010). *Community Participation and Regional Advocacy Project in the Russian Far East, Final Report.* Arlington, VA: MSI. At: https://pdf.usaid.gov/pdf_docs/PDACQ845.pdf.

Marlowe, D. and Kenneth J. Gergen (1969). "Personality and Social Interaction," In G. Lindzey and E. Aronson, eds., *Handbook of Social Psychology.* Second Edition, Vol. 3. Reading, MA: Addison-Wesley Publishing Co.

Marshall, Colin (2018). *Compassionate Moral Realism.* Oxford: Oxford University Press.

Matland, R. E. (1995). "Synthesizing the Implementation Literature: The Ambiguity-Conflict Model of Policy Implementation," *Journal of Public Administration Research and Theory* 5, 2: 145–174.

Mattes, Michaela and Burcu Savun (2010). "Information, Agreement Design, and the Durability of Civil War Settlements," *American Journal of Political Science* 54, 2: 511–524.

Maxwell, G. and D. Schmitt (1968). "Are 'Trivial' Games the-Most Interesting Psychologically?," *Behavioral Science* 13.

Michelmann, Hans J. and Panayotis Soldatos, editors (1990). *Federalism and International Relations: The Role of Subnational Units*. Oxford: Clarendon Press.

Minas, J., A. Scodel, P. Marlowe, and H. Rawson (1960). "Some Descriptive Aspects of Two-Person Non-Zero-Sum Games, II," *Journal of Conflict Resolution* 4.

Mislin, A. A., et al. (2011). "After the Deal: Talk, trust building and the implementation of negotiated agreements," *Organizational Behavior and Human Decision Processes* 115, 1: 55–68.

Mooney, R. L. (1963). "A Conceptual Model for Integrating Four Approaches to the Identification of Creative Talent," in C. W. Taylor and F. Barron, eds., *Scientific Creativity: Its Recognition and Development*. New York, NY: John Wiley & Sons.

Moore, Christopher (1993). "'Have Process, Will Travel:' Reflections on Democratic Decision Making and Conflict Management Practice Abroad," *NIDR Forum*, Winter: 1–12.

Murray, Henry A. (1938). *Explorations in Personality*. New York, NY: John Wiley and Sons, Inc.

Nathan, Laurie (2019). *The Ties That Bind: Peace Negotiations, Credible Commitment and Constitutional Reform*. Basel: Swisspeace.

National Paint and Coatings Association (NPCA) (1995). *Wood Furniture Regulatory Negotiation: A Summary*. Washington, DC: NPCA.

NATO/CCMS (1998). *Environment and Security in an International Context*. Edited by EcoLogic, EBR Inc., and the Center for Negotiation Analysis. Brussels: NATO.

Neirenberg, Gerald (1973). *Fundamentals of Negotiating*. New York, NY: Hawthorn Books.

Neulinger, John and Morris Stein (1971). "Personality Characteristics of Volunteer Subjects," *Perceptual and Motor Skills* 32.

Nicolson, Harold (1946). *The Congress of Vienna*. New York, NY: Harcourt and Brace.

Nicolson, Harold (1964). *Diplomacy*. New York, NY: Oxford.

Office of the Solicitor (1992). *Negotiated Rulemaking Handbook*. Washington, DC: US Department of Labor.

O'Leary, M., W. Coplin, H. Shapiro, and D. Dean (1974). "The Quest for Relevance: Quantitative International Relations Research and Government Foreign Affairs Analysis," *International Studies Quarterly* 18, 2.

Organization for Economic Cooperation and Development (2021). "COVID-19 spending helped to lift foreign aid to an all-time high in 2020, Detailed Note," April 13. At: https://www.oecd.org/dac/financing-sustainable-development/development-finance-data/ODA-2020-detailed-summary.pdf.

Osgood, Charles (1962). *An Alternative to War or Surrender*. Urbana, IL: University of Illinois Press.

Paquin, Stéphane (2020). "Paradiplomacy," in Thierry Balzacq, Frédéric Charillon, and Frédéric Ramel, eds., *Global Diplomacy: An Introduction to Theory and Practice*. London: Palgrave Macmillan.

Paterson, Matthew and Michael Grubb (1992). "The International Politics of Climate Change," *International Affairs* 68, 2: 293–310.

Pelcovits, N. (1976). *Security Guarantees in a Middle East Settlement*. Foreign Policy Papers 2, 5. Beverly Hills, CA: SAGE Publications.

Perton, Victor (1997). "Regulatory Review - The Next Wave?," Wellington, New Zealand: Parliament of Victoria. At: https://www.parliament.vic.gov.au/images/stories/committees/lawrefrom/regulatory_efficiency/next_wave.pdf.

Petzold-Bradley, Eileen, Alexander Carius, and Arpad Vincze (2001). *Responding to Environmental Conflicts: Implications for Theory and Practice.* Dordrecht: Kluwer Academic Publishers.
Price Benowitz LLP (2021). "FCPA Famous Cases," At: https://whitecollarattorney.net/fcpa/famous-cases/.
Pritzker, David M. and Deborah S. Dalton (1995). *Negotiated Rulemaking Sourcebook.* Washington, DC: Administrative Conference of the United States.
Program on Negotiation (2020). "Putting Your Negotiated Agreement Into Action," At: https://www.pon.harvard.edu/daily/negotiation-skills-daily/we-have-a-deal-now-what-do-we-do-three-negotiation-tips-on-implementing-your-negotiated-agreement/.
Pruitt, Dean (1981) *Negotiation Behavior.* New York, NY: Academic Press.
Pruitt, Dean (1987) "Creative Approaches to Negotiation," in D. Sandole and I. Sandole-Staroste, eds., *Conflict Management and Problem Solving.* London: Frances Pinter Publishers.
Pruitt, Dean G. and Peter J. Carnevale (1993). *Negotiation in Social Conflict.* Pacific Grove, CA: Brooks Cole.
Pruitt, Dean and M. Kimmel (1977) "Twenty Years of Experimental Gaming: Critique, Synthesis, and Suggestions for the Future," *Annual Review of Psychology* 28: 363–392.
Radio Free Europe (2021). "U.S. Iran Envoy Warns Tehran May Be Delaying Talks to Advance Nuclear Program," October 25. At: https://www.rferl.org/a/31528864.html.
Raiffa, H. (1982). *The Art and Science of Negotiation.* Cambridge, MA: Belknap Press.
Raiffa, H. (1991). "Contributions of Applied Systems Analysis to International Negotiation," in V. Kremenyuk, ed., *International Negotiation: Analysis. Approaches. Issues.* San Francisco, CA: Jossey-Bass Publishers.
Rapoport, Anatol and A. Chammah (1965). *Prisoner's Dilemma: A Study in Conflict and Cooperation.* Ann Arbor, MI: University of Michigan Press.
Reich, Robert (1981). "Regulation by Confrontation or Negotiation?," *Harvard Business Review,* May/June: 82–93.
Renner, Michael (1996). *Fighting for Survival.* New York, NY: W. W. Norton and Co.
Ross, Nick (2017). "*Civil Society's Role in Monitoring and Verifying Peace Agreements: Seven Lessons from International Experiences,*" Geneva: Inclusive Peace & Transition Initiative (The Graduate Institute of International and Development Studies).
Rubin, Jeffrey and Bert Brown (1975). *The Social Psychology of Bargaining and Negotiation.* New York, NY: Academic Press.
Rubin, Jeffrey and I. W. Zartman (1992) "*Review of the Experimental Research on Power,*" Laxenburg, Austria: International Institute for Applied Systems Analysis.
Sakr, N. (1977). "Economic Viability: 3 Major Constraints," *The Middle East* (28 February).
Sand, Peter, editor (1992). *The Effectiveness of International Environmental Agreements: A Survey of Existing Legal Instruments.* Cambridge: Grotius Publications Ltd.
Schelling, Thomas C. (1960). *The Strategy of Conflict.* New York, NY: Oxford University Press.
Scodel, A., J. Minas, P. Ratoosh, and M. Lipetz (1959). "Some Descriptive Aspects of Two-Person Non-Zero-Sum Games, I," *Journal of Conflict Resolution* 3.
Shaw, Jerry and Christen Thorslund (1975). "Varying Patterns of Reward Cooperation," *Journal of Conflict Resolution* 19, March.
Shefska, Zach (2020). "How is Negotiability Score Calculated?," At: https://help.yaamember.com/hc/en-us/articles/360056761413-How-is-Negotiability-Score-calculated-.
Sherif, Muzafer (1967). *Social Interaction: Process and Products.* Chicago, IL: Aldine Publishing.

Shinn, James and James Dobbins (2011). *Afghan Peace Talks: A Primer*. Santa Monica, CA: RAND Corporation.

Singh, J. P. (2000). "Weak Powers and Globalism: The Impact of Plurality on Weak-Strong Negotiations in the International Economy," *International Negotiation* 5, 3: 449–484.

Snyder, Scott (2000). "Negotiating on the Edge: Patterns in North Korea's Diplomatic Style," *World Affairs* 163, 1: 3–17.

Spangler, Brad (2003). "Decision-Making Delay," *Beyond Intractability*, July. At: https://www.beyondintractability.org/essay/delay/.

Spector, Bertram I. (1975). "*The Effects of Personality, Perception and Power on the Bargaining Process and Outcome*," Ph.D. Dissertation, New York University.

Spector, Bertram I. (1977). "Negotiation as a Psychological Process," *Journal of Conflict Resolution* 21, 4: 607–618.

Spector, Bertram I. (1992). "Developing the Negotiator's Tool Box: Practical Systems to Support Effective International Negotiations," *Control and Cybernetics* 21, 1: 21–35.

Spector, Bertram I. (1993). "*Post-Agreement Negotiation: Conflict Resolution Processes in the Aftermath of Successful Negotiations*," Potomac, MD: Center for Negotiation Analysis. Working Paper Series (September).

Spector, Bertram I. (1993a). "Decision Analysis for Practical Negotiation Application," *Theory and Decision* 34, 3: 183–199.

Spector, Bertram I. (1993b). "Introduction," *Theory and Decision* 34, 3: 177–181.

Spector, Bertram I. (1993). "Creativity in Negotiation: Directions for Future Research," Laxenburg, Austria: IIASA Working Paper WP-93-4 (January). Also published in Dutch in *Negotiation Magazine V*, 4: 153–162 (December 1992).

Spector, Bertram I. (1995). "Creativity Heuristics for Impasse Resolution: Reframing Intractable Negotiations," *The Annals of the American Academy of Political and Social Science* 542: 81–99 (November).

Spector, Bertram I. (1997). "Analytical Support to Negotiations: An Empirical Assessment," *Group Decision and Negotiation* 6, 5: 421–436.

Spector, Bertram I. (1997a). "*Policy Implementation, Conflict and Dispute Resolution*," Washington, DC: Management Systems International. USAID's Implementing Policy Change Project, Working Paper No. 11 (August).

Spector, Bertram I. (1997b). "Managing Disputes and Building Consensus: A Guide to Applying Conflict Resolution Mechanisms when Implementing Policy Change," USAID's Implementing Policy Change Project, Working Paper No. 9 (April).

Spector, Bertram I. (2001). "Transboundary Disputes: Keeping Backyards Clean," in I. William Zartman, ed, *Preventive Negotiation: Avoiding Conflict Escalation*. Lanham, MD: Rowman and Littlefield.

Spector, Bertram I. (2002). "Negotiation Readiness in the Development Context: Adding Capacity to Ripeness," in Ho-Won Jeong, ed, *Approaches to Peacebuilding*. New York, NY: Palgrave Macmillan.

Spector, Bertram I. (2008). "Perverse Negotiations: Bribery, Bargaining, and Ripeness," in Terrence Lyons and Gilbert Khadiagala, eds., *Conflict Management and African Politics: Ripeness, Bargaining, and Mediation*. London: Routledge.

Spector, Bertram I. (2020). "Ripe for Renegotiation?," *International Negotiation* 25, 1: 69–77.

Spector, Bertram I. and Anna Korula (1993). "Problems of Ratifying International Environmental Agreements," *Global Environmental Change* 3, 4 (December): 369–381.

Spector, Bertram I. and Joseph H. Moskowitz (1975). "Risk and Styles of Political Dissent Within the Executive Branch: Some Social Psychological and Personality Correlates," Unpublished manuscript, CACI, Inc.

Spector, Bertram I., Gunnar Sjöstedt, and I. William Zartman, eds. (1994). *Negotiating International Regimes: Lessons Learned from the United Nations Conference on Environment and Development (UNCED)*. London: Graham & Trotman.

Spector, Bertram I. and Lynn M. Wagner (2010). "Negotiating International Development," *International Negotiation* 15, 3: 327–340.

Spector, Bertram I. and I. William Zartman, editors (2003). *Getting It Done: International Regimes and Post-Agreement Negotiation*. Washington, DC: United States Institute of Peace Press.

Stedman, Stephen (2002). "Policy Implications," in Stephen Stedman, Donald Rothchild and Elizabeth Cousens, eds., *Ending Civil Wars: The Implementation of Peace Agreements*. Boulder, CO: Lynne Rienner.

Stein, Janice (1989). "Prenegotiation in the Arab-Israeli Conflict," in J. Stein, ed., *Getting to the Table*. Baltimore: Johns Hopkins University Press.

Stein, Morris I. (1963). "Explorations in Typology," In R. W. White, editor, *The Study of Lives*. New York, NY: Atherton Press.

Stein, Morris I. (1971). "Ecology of Typology," Paper presented at the Association of American Medical Colleges Conference on Personality Measurement in Medical Education, Des Plaines, IL.

Stein, Morris (1974) *Stimulating Creativity*. New York, NY: Academic Press.

Stein, Morris I. and John Neulinger (1968). "A Typology of Self-Descriptions," In M. M. Katz, et al., eds., *The Role and Methodology of Classification in Psychiatry and Psychopathology*. Washington, DC: Government Printing Office, Public Health Service Publication No. 1584.

Sunshine, Russell B. (1990). *Negotiating for International Development: A Practitioner's Handbook*. Dordrecht: Martinus Nijhoff Publishers.

Susskind, Lawrence E. (1997). "Environmental Mediation: Theory and Practice Reconsidered," in Martin Gillian and Winfried Hamacher, eds., *Lessons Learned in Environmental Mediation: Practical Experiences in North and South*. International Workshop. Geneva/Bonn: International Academy of the Environment and Deutsche Gesellschaft für Technische Zusammenarbeit (GTZ).

Swiss Federal Office (1993). *"Results of the Questionnaire Regarding Seven Environmental Conventions: Participation and Implementation,"* Bern: Federal Office of Environment, Forests and Landscape, International Affairs Division, March 25.

Szulc, T. (1974). "How Kissinger Did It: Behind the Vietnam Cease-Fire Agreement," *Foreign Policy* 15 (Summer).

Tardif, T. and R. Sternberg (1988). "What Do We Know About Creativity?," in R. Sternberg, ed., *The Nature of Creativity*. Cambridge: Cambridge University Press.

Taylor, C. (1988). "Various Approaches to and Definitions of Creativity," in R. Sternberg, ed., *The Nature of Creativity*. Cambridge: Cambridge University Press.

Terhune, K. (1968). "Motives, Situation, and Interpersonal Conflict Within Prisoner's Dilemma," *Journal of Personality and Social Psychology Monograph Supplement* 8. No. 3, Part 2.

Terhune, K. (1970). "The Effects of Personality in Cooperation and Conflict," In Paul Swingle, ed., *The Structure of Conflict*. New York, NY: Academic Press.

Ulvila, Jacob (1990). "Turning Points: An Analysis," in J. McDonald Jr. and D. Bendahmane, eds., *U.S. Bases Overseas*. Boulder, CO: Westview Press.

Ulvila, Jacob and Warren Snider (1980). "Negotiation of International Oil Tanker Standards: An Application of Multiattribute Value Theory," *Operations Research* 28: 81–96.

United Nations Conference on Environment and Development (1992, 1993). *Nations of the Earth Report, National Reports Summaries*, Volumes 1–3. Geneva: UNCED.

United Nations Department of Economic and Social Affairs (UNDESA) (2007). "*UN Millennium Development Goals Report 2007*," New York, NY: Inter-Agency and Expert Group on MDG Indicators, United Nations.

United Nations Development Program (1991). *Human Development Report.* New York, NY: Oxford University Press.

University of Edinburgh (2021). *Peace Agreements Database (PA-X, Version 5).* At: peaceagreements.org.

US Department of State (2019). "Treaties Pending in the Senate, October 22, 2019," At: https://www.state.gov/treaties-pending-in-the-senate/.

Van Arkadie, B. (1977). *Benefits and Burdens: A Report on the West Bank and Gaza Strip Economies Since 1967.* New York, NY: Carnegie Endowment for International Peace.

Verjee, Aly (2020). *After the Agreement: Why the Oversight of Peace Deals Succeeds or Fails.* Washington, DC: US Institute of Peace.

Vinacke, W. Edgar (1969). "Variables in Experimental Games: Toward a Field Theory," *Psychological Bulletin* 71.

Volcovici, Valerie, Kate Abnett and William James (2021). "U.N. Climate Agreement Clinched After Late Drama over Coal," *Reuters*, November 14. At: https://www.reuters.com/business/cop/un-climate-negotiators-go-into-overtime-save-15-celsius-goal-2021-11-13/.

Wagner, Lynn M. (2013). "A Forty-Year Search for a Single-Negotiating Text: Rio+20 as a Post-Agreement Negotiation," *International Negotiation* 18, 3: 333–356.

Walter, Barbara F. (1997). "The Critical Barrier to Civil War Settlement," *International Organization* 51, 3: 335–364.

Walter, Barbara F. (2002a). *Committing to Peace: The Successful Settlement of Civil Wars.* Princeton, NJ: Princeton University Press.

Walter, Barbara F. (2002b). "Re-Conceptualizing Conflict Resolution as a Three-Stage Process," *International Negotiation* 7, 3: 299–311.

Wanglai, Gao (2009). "Negotiating with China in Power Asymmetry: The Case of Sino-British Negotiations on the Handover of Hong Kong," *International Negotiation* 14, 3: 475–492.

Weisberg, R. (1988). "Problem Solving and Creativity," in R. Sternberg, ed, *The Nature of Creativity.* Cambridge: Cambridge University Press.

Werner, Suzanne and Amy Yuen (2005). "Making and Keeping Peace," *International Organization* 59, 2: 261–292.

White, Louise (1990). *Implementing Policy Reforms in LDCs: A Strategy for Designing and Effecting Change.* Boulder, CO: Lynne Rienner Publishers.

Whiting, A. (1972). "The Scholar and the Policy-Maker," in R. Tanter and R. Ullman, eds., *Theory and Policy in International Relations.* Princeton, NJ: Princeton University Press.

Winham, Gilbert (1979). "Practitioners' Views of International Negotiation," *World Politics* 32: 111–135.

World Bank (1997). *The Inspection Panel, Annual Report, August 1, 1996 to July 31, 1997.* Washington, DC: The World Bank.

Young, O. (1972). "The Perils of Odysseus: On Constructing Theories of International Relations," in R. Tanter and R. Ullman, eds, *Theory and Policy in International Relations.* Princeton, NJ: Princeton University Press.

Zahlan, A. (1976). "The Economic Viability of a West Bank State," *Middle East International* (November).

Zakaria, Fareed (1997). "The Rise of Illiberal Democracy," *Foreign Affairs* 76, 6: 22–43.

Zartman, I. William (1976, 1983a). "The Analysis of Negotiation," in I. William Zartman, ed., *The 50% Solution*. New Haven, CT: Yale University Press.

Zartman, I. William (1983b). "Reality, Image, and Detail: The Paris Negotiations, 1969-1973," in I. W. Zartman, ed., *The 50% Solution*. New Haven, CT: Yale University Press.

Zartman, I. William (1986). "Ripening Conflict, Ripe Moment, Formula, and Mediation," in *Perspectives on Negotiation: Four Case Studies and Interpretations*. Washington, DC: Center for the Study of Foreign Affairs, Foreign Service Institute, U.S. Department of State.

Zartman, I. William, editor (1987). *Positive Sum: Improving North-South Negotiations*. New Brunswick, NJ: Transaction.

Zartman, I. William (1993). "Decision Support and Negotiation Research: A Researcher's Perspective," *Theory and Decision* 34, 3: 345–351.

Zartman, I. William (1995). "Dynamics and Constraints in Negotiations in Internal Conflicts," in I. William Zartman, editor, *Elusive Peace: Negotiating an End to Civil Wars*. Washington, DC: The Brookings Institution.

Zartman, I. William, editor (1995). *Elusive Peace: Negotiating an End to Civil Wars*. Washington, DC: The Brookings Institution.

Zartman, I. William, editor (1999). *"Traditional Cures for Modern Conflicts: African Conflict Medicine."* Boulder, CO: Lynne Rienner.

Zartman, I. William (1999). "Negotiating Cultures," in Peter Berton, Hiroshi Kimura and I. William Zartman, eds., *International Negotiation: Actors, Structure/Process, Values*. New York, NY: St. Martin's Press.

Zartman, I. William (2000). "Ripeness: The Hurting Stalemate and Beyond," in Paul C. Stern and Daniel Druckman, eds, *International Conflict Resolution After the Cold War*. Washington, DC: National Research Council.

Zartman, I. William (2021). "Gray Peace: Is Part of a Peace Sufficient?," *International Negotiation* 26, 3: 359–365.

Zartman, I. William and Jeffrey Rubin, editors (2000). *Power and Negotiation*. Ann Arbor, MI: University of Michigan Press.

Zartman, I. William and Jeffrey Z. Rubin (2000). "Symmetry and Asymmetry in Negotiation," in I. William Zartman and Jeffrey Z. Rubin, eds., *Power and Negotiation*. Ann Arbor, MI: University of Michigan Press.

Zartman, I. William and Bertram I. Spector (2013). "Post-Agreement Negotiating within Multilateral Regimes," *International Negotiation* 18, 3: 325–332.

INDEX

Abraham Accords 19, 167
altruism 142–148
analogical thinking 29–32

Camp David Accords 18, 96–107
Camp Game simulation 35–53
caring 142–148
China 144, 151–152
citizen negotiation 111–119, 177–178
compliance with agreements 68, 171
confidence 5
conflict prevention 136–137
constituency development 136–137
corruption 152–153
COVID-19 147–148
creativity 3, 10–23, 28–32, 175
cultural impacts 58, 126

decision support systems (DSS) 91–109, 177
delay tactics 151
democratization of negotiation 129–139
development-induced conflicts 156–163
Druckman, Daniel 13, 27, 95

empathy 6, 141–142, 148, 161, 166, 178
engineering negotiations 4, 25–33, 156–163, 175
Environmental Protection Agency (EPA) 125–126
Euroregions 131–132
evolutionary negotiations 165–172, 179
experimentation 10–23, 170, 175

formula-detail 49, 166–168
freshness 13–17, 21, 23

Gabcikovo-Nagymaros dam 29, 31, 159

humanitarian negotiations 6, 9, 141–148, 152, 159, 178

implementation formulas 63–73, 75–89, 176–177
inclusion 6, 70, 111–119
international development assistance 141–148, 178
international donors 122, 130, 163
International Institute for Applied Systems Analysis (IIASA) 7
International Negotiation: A Journal of Theory and Practice 1, 6, 91

justice and fairness 142–148

learning 49–50
localization of negotiation 130–131

monitoring and oversight mechanisms 70
Murray, Henry 40–42

negative negotiations 150–154, 179
negotiability of nations 57–62, 176
negotiated rulemaking 120–128, 177
negotiation dynamics 3
negotiation reputation 5
negotiation system 2–3, 134–136

non-central government 129–139
non-governmental organizations (NGOs) 111–119, 134, 159, 163
North Korea 58
North-South divide 75–89, 141–148

Osgood, Charles 167
Oslo Accords 18–19

Panama Canal negotiations 17–18
Panama Papers 153
paradiplomacy 129–139, 178
partial peace 64
perceptions 40–53
personality 39–48
post-negotiation 63, 114–115, 168–169
power symmetry and asymmetry 76–78, 151–152
pre-negotiation 63, 114, 168–169
Processes of International Negotiation (PIN) project xiii, 7
psychology 4, 34–56, 176
psychology of regret 171

ratification 66, 78–89
readiness 113, 115
regimes 166–170

regulatory negotiations 120–128
ripeness 13, 48, 112–113, 122
Russia 116–119

Sherif, Muzafer 88
situational factors 26–28, 134
Spector, Bertram 29–32, 35–53, 66, 79–89, 93–94, 96–107
Stein, Morris 12–13, 20, 40–52

technology 5
trust-building 69, 166–167
two-person negotiation model 35, 53

UNCED 75–76, 80, 169–170
United States Agency for International Development (USAID) 116, 157, 159, 160, 163

values 6, 141–148, 178
Vietnam Paris negotiations 16–17

West Africa 158–159
World Bank 59–60, 145–146, 159

Zartman, I. William 10, 16, 64, 143, 152

Printed in the United States
by Baker & Taylor Publisher Services